STANLEY COMPLETE
FLOORING

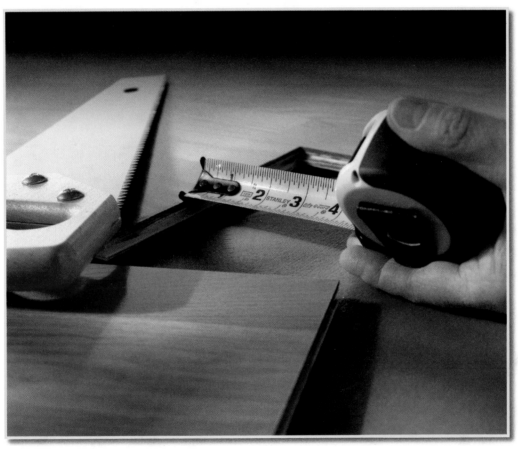

Meredith® Books
Des Moines, Iowa

Stanley Complete Flooring
Editor: Larry Johnston
Senior Associate Design Director: Tom Wegner
Copy Chief: Doug Kouma
Copy Editor: Kevin Cox
Contributing Editors/Writers: Amber Dawn Barz and
    Jan Soults Walker, Writing and Editing Services, Inc.
Publishing Operations Manager: Karen Schirm
Edit and Design Production Coordinator: Mary Lee Gavin
Editorial and Design Assistant: Diana Meinders
Book Production Managers: Marjorie J. Schenkelberg,
    Mark Weaver
Imaging Center Operator: Jonathan Sands
Contributing Copy Editor: Steve Hallam
Contributing Proofreaders: David Krause, Jodie Littleton,
    Cheri Madison
Other Contributor: Janet Anderson

Additional Editoral Contributions from
    Art Rep Services
Director: Chip Nadeau
Designer: Shawn Wallace, Evolutionary Studios, Inc.
Photographer: Mike Dvorak Photography
Illustrator: Dave Brandon

Meredith® Books
Editorial Director: Gregory H. Kayko
Art Director: Gene Rauch
Managing Editor: Kathleen Armentrout
Brand Manager: Mark Hetrick

Director, Marketing & Publicity: Amy Nichols
Executive Director, Sales: Ken Zagor
Director, Operations: George A. Susral
Director, Production: Douglas M. Johnston
Business Director: Janice Croat

Vice President and General Manager, SIM: Jeff Myers

Meredith Publishing Group
President: Jack Griffin
Executive Vice President: Doug Olson

Meredith Corporation
Chairman of the Board: William T. Kerr
President and Chief Executive Officer: Stephen M. Lacy

In Memoriam: E. T. Meredith III (1933–2003)

Special thanks to:
A1 Tool Rental
Bill Voss Remodeling
CannonDale Flooring
Carpet Mill Connection
Ceramic Tile Works
Cutting Edge Tile / North Prairie Tile
Dave's Floor Sanding, Maple Grove, Minnesota
Floor Center
Homes by Thomas R. Briggs
Marmoleum Click by Forbo Flooring Systems
Dave Morse Mesquite and More
Mo and Milo Iglesias
Mound True Value Hardware and Paint
Nob Hill Decorative Hardware Minnesota
Reflex Moldings USA
RBC Tile
Sun Touch
Tom and Matt Austin
Tile Shop
Tim the Carpet Guy
Tool Equipment Sales and Rental

All of us at Meredith® Books are dedicated to providing you with the information and ideas you need to enhance your home and garden. We welcome your comments and suggestions about this book. Write to us at:

Meredith Corporation
Meredith Books
1716 Locust St.
Des Moines, IA 50309-3203

If you would like more information on other Stanley products, call 1-800-STANLEY or visit us at: www.stanleyworks.com
Stanley® and the notched rectangle around the Stanley name are registered trademarks of The Stanley Works and subsidiaries.

Note to the Readers: Due to differing conditions, tools, and individual skills, Meredith Corporation assumes no responsibility for any damages, injuries suffered, or losses incurred as a result of following the information published in this book. Before beginning any project, review the instructions carefully, and if any doubts or questions remain, consult local experts or authorities. Because codes and regulations vary greatly, you always should check with authorities to ensure that your project complies with all applicable local codes and regulations. Always read and observe all of the safety precautions provided by manufacturers of any tools, equipment, or supplies, and follow all accepted safety procedures.

CONTENTS

CONTENTS

HOW TO USE THIS BOOK

Your success with any of the flooring projects described in this book depends on how familiar you are with all of its aspects, so start by reading the first three chapters. The first two chapters concentrate on design tips and methods for selecting materials—information that will help you choose the right materials for the practical aspects of your project and its style. The third chapter contains information that will help you carry out essential preparation tasks. After that you're ready to apply your new knowledge to a specific material, so find the chapter that describes the flooring you have chosen to install.

Each project comes with a general introduction and a "Prestart Checklist" that will give you an idea of how much time the project will take and what tools, skills, and materials you will need to get started.

Understanding your limits and the constraints on your time will go a long way toward making your work enjoyable and safe. Plan your time carefully—if necessary make a list of the stages of your work.

What if ...?

Because no two projects are alike, you may encounter unique conditions. So if the steps shown for any task don't conform to your situation, check the lower half of the page for boxes that provide additional information.

Those labeled "What if ... ?" help you apply techniques to specific needs. You'll also find "Stanley Pro Tips" and "Safety First" boxes. These items contain tricks of the trade and information you need to keep in mind so your work proceeds safely.

Know your limits

Review the "Prestart Checklist" at the beginning of each project to get an idea of how much time it will take and allow a little extra if you're new to the business of do-it-yourself home maintenance.

Prepare contingency plans, especially if you're working on a kitchen or bath. Those rooms could be unusable while you work on them. Taking showers in the spare bathroom or having a family night out at everyone's favorite restaurant may be the thing to relieve some of the stress caused by the inconvenience and disruption of the family routine.

SAFETY FIRST
Plan for safety from the start

Installing flooring is relatively safe. Depending on your project, however, you may use power tools and work with materials that can pose safety hazards. Use these steps to keep safe:
■ Set goals, allow enough time to complete them, and take breaks. Nothing detracts from safety more than fatigue and frustration.
■ Make the workplace comfortable. Keep tools spread out but close by. Buy a good tool belt or bucket belt and put each tool back in the same place after using it. Not having to look for a tool saves time and reduces frustration.

■ When sawing wood, tile, or other dust-producing material, or when engaging in any activity that produces airborne dust, wear a respirator or high-quality dust mask.
■ Eye protection is a must when sawing or chiseling any material. Choose safety glasses that offer protection on the sides.
■ When working with mastics and other fume-producing chemicals, provide plenty of ventilation. Wear a respirator if necessary.
■ Save your knees—wear knee pads. Make a habit of wearing gloves while working. Gloves

not only protect your hands from abrasions and cuts, they'll give you a better grip on tools and materials.
■ Make sure you have all the materials and tools you need on hand before you start a project. Running to the home center or hardware store in the middle of a project interrupts the work and can increase your frustration.

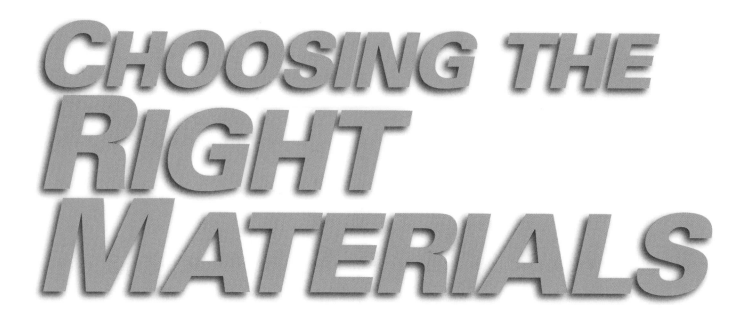

CHOOSING THE RIGHT MATERIALS

Of all the surfaces in a room, floors take the most abuse: a constant parade of feet—some wearing dirty or wet shoes, the occasional sink or tub overflow, misdirected shower sprays, and spilled food and drinks. Fortunately there are plenty of flooring materials that can stand up to abuse and do so with style.

Of all the aspects of a remodeling job, you may find nothing more rewarding than installing your new flooring. Floors almost always set the tone for a room, as either the dominant design feature or a neutral backdrop for the furnishings and the rest of the decor. The right choices also make a room look truly finished.

The materials you choose affect the comfort of a room, so you'll need to pay attention to more than aesthetics when selecting materials. Tailor your choices to your needs, just as you would when selecting finishing materials for any room in your home.

Carpet, for example, is very comfortable underfoot. It makes a great surface for a bedroom. If you have children, a material less prone to staining might be a better choice for the family area or dining room. In the bathroom you'll want a watertight surface. If you spend a lot of time in the kitchen, durability and comfort will also be considerations.

As you plan your flooring, you'll need to think about the subflooring below. If you are certain it is in good shape, you may be able to just lay the new material over it. If however, you are considering making a surface change, from carpet to laminate for example, you may need to shore up the subfloor by either replacing sections of the floor or by pulling up the entire underlayment and replacing it with a product designed to complement your new surfacing selection.

Even if the subfloor is in good shape, ceramic tile and stone call for an extra measure of caution and typically require a layer of backerboard installed between the subfloor and the finish material.

Make your home as beautiful and as easy to care for as possible with flooring materials that match your tastes and lifestyle.

CHAPTER PREVIEW

Gallery of ceramic and porcelain tile
page 8

Gallery of natural stone tile
page 10

Gallery of wood and engineered wood
page 12

Introduce warmth and comfort to every room in your home with attractive and practical flooring.

Gallery of laminate planks and tile
page 14

Gallery of bamboo and cork
page 16

Gallery of resilient flooring
page 18

Gallery of carpeting
page 20

Gallery of painted floor finishes
page 22

Gallery of concrete
page 24

Gallery of transitions
page 26

GALLERY OF CERAMIC AND PORCELAIN TILE

Clay-base ceramic tiles are an ideal choice for kitchens, baths, basements, porches, laundry rooms, and other moisture-prone areas. Floor tiles are extremely durable; water-, stain-, and wear-resistant; and easy to care for. An array of colors, patterns, shapes, and sizes is available. Tiles larger than 12 inches square are currently the most popular choice.

Tile ratings
All tile feels hard, but some types of tile are actually harder than others. The body of a tile, sometimes called the bisque or biscuit, is produced to meet a specific need or use. Although thickness is one gauge of strength, composition of the tile and the temperature and duration of firing also determine its strength. To help you determine whether the tile you are considering is appropriate for a particular location, check the tile's rating, as determined by the Porcelain Enamel Institute. Hardness ratings are as follows:
■ **Group I, Light traffic.** These tiles may be used on residential bathroom floors such as a guest bath where bare or stocking feet are the norm.
■ **Group II, Medium traffic.** These tiles are designed for use in interiors where little abrasion occurs. They are not recommended for kitchens, entries, or stairwells.
■ **Group III, Medium-heavy traffic.** These tiles can be used anywhere inside a home, including kitchens and baths.
■ **Group IV, Heavy traffic.** These tiles are very hard and can be used in homes or in light to medium commercial areas.
■ **Group V, Extra heavy traffic.** These tiles can be used anywhere.

Underlayment
To prevent chipping and cracking, tile must be installed over a firmly supported subflooring. Broken tiles cannot be repaired, but they can be replaced. Tile grout, if left unsealed, can be difficult to clean.

Warm solutions
Tile can feel cold underfoot, but it can be warmed with radiant or hydronic heating coils (see pages 76–81).

Traction and shine
Whatever tile you choose, glossy finishes have a tendency to show finger- and footprints and can be slippery when wet. For better traction choose a honed finish.

Mosaic tiles like these come in sheets (about 4×4 inches or larger), which make laying the small tiles much easier than you might think. You can find mosaics in an array of colors and patterns.

This porcelain tile floor pattern features a tumbled, handcrafted appearance that was inspired by the look of natural travertine stone.

STANLEY PRO TIP: **Choosing the right flooring materials**

Whatever flooring material you choose, it should be serviceable for your lifestyle. Take the following into account before you decide:
■ Cleanability. For easy-care flooring choose vinyl, laminate, or ceramic tile—smooth surfaces that clean up with a sweep and a rag. Other materials will require a bit more upkeep to maintain their good looks.
■ Durability. With the ability to endure an onslaught of abuse from children, pets, and heavy traffic, ceramic and stone tile, laminate, and concrete rank at the top. Although marks will show on hardwood, the surface can be refinished.

■ Longevity. Standing the test of time are stone and ceramic tiles, hardwood, cork, and concrete. Most other flooring materials will eventually need replacing.
■ Moisture resistance. For rooms prone to highly humid conditions, such as kitchens and baths, use materials that are more water-resistant, such as tile, vinyl, and certain types of laminate (check manufacturers' warranties).
■ Allergens. If you're particularly sensitive and concerned about your home's indoor air quality, choose a hard flooring material, such as ceramic tile or hardwood, that contains few crevices or grooves to harbor dust mites and allergens.

Terra-cotta tiles look as though they might have been a part of this kitchen for decades. Stone-look insets and a matching border draw attention to the room's angled configuration.

Larger-dimension tiles are currently the hottest selling stone floors. Combine different shapes to create additional pattern interest.

Style of floor tile

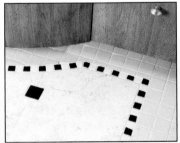

Some ceramic tiles closely mimic the look of stone. Mix and match them to create eyecatching borders and patterns.

Ceramic tiles offer more color options than any other flooring material. Accent borders provide an excellent way to tie together the colors in a room.

Vintage shapes and patterns can connect a room to the past. These new, hexagon-shape tiles were first introduced in the early 1900s.

Slate-look tiles protect the floor in this eating area that connects to a patio dining center.

GALLERY OF NATURAL STONE TILE

Stone tiles are sliced from boulders into a variety of sizes and shapes. Not all stones are suitable for use as a flooring material. Some are practically indestructible. Others may contain soft spots, fissures, and other imperfections that diminish performance. Porous stone tiles may warp from exposure to water or moisture. These may have to be installed with an epoxy adhesive and grout. Colored grout can pose a danger to some stone tiles as it can stain the tiles permanently.

The color and appearance of a single stone tile won't represent the entire batch required to surface a floor—even if all the tiles were cut from the same block of stone.

The finish on stone tiles must be carefully chosen and matched to the anticipated wear. For example a highly polished marble will dull on the floor in a beach house. For that reason you might want to limit highly polished tiles to areas where soft footwear is generally worn, such as in a bedroom. Whatever stone you choose, glossy finishes have a tendency to show finger- and footprints and can be slippery when wet. ≠For better traction, choose a honed finish.

Types of stone
Some stones are naturally hard and nonporous, and therefore maintenance free.

■ Granite is the most durable natural stone—it can withstand heat and moisture, and is impervious to stains. Rare colors and unusual patterns of granite cost significantly more than more commonly occurring grays and beiges.

■ Soapstone starts out as a light gray color and then mellows to a dark charcoal after oiling and aging. Like granite it can withstand heat and moisture and doesn't stain when oiled regularly.

■ Slate is slightly more porous that granite but is also durable.

■ Marble, travertine, and limestone are porous stones, so they must be sealed regularly to reduce staining.

Rough-hewn travertine stone lends a rustic appearance to this kitchen hearth. The honed finish ensures traction underfoot and disguises footprints and spills.

STANLEY PRO TIP: **Warm floors**

Stone and tile floors can feel pretty cold against bare feet, especially in northern climates. With a little forethought you can take the chill out of these floors by installing a radiant or hydronic heating system below your new flooring. (Stay away from underfloor heating if you're installing a solid wood floor; the change in temperature causes too much expansion and contraction and can cause permanent gaps and bulges in the flooring.)

Radiant heating systems typically have a network of electrical heating cables or hot-water-filled tubes installed between the subfloor and finish floor. Most systems can be installed across the entire floor or confined to a specific area such as the space in front of a vanity or tub. Like other heating systems a thermostat that can be turned on or off, up or

down, controls the temperature.

Radiant heating systems are available for purchase from most home centers.

White and tan marble tiles create a subtle floor pattern in this sunroom.

These 16-inch-square limestone tiles bring a soothing look to this bath floor and shower.

Black and white marble tiles laid on the diagonal create contrast in this white kitchen.

Traditional marble tiles give this new bath a timeless look.

GALLERY OF WOOD AND ENGINEERED WOOD

Choosing wood flooring has become a more complicated task than in previous decades. Walk down a wood flooring aisle in a flooring store or home center today and you'll see wood flooring available in solid wood or engineered wood, in strips or planks, or in random widths. You can install it by floating, nailing, or gluing. You can purchase it prefinished or unfinished.

Here's a rundown of the major differences.
■ Solid hardwood flooring lasts longer than many other flooring options and can be refinished five or six times—or even restained to change its appearance.

Today's polyurethane finishes allow installation in kitchens and half baths, as long as you take precautions to minimize water spills. Wood flooring is available in strips, planks, and parquet squares.

Unfinished flooring gives you almost unlimited color stain options. The drawback: Unfinished flooring must be sanded and finished after installation, which puts the room out of service for several days.

Prefinished flooring features a factory-applied finish that remodelers sometimes favor because it eliminates sawdust and finish vapors, and the room can be used within 24 hours of installation. The color options for prefinished flooring are not as varied as for unfinished flooring.
■ Engineered woods are considered more stable for kitchen and bath applications. This type of flooring consists of two or more layers of wood pressed together, similar to plywood. The top layer consists of a hardwood veneer, while the lower layers are typically softwood. Engineered planks are almost always prefinished. Like prefinished hardwood floors the color options are not as varied as for unfinished flooring.

Both solid and engineered woods are available in the following forms:
■ Strip flooring is available in widths of 2¼ inches or less.
■ Plank flooring is available in widths of 3 inches or more.
■ Random width flooring is installed in a pattern featuring three different widths installed in succession. The first row, for example, might be made of boards 8 inches wide, the second row of boards 5 inches wide, and the third row of boards 3 inches wide.

These cherry planks complement the kitchen's color scheme and warm the contemporary decor.

These hardwood planks were finished onsite and match the flooring in adjacent rooms.

These natural maple planks were prefinished, which eliminated a lot of the dust and mess associated with finishing a wood floor onsite.

Natural pine planks lend a casual country look to this bedroom. Because the wood is relatively soft, you'll notice wear faster than with other wood types.

STANLEY PRO TIP: **Wood color, pattern, and species**

A dark wood floor absorbs light and can make a room appear smaller. When paired with a light wall color, dark floors visually anchor the space. A light wood floor, on the other hand, can make a small room appear more spacious.

Parquet provides the warmth of wood with a tile-like pattern. Inlay designs and borders can be used to draw attention to a particular area and help define a large space.

■ Oak is light brown wood with highly visible grain patterns. Red oak has a pinkish tinge. The grain in white oak is less pronounced, and white oak is actually browner than red oak.

■ Maple and birch are both lighter in color than oak with lighter grain lines. These woods are more difficult to finish as they burn easily during sanding.
■ Ash is whiter than oak but similar in appearance. It does not take stain as well as oak.
■ Walnut and cherry are tough but softer than oak. Walnut finishes easily. Like maple and birch, cherry surfaces tend to burn when sanding.
■ Pine and fir are softer woods and dent easily.

Solid hardwood planks can be stained and finished multiple times in a variety of colors and patterns to match any decor.

GALLERY OF LAMINATE PLANKS AND TILE

Slightly less expensive than its wood counterpart, laminate plank flooring looks like traditional wood and can be installed over existing flooring. It is durable and easy to maintain but it can't be sanded and refinished as traditional wood planks can. Some laminate planks have a slight hollow feel underfoot.

Like laminate countertops laminate floors are made of layers: a clear, protective top layer; a second layer that is printed to look like the flooring of your choice (typically oak, pine, cherry, maple, or stone); a third core layer made from a wood product such as plywood; and a fourth layer that creates a stable surface that won't warp. Laminate comes in two shapes—planks and tiles.

Laminate often works in places where wood doesn't—in basements, over concrete, and over many existing floors. It's tough and doesn't dent, and the color is consistent from one board to the next.

Not all laminates are suitable for use in moisture-prone rooms, however, so be sure and check the manufacturer's warranty before purchasing it. Unfortunately, it cannot be refinished if damaged, but individual planks or tiles can be replaced.

Floating floor
Instead of being nailed down, laminate flooring floats above the subfloor. The edges of the planks or tiles either snap together or glue together to form one large piece. It is held down only at the edges by baseboard or shoe molding.

Laminate floors are installed over a foam underlayment which makes the floor quiet and somewhat soft underfoot.

Laminate goes down relatively quickly and is durable enough for active families with children and pets.

This rich, dark laminate captures the look of cherry planks. When laminate is used the color and pattern will remain consistent across the room.

STANLEY PRO TIP

Installation locations

Laminate flooring can be installed above or below grade. It installs quickly and easily and is easy to keep clean. It is ideal for installation over vinyl floors and floors that may contain asbestos, as it can be installed without disturbing the original floor. Glued-together planks are often suitable for bath installations; snap-together planks are usually not. If you are planning to install laminate in the bath, check with the manufacturer to be sure your product is approved for damp areas. Never install laminate over a floor that has a drain or a sump pump.

These laminate tiles resemble limestone but provide more give, so they are more comfortable underfoot.

These laminate tiles mimic the look of slate but feel much softer underfoot than actual stone.

It is difficult to tell these maple-look laminate planks from actual hardwood. The pale color reflects light and complements the cabinetry.

GALLERY OF BAMBOO AND CORK

Technically a grass, not wood, bamboo is nearly as hard as maple or oak and grows much more quickly. Bamboo plants mature in three years, making it an excellent choice for the environmentally conscious. It's available prefinished and as an engineered plank and installs in the same variety of ways as wood floors.

These bamboo planks, stained to match the built-in desk, emulate thin hardwood strips.

Cork
Old-fashioned cork flooring is also making a comeback—it is comfortable underfoot, environmentally friendly, and easy to care for. Because cork is a natural product (it comes from the bark of a cork tree), each tile displays a unique color, pattern, and texture. The cork can also be mixed with dye to create tiles in a variety of colors.

The comfort of cork comes from the millions of tiny air cells in the surface, an attribute that also makes cork an excellent choice when sound deadening is important. It recovers quickly from denting and its air-insulating cells help keep the floor warm in winter and cool in the summer.

Bamboo floors provide the durability of hardwood and look somewhat like narrow hardwood strip flooring. Like hardwood the natural material can be finished in a variety of shades.

Cork flooring sheets warm the floor of this kitchen. A high-gloss finish reflects light. The material is relatively easy to install and extremely comfortable underfoot.

Cork flooring is available in tiles (left) or sheets (above) and in a variety of colors and subtle patterns. It can be stained to match most decors. Like bamboo it makes an excellent choice for the environmentally conscious consumer.

GALLERY OF RESILIENT FLOORING

Resilient vinyl flooring is flexible, water- and stain-resistant, and easy to maintain. Because the flooring is relatively soft, it helps muffle noise and is easy on the feet and legs. Its downfall is that it can dent and sharp knives may cut through the surface. Resilient flooring includes all synthetic, resin-based floor coverings. It includes vinyl tiles and sheet flooring and linoleum. Sheets up to 15 feet wide eliminate seams in many rooms. Most warranties last no longer than 10 years.

Vinyl
Vinyl floor coverings are durable and suitable for any room in the house. You'll find vinyl available as sheets or tiles in two categories:
■ Rotogravure vinyl features a knobby texture as well as pattern and color printed on the finish side only. This knobby texture can be difficult to clean.
■ Inlaid vinyl features pattern and color through the thickness of the material. It's typically much more durable than rotogravure vinyl and will look good and last for many years.
  Sheet vinyl is a popular choice for bathrooms, kitchens, laundry rooms, entryways, hallways, and rec rooms. It comes in many patterns and styles. Vinyl tiles can be used in many of the same applications; however, dirt-collecting seams can make a vinyl tile floor difficult to keep clean. The multiple seams can also allow liquid spills to filter between tiles, loosen them, and damage the subfloor.

Linoleum
Made from organic materials linoleum is known for its bright colors and long wear. Extremely popular in the 1950s, its earth-friendly, nonallergenic nature is making it a popular choice again.

Affordable vinyl tiles come in dozens of colors that inspire custom designs— this black and white checkerboard is a kitchen classic. The material is also available in sheet form.

Vinyl can be laid in a variety of ways to create patterns and borders.

 PRO TIP

Chlorine

Don't buy resilient flooring if the room where you are installing it will encounter foot traffic from a chlorinated swimming pool; chlorine can ruin the flooring.

Brightly colored vinyl tiles enliven this entrance and define the color schemes in the adjoining rooms.

Linoleum tiles bring a nostalgic look to this kitchen floor.

Types of resilient flooring

Stone look-alike vinyl is affordably priced and can be found in home centers and flooring stores.

This hexagon-like pattern mimics the look of stone and disguises dust and footprints.

You can find vinyl that resembles wood in home centers and flooring stores. It feels softer underfoot than wood but is appropriate for use in baths and other moisture-prone areas.

GALLERY OF CARPETING

For warmth and softness underfoot, carpet is your choice. Carpet has two layers—face pile and backing. Because the face pile (or yarn fibers) is subject to all the wear and tear, it's your key consideration. Backing is almost never seen once the carpet is installed, but it plays a role in the overall quality.

Carpet face pile comes in two variations: cut and loop. In cut-pile carpets individual yarns stand up straight from the backing. In loop-pile construction the yarn comes out of the backing, loops over, and returns into the backing. Loop-pile carpets with a level surface are called level loops. If the loop height varies, the carpet is a multilevel loop. Most loop piles will perform better than cut piles in the long term because the loops help evenly distribute the impact of foot traffic.

Cut-and-loop or cut/uncut carpets combine both pile types to add surface texture and often blend multiple yarn colors. Sometimes referred to as "sculptured," these multitexture, multicolor carpets hide footprints and soil well.

If your room is less than 15 feet wide, you can install carpeting without having any seams.

Block-printed carpet squares lend a contemporary look to this gathering area and make the floor appear to be a kid-friendly play area.

This textured multilevel loop carpeting lends a casual look to any room.

Weight and wear

Generally the heavier the carpet, the better it will hold up. However don't select a product based on weight alone. When comparing different varieties consider the carpet's density, pile height, and fiber type. Many carpets come in good, better, and best choices. Although the carpets in each category look very much alike, the difference is usually weight. A retailer might offer a textured saxony in 28, 34, and 40 ounces, for example. If you're budget conscious select the heavier product for high-traffic areas and the lower-weight carpet for less-used rooms.

Humidity

Because carpet absorbs water, stains easily, and promotes mildew growth, it is usually not recommended for bath installations, particularly in areas adjacent to the toilet, tub, or shower.

Fiber

Carpet is typically made from one of four fibers: nylon, olefin, polyester, and wool. Wool is typically the most expensive (although it is not washable), followed by nylon, olefin (also referred to as polypropylene), and polyester, respectively. Nylon and other synthetics are washable.

Printed patterns are available on wall-to-wall carpeting. Many are special order so be sure to allow extra time in your schedule for shipment.

By seaming together two different colors of the same style of carpet, you can create borders and patterns as shown in these stripes.

Installing a carpet runner on wooden steps provides a great transition between a hardwood-clad main floor and a carpeted second floor.

GALLERY OF PAINTED FLOOR FINISHES

Paint is the least expensive flooring option and the easiest to change—whether you tire of it or it starts to look tired. The key to making a painted floor look good for longer than a few months is choosing the right products—primer and paint designed specifically for flooring. Depending on the product you choose, top coating with polyurethane may also be required.

Painting a floor is a relatively easy do-it-yourself project; the majority of time involved is spent masking and draping the surfaces you wish to keep paint-free.

Look for a floor paint finish that is washable, scrubbable, and moisture resistant. If you want to cover a porcelain, plastic, or tile surface, look for an epoxy paint designated for that specific purpose.

SAFETY FIRST
Paint

Many paints and finishes release low levels of toxic emissions into the air for years after application. These toxins, called Volatile Organic Compounds (VOCs), were once essential to the performance of the paint.

Consumer demand and new environmental regulations have led to the development of low-VOC and zero-VOC paints and finishes. These new products, available from most paint manufacturers, are durable and cost-effective, and the reduced emissions benefit everyone including those with allergies and chemical sensitivities. The paints also reduce landfill, groundwater, and ozone-depleting contaminants. The paints have little odor during application and no odor once cured, so painted areas can be occupied sooner.

To determine whether the paint or finish you are purchasing is low-VOC, read the label. The VOC content is listed in grams per liter and can range from 5 to 200. A product with the lowest VOC content yields the lowest health and environmental risk.

Stair treads once covered by worn carpeting take a new look with simple sanding, priming, and painting. Freehand vines and doodads disguise nail holes and other imperfections. Polyurethane protects the design.

Painting the wood planks on this sunroom floor brightens the room. A high-gloss top coat reflects additional light.

Cleaning, priming, and painting plywood subflooring creates a rustic background for this master bedroom floor. The overlay design was done freehand using an artist's brush and thinned latex paint. Slight wobbles in the final outcome add character and the appearance of age. Several coats of polyurethane protect the finish.

These stripes are painted on a concrete floor. You can paint stripes by using painter's tape to define the stripes' borders.

From a distance this painted floor resembles mosaic tiles. A putty-color base coat and sponge-painted squares form the intricate design, created in just a weekend.

GALLERY OF CONCRETE

As styles evolve so does the variety of flooring options. Concrete can stand up to the highway, so it's no wonder that it's becoming a popular hardwearing surfacing material for the home. Easy to clean and versatile, concrete also mimics the look of stone at a lower cost. Although it always has a rough-hewn quality, it can be dyed, scored, and textured to create many interesting looks. Hairline cracks are commonplace and may appear as the material ages.

Before it is fully cured, concrete can be stamped to create any sort of surface texture. Decorative tiles and metals can be inlaid for a custom look. Because concrete is porous it must be sealed for protection against embedded dirt and stains.

Concrete floors and counters bring an industrial look to this kitchen. Scoring the material reduces cracking.

Before it cures concrete can be stamped to create unusual patterns and designs. These starfish patterns add whimsy to the floor of a child's bath.

Concrete floors are easy to maintain. Scored in 3-foot squares, concrete resembles larger stone tiles. The material can feel cold underfoot but warms in sunshine.

This concrete was stained to mimic tan limestone. The material can be stained and stamped to resemble brick, terra-cotta tiles, or most any sleek surface.

GALLERY OF TRANSITIONS

Changing flooring materials within the same room or between rooms with large openings requires some forethought and planning. The materials not only need to look good together, you'll need to choose an edging or transition that makes the change as attractive, comfortable, and level to walk across as possible.

A combination of wood planks, carpet inlays, and area rugs defines the activity areas in this traditional home.

A row of slate tiles separates an entry hall and a formal dining area.

Classic marble tiles used in the master bath transition to warm wood floors in the adjacent bedroom and sitting area.

A tiled bath floor connects to a carpeted bedroom.

Concrete transitions to bamboo in this serene Asian-style bath.

PLANNING YOUR PROJECT

Nothing contributes more to the success of your flooring project than careful planning. Planning helps you produce attractive, professional-looking results, and it organizes the job. A well-drawn, detailed layout plan will help you create a more accurate cost estimate than sketches or generalized notes.

One aspect of a flooring update, however, can't be solved with graph paper and a ruler—the disruption and mess. To minimize the stress anticipate debris disposal. Collect sturdy cartons for hauling out the old flooring. Check with your local municipality to determine the proper way to dispose of the old floor. Order your replacement flooring early and get all the preparation out of the way by the delivery date. If you won't be done by the time the flooring arrives, plan where to store the boxes or rolls.

If you are redoing the kitchen floor, make alternate arrangements for meals for a few days, allowing time for removing the old floor, installing the new, and cure time if required. Coordinate the temporary removal of bathroom fixtures with your family's daily schedule.

Use this list to keep your flooring project organized from start to finish:

■ Measure all the rooms you are reflooring and calculate their areas.
■ Create a scaled drawing that includes each flooring material.
■ Estimate material quantities, including underlayment and other preparation materials such as adhesives, grouts, fasteners, and transitions. Be sure to include any trim pieces.
■ Make a list of the tools you'll need. Purchase or rent them. Plan your work so you can return rented tools within 24-hour increments to minimize costs. Nothing stalls a project—or your enthusiasm—more than running back and forth to the hardware store or rental center.
■ When shopping for flooring visit several suppliers to get the best deal, then estimate your total costs.

Careful planning is the key to every successful flooring installation.

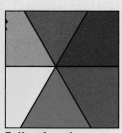

These durable slate-look ceramic tiles make an excellent choice for a front foyer. The tiles disguise footprints and make an attractive transition to the carpet in adjoining rooms.

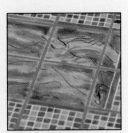

Understanding scale and pattern
page 38

Understanding texture
page 40

Basic tools
page 42

Safety first
page 46

MAKING A DIMENSIONAL LAYOUT DRAWING

A dimensional layout drawing puts on paper all the details of the surfaces you'll be reflooring. It shows the layout of the material—such as tiles or planks. The drawing allows you to plan precisely, assists a supplier in helping you make estimates, and will lead you to answers to other questions about your project. The making of a drawing is a straightforward procedure. The process begins with a rough sketch on which you post the measurements of the room. Then you make a scale drawing based on the sketch and measurements. In the final stage you use tracing paper to draw in the flooring pattern or to experiment with options.

PRESTART CHECKLIST

☐ **TIME**
About an hour to sketch and measure a basic 12×12 room. Time for making a dimensional layout plan will vary with the complexity of the design and the number of alternative layouts drawn.

☐ **TOOLS**
Sharp pencils, measuring tape, ruler, architect's scale, plastic drawing square

☐ **SKILLS**
Measuring and sketching accurately

☐ **PREP**
Selection of flooring materials

☐ **MATERIALS**
Large sheets of graph paper and tracing paper, masking or drafting tape

Before you measure the room, make a rough sketch of its contours. Start in a corner and measure to the nearest ⅛ inch the length of every surface where it changes direction. Post the measurements on the sketch as you go. Note the dimensions of appliance recesses, cabinets, and built-in furnishings.

TYPICAL DIMENSIONAL DRAWING

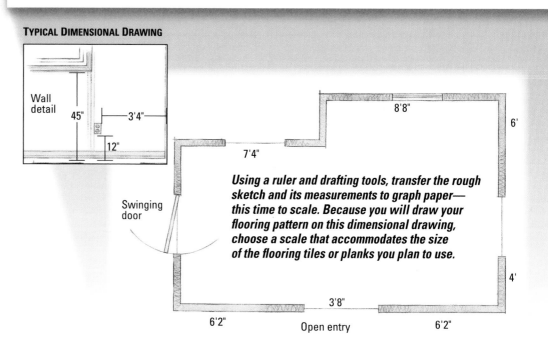

Using a ruler and drafting tools, transfer the rough sketch and its measurements to graph paper— this time to scale. Because you will draw your flooring pattern on this dimensional drawing, choose a scale that accommodates the size of the flooring tiles or planks you plan to use.

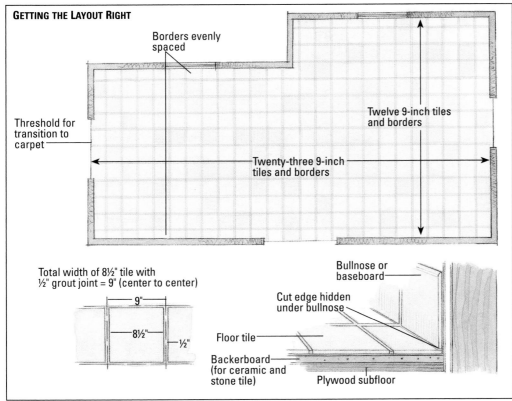

GETTING THE LAYOUT RIGHT

Borders evenly spaced

Threshold for transition to carpet

Twelve 9-inch tiles and borders

Twenty-three 9-inch tiles and borders

Total width of 8½" tile with ½" grout joint = 9" (center to center)

9"

8½"

½"

Bullnose or baseboard

Cut edge hidden under bullnose

Floor tile

Backerboard (for ceramic and stone tile)

Plywood subfloor

Tape your dimensional drawing securely to your work surface, then tape a piece of tracing paper over it. Carefully draw your flooring layout on the tracing paper. Experiment with various designs, using new sheets of tracing paper until you arrive at the layout that looks best in the room. Whenever possible hide the edges of cut tiles or planks under toe-kicks, along an inconspicuous wall, or under a countertop backsplash. Doorways should start with a full tile or plank. If not revise the layout.

revise the layout.

REVISE THE LAYOUT
Uneven borders and rows

If your first layout results in unevenly spaced borders and end rows, consider revising your layout. Remove the partial pieces and the full flooring tiles on each axis. Redraw the layout with the remaining section of full tiles centered in the room. This will leave enough space for wider tiles at the borders. Measure to the edge and divide by 2. In this example seventeen 2-inch border tiles and fifteen 12-inch full tiles were removed, leaving a space of 14 inches ÷ 2 = 7 inches, or more than a half-tile at each border.

This method also allows you to make more accurate material estimates. If you count the tiles in the first layout, you'll find there are 55 full tiles and 17 cut tiles. Counting the tiles in the final layout results in an estimate of 40 full and 32 cut tiles.

Preliminary layout with uneven borders

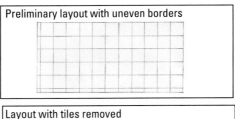

Layout with tiles removed

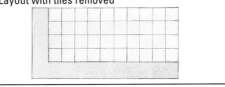

Final layout with borders

Laying out irregular shape tiles

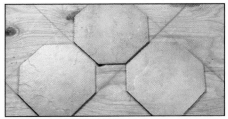

Almost all irregularly shaped tiles have a reference point you can use to anchor your dimensional layout. Use a ruler to lightly draw in layout lines and space them to conform to the tile-grout dimension. Cut a thin cardboard template scaled to the overall configuration of a square of the tile and use the template to draw trial layouts.

Most irregular tiles are sold by the square foot. To make material estimates divide the total area by the coverage per carton.

MAKING A DIMENSIONAL FLOOR PLAN

One of the most common problems in planning a floor installation is out-of-square walls. Walls seldom define a room squarely, but you can make paper-and-pencil adjustments much more easily than you can rebuild a wall.

To determine if the area is square, use the 3-4-5 triangle method (illustrated below). Snap a chalkline on the floor or tack a mason's line at the midpoints of each pair of opposite walls. From the intersection measure out on one line a distance of 3 feet. Tape the line at that point and measure and tape a distance of 4 feet on the other line. Now measure the distance between the tapes. If it's 5 feet exactly, the floor is square. Adjust the lines, if necessary, until they are perpendicular. Now measure from the lines to the out-of-square walls at each end and post this measurement on your drawing.

Wavy walls may also affect your drawing. Check them with a 4-foot level and represent the condition on your drawing as accurately as possible.

Check the floor to determine if it is level and flat. If the floor is not level, it won't affect the final look unless you are also tiling a wall. But floors must be reasonably flat (within ⅛ inch in 10 feet) to keep the tile from cracking. For more on leveling floors, see pages 53 and 57.

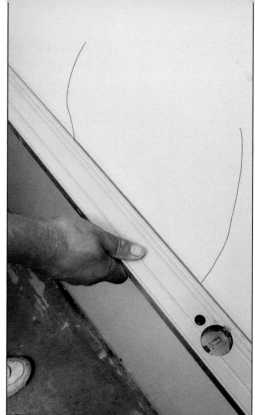

Wavy walls will affect the contour of the edge tiles on floors. Use a 4-foot level to check the lower surface of the wall near the floor. It's possible to remedy minor variations in the surface in many ways.

CHECKING FOR SQUARE WITH 3-4-5 TRIANGLE METHOD

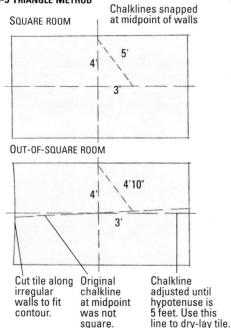

SQUARE ROOM

Chalklines snapped at midpoint of walls

5'
4'
3'

OUT-OF-SQUARE ROOM

4'10"
4'
3'

Cut tile along irregular walls to fit contour.

Original chalkline at midpoint was not square.

Chalkline adjusted until hypotenuse is 5 feet. Use this line to dry-lay tile.

WHAT IF...
The floor is not square?

An out-of-square floor surface will require tapered tiles on at least one edge. Place the tiles on your layout plan to make the tapered tiles less noticeable. Modify the grout width, hide cut edges under toe-kicks, or arrange your layout so the tapered edges fall behind furniture (left). Try a diagonal layout (right) or a larger, irregular tile to hide the tapered edges. In extreme cases you can shim out the wall and rebuild it.

Laying out different configurations

RECTANGULAR ROOM

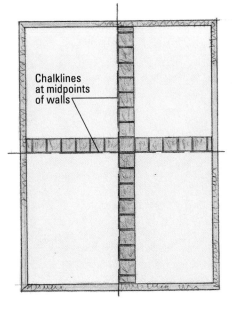

Chalklines at midpoints of walls

L-SHAPE ROOM

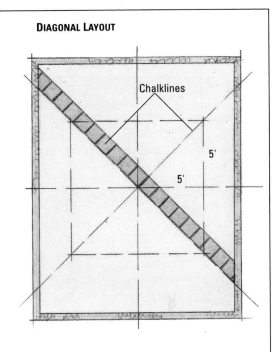

Chalklines

Doorway

DIAGONAL LAYOUT

Chalklines

5'

5'

In a rectangular or square room, pencil in reference lines at the midpoints of the walls and draw in tiles on both axes. If you have the tiles, lay them out on the floor to make your drawing more accurate. Adjust the placement of the lines so the pattern ends in even borders if possible.

When laying out an L-shape room, position the lines so they carry from one room to the other. Adjust them so the layout results in even borders if necessary.

To establish lines for a diagonal layout, first pencil in lines at the midpoints of the room. Then on each axis mark an equal distance from the intersection. Extend these points until the extensions intersect. Draw diagonal lines from the intersections through the midpoint.

Hide or fix the problem

Wavy walls can result in edge tiles with uneven cuts. If the problem is not severe, the cuts may not be noticeable.

When drawing a layout plan, try the following solutions. Minor variations in a wall surface may actually "disappear" if hidden under a baseboard.

More severe depressions in a wall can be leveled with a skim coat of thinset prior to tiling the floor (page 60). Feather the edges of the skim coat to blend in with the level surface. Skim-coating, however, requires proper preparation of the wall so the mortar will stick (pages 60–61). You will also have to tile the wall, paint it, or cover it with another material.

STANLEY PRO TIP
Plan full tiles in doorways

When you are preparing a dimensional layout plan, draw the tiles in so a full tile will fall with its edge in the center of a doorway. If you can't set a full tile in the doorway because your plan already incorporates wide border tiles, you may be able to minimize the effect of a cut tile with a threshold in the doorway (page 111 or 169).

If the tile continues into an adjoining room, center a tile at the doorway, if possible, so an even portion falls in each room.

WHAT IF...
The floor is not level?

Tapered, cut tiles

An out-of-level floor creates tapered wall tiles at the floor. A diagonal wall layout may hide a minor condition. For severe problems install a wallcovering other than tile or level the floor.

FLOORING AND INTERIOR DESIGN

Once your layout drawings are complete you'll need to make color, pattern, and textural decisions.

Designers often refer to the floor as the "fifth wall" because it plays a major role in the overall look of a room. A dark color floor, for example, can anchor a large room and make it feel smaller and cozier. A light floor, on the other hand, reflects more light to make a small room feel more spacious. Because of this the choice of floor color is an important design decision. You can always paint the walls a different color, but you'll likely live with your flooring choice for years to come.

In this room a pale neutral carpet provides cool contrast against the deep terra-cotta color walls.

A beige carpet runner lightens the look of the dark cherry treads.

A dark wood floor balances the sunny yellow and blue color scheme used in this living area. The cherry-stained wood makes the large room feel cozier.

Creamy white tile floors complement the white cabinets. Sage green walls add appealing color.

Dark gray slate floors contrast with the white walls and cathedral ceiling of this family room. The combination of cool colors creates a soothing and serene ambience.

This Brazilian cherry floor brings warmth to a bright white dining room furnished with black painted chairs and a matching table.

Pale color carpet tiles combine with white walls to make this gathering area feel spacious and airy.

FAIL-SAFE COLOR COMBINATIONS

Used in an appropriate manner, color is the glue that holds your home's decorating scheme together. Whether you prefer warm, vibrant colors; cool, serene colors; or a combination of the two, there is a color scheme that will work for you.

One of the easiest ways to decide on a color scheme is to flip through the pages of books and magazines geared toward interior design. Flag the spaces featuring the colors that appeal to you. Look at them again in a few days and again at the end of the week. Are you drawn to the same locations each time? If so these are the colors you are most likely able to live with.

Not sure what combination of colors you like the best? Use a favorite piece of pottery, an oil painting, a framed print, or a colorful area rug as your inspiration. If the colors look great together in the art piece, they will look great together on the walls and floor of your home.

If you prefer using a more scientific approach to selecting colors, the color wheel offers several ways to find an attractive palette. Many interior design schemes are based on the groupings of primary, secondary, analogous, complementary, and monochromatic color combinations.

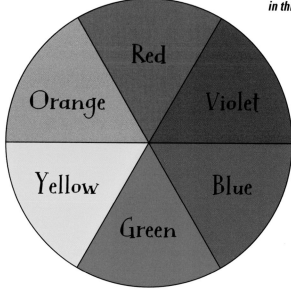

SECONDARY COLOR SCHEME

The secondary colors are orange, green, and violet. Green comes from an equal combination of blue and yellow, orange from equal amounts of yellow and red, and violet from equal amounts of red and blue. Like primary colors, secondary colors work well together. If you can't envision your room filled with bold orange and green, pair up shades of the colors, such as the peach and olive used in this kitchen.

ANALOGOUS COLOR SCHEME

Analogous colors are colors that appear nearest to one another on the color wheel. For example blue-green, green, and green-yellow are analogous colors. Because these adjacent colors share a component color, they always look good with each other. The analogous colors of green-yellow, yellow, and yellow-orange create a lively, upbeat ambience in this room.

PRIMARY COLOR SCHEME

If you love vibrant hues, consider using a classic primary color scheme—red, yellow, and blue. Each is a pure color that can't be created by mixing other hues. Choose your favorite of the three and balance it with wood tones and neutral accents, or as shown in this bedroom, pair any two of these colors together. For an even stronger color statement, combine all three; they work well with any decorating style.

COMPLEMENTARY COLOR SCHEME

Opposites on the color wheel—red and green, orange and blue, and violet and yellow—are complementary colors. When these colors are used together, they make each other appear brighter and more intense. In this kitchen the colors are similarly grayed for a rich appearance.

MONOCHROMATIC COLOR SCHEME

A color scheme using a single color in varying intensities is called a monochromatic color scheme. These one-color schemes are most interesting when combined with a variety of textures and patterns, such as with this textured carpet, suede chairs, and cotton draperies.

BLACK AND WHITE COLOR SCHEME

In this fail-proof color scheme, you won't find any of the colors on the color wheel—only black and white. The concept is total contrast and the look is always dramatic— the more black, the more drama.

Flooring color and longevity

If you tire of color easily, choose a neutral color for the flooring and reserve the brighter colors for painted surfaces and accent pieces that you can easily change.

UNDERSTANDING SCALE AND PATTERN

How spacious a room feels is as important as its actual dimensions. As discussed on page 34, you can make a small room appear larger by choosing pale colors that reflect light and a large room feel smaller by choosing dark colors that absorb light. Similarly smaller rooms appear larger and larger rooms feel more intimate when you alter the scale of the elements in the room. The flooring materials you select play a significant role in the perception of the scale. For example small, subtle patterns, such as 4-inch-square tiles in a pale cream shade, make a room appear more spacious than large, bold patterns, such as a 16-inch-square black-and-white checkerboard tile.

Strip flooring laid parallel to the longest wall moves the eye forward, while parquet squares and perpendicular planks retain the focus within the space. Irregular shapes in an otherwise symmetrical flooring installation have a tendency to stop the eye and draw attention to themselves. A border installed around wall-to-wall carpet, on the other hand, creates a sense of motion and space.

Using the same flooring throughout your home achieves a more spacious appearance because the eye perceives each space as connected and more expansive. If it is impractical to use the same flooring throughout, you can achieve a similar effect by choosing materials in the same color.

Similarly shiny surfaces reflect more light and lend a more spacious feel than honed surfaces, which absorb more light.

Large-scale ceramic tiles are a few shades lighter than the cabinet finish, reinforcing the sleek, clean look. The busy pattern of the granite counter remains understated because of its tone-on-tone coloration.

Wide plank floors complement the scale of this commodious kitchen and create a design base for the soaring ceiling.

Lightly finished maple flooring offers a neutral base and a subtle floor pattern for this traditional living room and allows the area to appear even more spacious. A subtly patterned rug defines the conversation area.

Making pattern work

Because pattern is a powerful design tool, it can be intimidating. Use these simple guidelines for choosing and mixing patterns to remove the guesswork:

■ Pattern has weight. To keep a room in balance, distribute pattern evenly around a room. The exception? You can place all the pattern in one part of the room to draw attention to the area, such as a seating area, as long as that cluster of pattern is balanced by weighty furnishings or architectural features across the room.

■ Pattern provides harmony. For a pleasing appearance select patterns within the same color family. The patterns don't all have to be the same color, but there should be a thread of continuity.

■ Keep scale in mind. Small prints work well in small spaces. Large patterns complement the scale of a large room.

Colorful tiles in a bold pattern lend drama to this master bath. The deep tones absorb light and make the large room feel more intimate.

Staining existing wood planks two different tones creates a subtle diamond pattern and emphasizes the floor as the focal point of the room. Small-scale monochromatic patterns on the furnishings prevent the patterns from clashing.

A small checkerboard pattern of sand and black marble tiles grounds the white bath and complements the period styling.

UNDERSTANDING TEXTURE

Texture is one of the most subtle design tools. Though not as dramatic as bold color or lively pattern, its presence adds a visual and tactile element to your flooring design. How your flooring looks and feels is paramount to a successful installation. The key to successfully using texture is in diversity. Think of pairing opposites: hard and soft, nubby and smooth, rough and slick, fuzzy and silky, coarse and fine. Mix things by topping your smooth wood floor with a nubby textured rug. Contrast a honed brick floor with a sleek stone countertop.

Wall-to-wall carpeting, a vintage rug, and soft flowing fabrics lend a romantic look to this bedroom suite.

Smooth limestone floors combine with earthtone tile wainscoting and handcrafted rice wallpaper to wrap this bath in luxurious texture.

Texture and mood

The use of texture impacts the ambience of a room. Grouping soft, fine textures casts a romantic, luxurious feel. Rugged, hard textures, on the other hand, achieve a down-to-business attitude. When planning your mix consider the mood you want to create and rely on textures that will impart that attitude for your flooring, countertops, and furnishings.

Stone tile floors laid irregularly contrast with the carved chairs and the sleek, arched French doors dressed in classic silk.

BASIC TOOLS

You probably already have some basic carpentry tools around the house. To handle the demands of your flooring installation, make sure the tools you have are good quality and in good condition. The tools shown provide a useful starter kit for any avid do-it-yourselfer.

Use a **carpenter's level** to see if your floors are level. A **torpedo level** works for short sections. A **16-ounce framing hammer** is essential—heavy enough to drive framing and other large nails, yet light enough for trimwork. Add a **22-ounce hammer** for heavy work. A **tape measure** provides a compact ruler for all measuring tasks. A 25-foot model is standard.

The installation of many types of flooring requires a number of tools and supplies. To protect your investment store tools in toolboxes when not in use. Keep like tools together in individual carriers so they are easier to find when you need them.

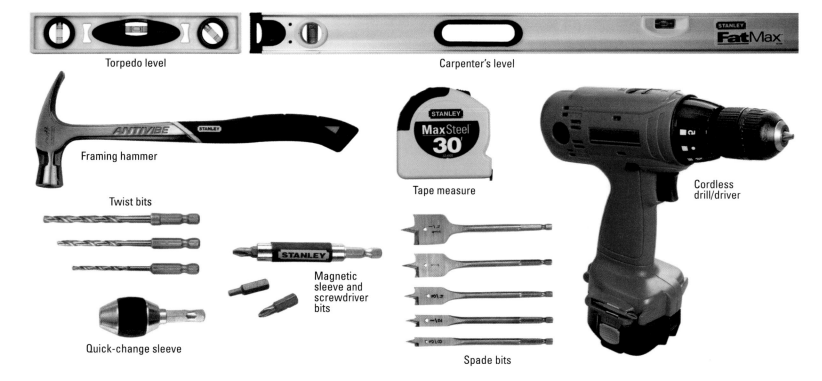

Torpedo level

Carpenter's level

Framing hammer

Tape measure

Cordless drill/driver

Twist bits

Magnetic sleeve and screwdriver bits

Quick-change sleeve

Spade bits

Use a ⅜-inch **variable speed electric drill** to bore holes. For installing screws buy a **magnetic sleeve** and several **screwdriver bits**. A **cordless 18-volt drill** is portable and keeps the workplace free of extension cords. Buy several **spade bits** for drilling holes. When you need the extra reach, attach spade bits to a **bit extender**. A **quick-change sleeve** speeds switching **twist bits** for smaller holes. Make finder holes with a **long bit**. For cutting holes larger than 1 inch, buy a **hole saw**. Renting or buying a **hammer drill** will speed tough-to-bore holes in concrete.

A **stand-up flashlight** will illuminate cramped, dark quarters. You'll find a **nail set** handy for finishing nails below the surface of moldings and extending your reach into hard-to-hammer places.

A **chalkline** marks long, straight lines. A **stud finder** finds studs in the walls. Get one that locates the stud by sensing its density, not the presence of nails.

For cutting miters in trim, you'll need either a **miter box** and backsaw or a power **mitersaw** equipped with a fine-cutting blade. A **coping saw** is indispensable for cutting moldings at inside corners. A pair of heavy-duty **metal snips** comes in handy for a variety of cutting tasks, including the installation of metal studs.

Bit extender

Long bit

Hammer drill

Electric drill

Stand-up flashlight

Nail set

Hole saw

Chalkline

Coping saw

Miter box and backsaw

Metal snips

Stud finder

BASIC TOOLS _continued_

Demolition tools

To cut away a small section of concrete, a **small sledgehammer** and **cold chisel** may be all you need. To chisel out a large area, rent an **electric jackhammer** and **jackhammer chisel**. For cutting through subflooring or framing, a **reciprocating saw** is indispensable. Its long blades reach in to cut awkward spots and can even slice through nails and screws. Several types of blades are available, including metal-cutting blades. Buy several; they often break.

For pulling nails nothing beats a **cat's paw**. A **12-pound sledgehammer** is useful for demolition and for nudging wayward walls into position. A **flat pry bar** will enable you to disassemble most nailed-together framing members. Occasionally you may need a longer **ripping bar** for heavy-duty work.

DEMOLITION TOOLS

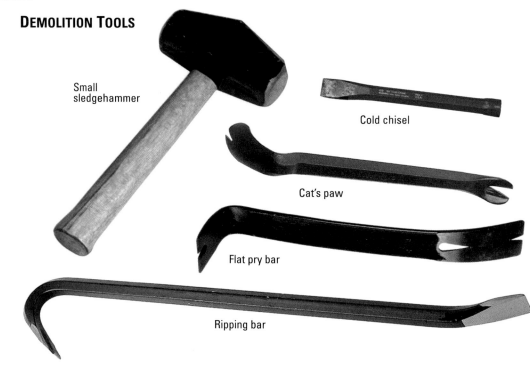

Small sledgehammer

Cold chisel

Cat's paw

Flat pry bar

Ripping bar

12-pound sledgehammer

Reciprocating saw

Jackhammer chisel

Electric jackhammer

A **combination square** allows you to mark boards for crosscutting. A **layout square** does many of the same tasks and can serve as a guide when crosscutting with a circular saw or jigsaw. Use a **framing square** for larger layouts. A **T-bevel** transfers angles from one place to another.

If you need to cut away a small portion of drywall or plaster, a **drywall saw** is adequate. A full-size **hacksaw** is useful for cutting and removing rusted fittings and old sections of pipe (a possibility if you'll be removing appliances or fixtures). Have a **close-work hacksaw** for working in tight areas. Most use full-size hacksaw blades as well as shorter metal-cutting blades.

A **utility knife** does everything from sharpening pencils to cutting carpet.

Keep plenty of blades on hand and change them often so you always have a sharp edge.

Use a **circular saw** for cutting framing lumber and, with a metal-cutting blade, for cutting metal pipes. For quick work a **toolbox handsaw** packs a lot of cutting capability into a compact size. For cutting subflooring and wood flooring planks, use a **jigsaw**.

T-bevel

Combination square

Jigsaw

Layout square

Framing square

Toolbox handsaw

Close-work hacksaw

Drywall saw

Circular saw

Utility knife

Hacksaw

SAFETY FIRST

Safety equipment is essential. You need to protect yourself from dust, debris, and excessive noise. Wear goggles or safety glasses, a dust mask or respirator, and earplugs or sound-deadening muffs. Wear work gloves to protect your hands from abrasions and splinters—but don't wear them when operating power tools. Leather work boots protect your feet better than tennis shoes.

Use common sense: Don't work when you are tired or distracted. Make sure the area where you will be working is well lit and don't attempt to accomplish tasks by yourself that require a partner. Tuck in loose-fitting clothing and tie back long hair. Remove rings and other jewelry and choose clothing free of ties or flaps that could get caught up in a power tool. Don't use corded power tools in wet or damp locations.

Always use sharp tools and always cut away from your body, never toward it. Clamp the pieces you plan to cut to a solid support. Never saw anything by supporting it with only your hand or leg.

When operating a tablesaw avoid cutting short pieces. Beware of kickback—this occurs when a blade tooth catches a cutoff piece trapped between the saw fence and the blade and hurls it back toward you at high speed.

When cutting curves with a saber saw or tiles with a tile saw, don't wrap your fingers underneath the workpiece in line of the cut.

Make sure the adjustment on power tools is secured in the proper position before plugging them in. Give locking knobs a final check before turning on the tool.

Keep the work area neat and swept clean. Don't leave tools on the floor—put them away when they are not in use.

Protect your hands from splinters by wearing work gloves. Protect your knees from unnecessary strain by wearing knee pads.

Preparing a subfloor may require a variety of do-it-yourself skills, from driving in screws with a special drill bit to sanding bits of concrete from a basement or garage floor.

Skills and safety

Before tackling a major flooring project, evaluate your do-it-yourself skills. If you are organized, comfortable following instructions, willing to learn, and handy with tools, you can successfully complete the projects in this book.

Note that many of the flooring projects outlined in this book are labor intensive. Materials can be heavy and cumbersome to move. If your project requires demolition and surface preparation, be prepared to get dirty and, once you're finished, do some major room cleanup. If you have any reservations about your ability to complete the project, hire a professional to do the work.

Cutting tile

A wet-saw tile cutter can discharge chips and larger pieces of tile at high speed, so eye protection is a must. Wear ear protection to guard against damage from the noise of the saw.

Cutting wood and laminate

Whether you are using a saber saw, chop saw, tablesaw, mitersaw, or circular saw, the newly sawn edges of wood and laminate will be razor sharp, so be careful handling the cut pieces.

PREPARING THE ROOM

Getting ready to lay new flooring could include some demolition. If you are planning to combine two rooms into one, for example, you'll need to remove a stud wall or two and tear up old flooring before laying the new continuous flooring. Demolition is hard, messy work, but it can be rewarding. It moves along quickly, progress is instantly visible, and knocking things apart can be satisfying.

Demolition with forethought

Before you start tearing things up, decide whether you want to salvage any building materials. Wood moldings, for example, can be difficult to match. But even if they are readily available, you can save money by reusing the old ones. You can also reuse framing lumber after you remove the nails. After deciding what to salvage, your primary objective will be to contain dust and debris.

Dust control

Some easy methods will help you isolate the worksite from the rest of the house.

■ If you are tearing out a wall or doing other dirty work in a room where you want to save the flooring (such as wood flooring that you want to try to match for the new adjoining space), protect it with reinforced plastic tarps. Tape the tarp to the floor to keep it in place. Set a small rug (a carpet sample works well) just outside the door of the work area to remove debris from your shoes. Slip into a pair of slippers and leave your work shoes behind at the end of the day.

■ Lay tarps on floors of adjoining rooms where you don't plan to work to protect existing flooring that you plan to keep.

■ Tape plastic over doorways you won't use or tack up an old bedsheet as a curtain for doorways you will go through.

■ If the demolition room has a window, open it and set a box fan in the opening to blow out airborne dust.

■ Keep dust from spreading into other rooms by taping cardboard over heat and return-air ducts. Remove the vent covers, wrap them with plastic, and reinstall when the job is complete.

Cleanup

If the work area is small, bag debris and put it out with the trash. Construction debris is heavy; don't overfill containers. Use heavyweight or doubled bags. Rent a roll-off waste container for debris if your project is especially large.

A shop vacuum makes quick work of construction dust, but most standard filters can't deal with the fine dust generated by demolition. To trap these fine particles, use bags made to fit over the regular filters. You might be able to retrofit your vacuum with an aftermarket filter.

In some places you can donate salvaged building materials to groups that recycle them.

CHAPTER PREVIEW

Removing old surfaces and framing
page 50

Preparing a slab floor
page 52

Framing sleeper floors
page 54

Preparing for tiled floors
page 56

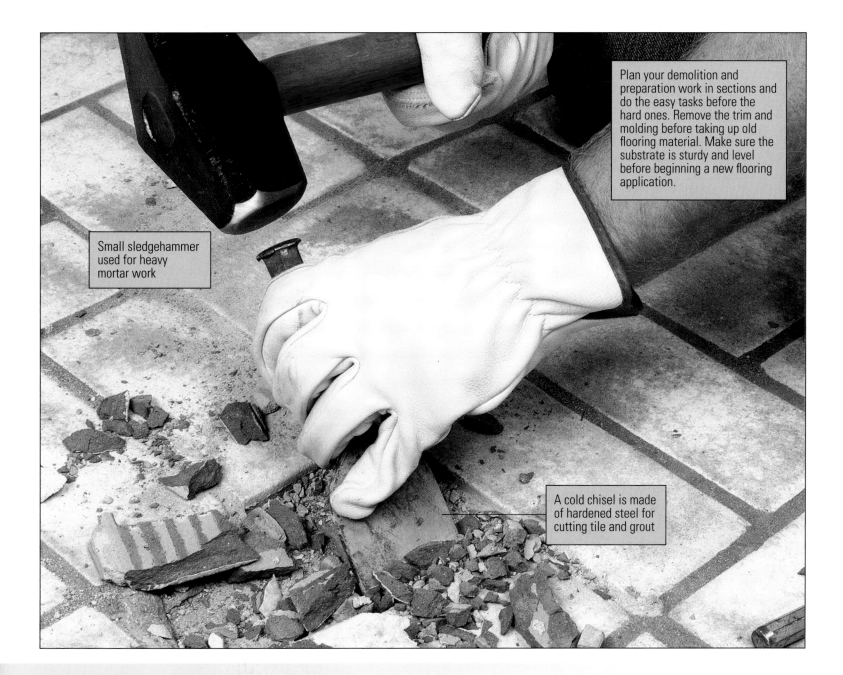

Plan your demolition and preparation work in sections and do the easy tasks before the hard ones. Remove the trim and molding before taking up old flooring material. Make sure the substrate is sturdy and level before beginning a new flooring application.

Small sledgehammer used for heavy mortar work

A cold chisel is made of hardened steel for cutting tile and grout

Installing cement backerboard
page 58

Installing new underlayment
page 63

Removing molding and baseboards
page 64

Removing appliances
page 66

Removing fixtures
page 68

Preparing a wood subfloor
page 74

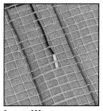
Installing electric radiant heat
page 76

REMOVING OLD SURFACES AND FRAMING

Taking off baseboards is the first step in demolition. Slide a wide putty knife under the trim and jiggle until you can insert a flat pry bar behind the wood. Move along the trim with the pry bar, keeping the putty knife behind it for added leverage.

Before you remove old drywall, make sure you won't damage utility lines. Tap the wall with a screwdriver handle to find a spot that sounds hollow. That's the place to make your first hole with the hammer.

Use a heavy-duty paint scraper or chisel to remove construction-adhesive residue. Soften stubborn spots with construction-adhesive remover.

When taking out old framing, you can beat the studs with a sledgehammer. But cut the nails if you plan to reuse the lumber. After removing the studs pry off the top and bottom plates.

PRESTART CHECKLIST

☐ **TIME**
Trim and molding: About 10 minutes per lineal foot
Drywall: 1–2 hours, 4×8 sheet
Framing: 5–15 minutes per framing member
Flooring: 30–45 minutes per square yard

☐ **TOOLS**
Hammer, pry bar, utility knife, groove joint pliers, cordless drill, reciprocating saw, floor scraper, small sledgehammer, cold chisel, putty knife heat gun, spray adhesive remover

☐ **SKILLS**
Prying, pulling nails, removing screws, cutting, scraping

☐ **PREP**
Isolate worksite to contain the mess; determine utilities contained within the wall

Remove sheet flooring

Insert a floor scraper or wide putty knife under the sheet at a corner and pry it up. Work down each strip of the material, rolling the strip as you go. Use a hair dryer to soften the adhesive. Spray adhesive remover, let it work, and scrape the residue from the floor.

Remove ceramic tile

Crack one tile with a small sledgehammer and cold chisel to make a starting point in the middle of the floor. Break out the remaining area and chip out the grout along the edge of an adjacent tile. Tap a wide chisel under the edge of the tiles and pop them off the floor.

Remove drywall

1 Use a hammer to punch a hole in the drywall between the studs. (If the surface is tiled, it may help to first shatter one or two tiles in the center of the wall.) Enlarge the hole until you can put your hand or the end of a pry bar into it.

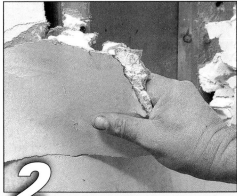

2 Grab an edge of the hole you made and pull off the drywall. To remove large sections space your hands as far apart as possible. Use a pry bar if necessary. Pull the remaining nails. Check for rot and mold.

Remove resilient tile

Warm the adhesive with a heat gun. If you don't have a heat gun, use a hair dryer set on high heat. Warm a corner first, insert a floor scraper or wide putty knife, and with the heat on lift up the tile. Scrape the adhesive from the floor with a floor scraper.

Remove carpet

Grab a corner of the carpet with groove-joint pliers and pull it off the tack strips. Pull it off the entire floor. Cut the pad into strips with a utility knife and pull the strips from the floor. Work a pry bar under the tacking strips and pry loose.

Remove wood framing

1 With a reciprocating saw cut through the nails between the bottom of the stud and the plate. Use a metal-cutting blade.

2 Knock the bottom of the stud sideways with a hammer to free the bottom. With the bottom loose, twist and lever the stud free of the nails that hold it to the top plate. Remove the nails as you go.

PREPARING A SLAB FLOOR

No matter what kind of finished flooring you plan to install, the substrate must be properly prepared. In the case of a concrete slab, it should be solid, smooth, and level. Inspect its condition before you build new framing (if needed) and install any flooring materials. First look for large cracks and sagging sections. If they're present the base is not adequate. You'll need to remove sagging sections and pour new concrete.

Cover isolated, inactive cracks with an isolation membrane. Completely cover new concrete and any other floors you suspect might develop cracks. Fix active cracks—those that are growing longer or wider—instead of covering them up. Active cracks can indicate serious structural problems and can pull the floor apart.

PRESTART CHECKLIST

☐ **TOOLS**
Repair surface:
4-foot level, sledgehammer, cold chisel, carpenter's pencil, margin and mason's trowels, grinder, masonry-grit abrasive wheel, vacuum, brush, mop
Repair structural defect:
sledgehammer, crowbar, wheelbarrow
Install membrane: roller, mason's trowel

☐ **SKILLS**
Using a level, troweling, grinding with a power grinder

☐ **PREP**
Remove finished flooring

☐ **MATERIALS**
Repair surface: hydraulic cement or thinset, muriatic acid, rubber gloves
Repair structural defect: gravel, reinforcing wire, concrete mix, 2×4 screed
Install membrane: membrane, adhesive

1 Divide the slab into imaginary 6-foot sections and check each section with a 4-foot level. Mark cracks, high spots, and other defects with a carpenter's pencil. Cracks may be a sign of a structural defect that will require a professional to correct. Others may be D-I-Y repairable.

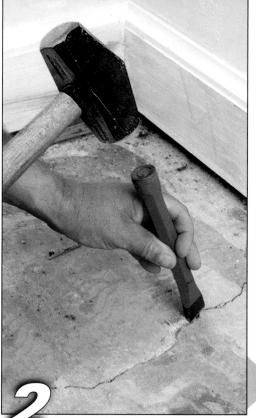

2 Use a small sledgehammer and a cold chisel to open small cracks so you can fill them. If possible angle the chisel into each side of the crack to create a recess wider at the bottom of the crack than on the top. This will help hold the patching cement securely.

Apply an isolation membrane (slip sheet) over cracks

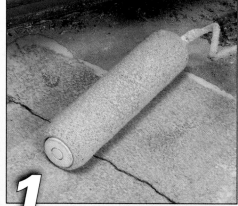

1 Apply the membrane adhesive equally on both sides of a crack or expansion joint. Use a roller to apply the adhesive and spread on a light but even coat.

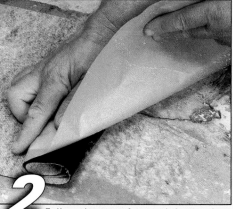

2 Follow the manufacturer's instructions to apply the membrane to cured or wet adhesive. Apply the membrane over the adhesive, following the contour of the crack across the surface.

3 Wash out the crack with water and fill it with quick-setting hydraulic cement or thinset. Use a margin trowel or mason's trowel and feather out the edges until the patch is level with the surrounding surface.

4 To fill depressions in the slab, pour a small amount of thinset or self-leveling compound into the depression and trowel level. Add thinset or compound until the surface is level and feather the edges of thinset even with the floor.

5 Grind down high spots using a grinder equipped with a masonry-grit abrasive wheel. A right-angle grinder makes this job go quickly. Hold a vacuum hose near the grinder to remove the dust as you work. Vacuum and damp-mop the surface thoroughly.

Repairing structural defects

Large holes, cracks with uneven surfaces, and sunken areas are signs of structural defects in a slab. Repair these defects before installing new flooring materials.

For most repairs you'll have to break the concrete into manageable pieces and remove it. The remaining hole must be excavated an additional 4 inches and filled with a 4-inch gravel layer. New concrete calls for reinforcing wire and screeding (leveling) with a long 2×4. Let the patch cure for three to seven days.

Fixing structural defects in a slab is a formidable job. Consult with a specialist before tackling it. Contracting the work is often more cost effective.

SELF-LEVELING COMPOUNDS

Self-leveling compounds, technically not a substrate, are used to level depressions in slabs and subfloors. Most call for only light mixing with water and level themselves when poured. Quick-setting brands allow tiling within hours.

Self-leveling compounds work best when applied in thicknesses of less than 1 inch. If using a compound to fill a deeper depression, make more than one pour, following the manufacturer's directions.

Pour the compound after completing the repair work. This sequence ensures the compound stays clean and ready for tiling.

Commercially applied gypsum-based compounds are excellent for leveling floors on which surface radiant heating systems have been installed.

FRAMING SLEEPER FLOORS

You can install laminate, engineered wood, resilient flooring, and many other finished flooring materials directly over a dry concrete slab. However a wooden subfloor helps insulate the flooring from the cold concrete. It also adds a little cushion to the hard surface of the concrete. A wooden subfloor will not cure moisture problems. Moisture that comes up through the slab will ultimately find its way into your finished floor. Cure the moisture problem before you install the floor.

Headroom, especially in a basement, may be at a premium. To make low flooring framing that will conserve headroom, lay pressure-treated 2×4s (sleepers) flat and cover them with ¾-inch tongue-and-groove OSB underlayment or exterior plywood.

Prepare the slab by vacuuming it, then seal with an asphalt primer and a layer of asphalt mastic. Lay a moisture barrier (6 mil polyethylene is often used) and mark the plastic sheet with a felt marker so you can position the sleepers on 16-inch centers.

PRESTART CHECKLIST

☐ **TIME**
About 8 hours for a 10×10 floor

☐ **TOOLS**
Circular saw, level, powder-actuated gun, cordless drill

☐ **SKILLS**
Measuring and marking, cutting lumber, installing mastic and waterproofing membrane using powder-actuated fasteners

☐ **PREP**
Clean and repair floor

☐ **MATERIALS**
Polyethylene membrane, tape, powder-actuated fasteners, shims, screws, ¾-inch tongue-and-groove OSB underlayment or exterior plywood, pressure-treated 2×4s

1 Prepare the floor by vacuuming and installing a waterproofing membrane on asphalt mastic. Overlap the seams of the plastic sheet at least 6 inches and tape the seams with the tape recommended by the manufacturer. Starting with a ¼-inch gap along the walls, mark the sheet with a felt marker at 16-inch intervals. Snap chalklines to help you position the sleepers. Set out the sleepers along the perimeter of the room and in their approximate locations across the rest of the floor, cutting them to length as necessary.

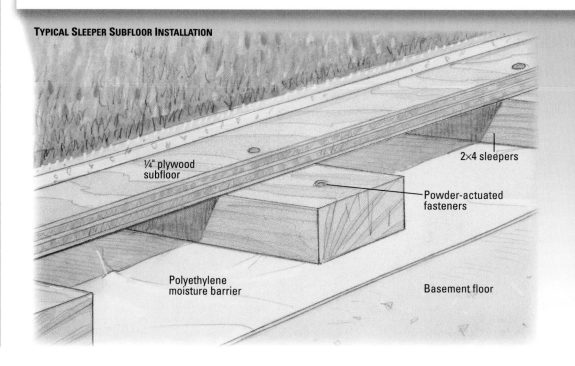

TYPICAL SLEEPER SUBFLOOR INSTALLATION

¼" plywood subfloor

2×4 sleepers

Powder-actuated fasteners

Polyethylene moisture barrier

Basement floor

2 After making sure that the floor is level, use cedar shims to level the sleepers. Fasten the sleepers (through the shims) with powder-actuated fasteners.

3 Set the first sheet of underlayment (tongue to the wall) with the long side perpendicular to the sleepers and ½ inch from the wall. Fasten the sheet with 2½-inch coated screws every 6 inches along the walls and every 8 inches across the sheet. Don't drive screws at the grooved edge yet.

4 Install the remaining sheets in the first row along the wall with a ⅛-inch gap between the ends. In the second row start with a half-sheet (then a full sheet for the third row) so the joints will be offset. Fit the tongue of one sheet into the groove of the other and screw it to the sleepers.

LEVEL THE SLEEPERS

Lay a 4-foot level across the sleepers to make sure they lie on the same plane. Insert cedar shims to raise the sleepers at low spots.

Work faster and easier with a powder-actuated nailer

A powder-actuated nailer drives nails into concrete quickly and easily. There's less chipping of the concrete surface.

You can buy a powder-actuated nailer at most home centers or rent one from rental outlets. A nailer is handy for anchoring both wood or metal framing to masonry.

An explosive charge drives a hardened nail into the concrete. Some types operate by pulling a trigger, others by hitting the firing pin with a hammer. Concrete nails (which break or bend if not hit squarely) and hardened screws (which take some time to install) are slower and less secure than powder-driven nails.

Wear ear and eye protection when using a powder-actuated nailer. Plant the tip of the nailer firmly against the wood before pulling the trigger or striking the firing pin.

STANLEY Pro Tip

Locating the first sheet

Because walls are seldom perfectly straight, measure 49 inches from the wall and snap a chalkline. Position the edge of the first sheet along the line.

This will give you enough clearance along the length of the room so you can line up the inside edges (the grooved edges) of the plywood sheets.

In some places you will have more than a ¼-inch gap along the wall, but you can cover with baseboard and shoe molding.

PREPARING FOR TILED FLOORS

Ceramic and stone tile are the most stable finished floor coverings. But for better stability and water resistance, lay a substrate of cement backerboard. Shown here is a basic overview of laying backerboard, with details for cutting and installation on pages 58–61.

If you decide not to use cement backerboard, ensure that the wood subfloor or cement slab is level by adjusting high and low spots as shown.

Verify the accuracy of your dimensional layout plan by setting a row of tiles in each direction in a dry run on the floor.

Leave outswinging doors in place. Remove inswinging doors as needed.

PRESTART CHECKLIST

☐ **TIME**
About 30–45 minutes per square yard to prepare and set tile.

☐ **TOOLS**
Angle grinder (slab) or belt sander (wood floor), chalk line, margin trowel, notched trowel, straightedge, utility knife, carbide scriber, snap cutter or wet saw, nippers, masonry stone, grout knife, caulk gun, grout float, hammer, cordless drill, putty knife, tape measure, china marker or felt-tip pen

☐ **SKILLS**
Power sanding, snapping chalklines, driving fasteners, troweling

☐ **PREP**
Repair structural defects

☐ **MATERIALS**
Bucket, thinset

DIMENSIONAL KITCHEN DRAWING

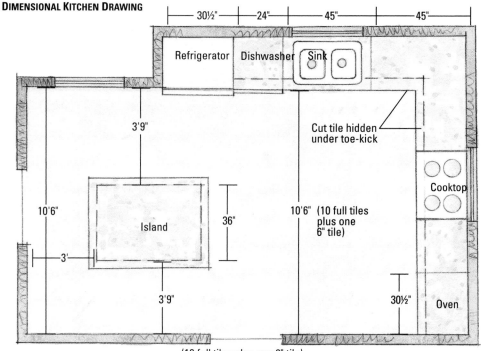

A dimensional drawing for a kitchen floor includes spaces that currently house appliances. When you note dimensions on the plan, add the thickness of any baseboard that you will remove. Measure up to the edge of toe-kicks under the cabinets.

DIMENSIONAL BATHROOM DRAWING

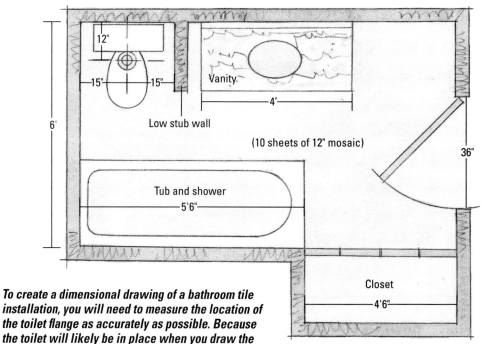

To create a dimensional drawing of a bathroom tile installation, you will need to measure the location of the toilet flange as accurately as possible. Because the toilet will likely be in place when you draw the plan, you will not be able to see the flange. Estimate its location: Measure from the side wall to half the width of the toilet base and from the back wall to about one-fourth of its length.

Installing backerboard

1 Examine the floor carefully and mark defects—high spots, indentations and depressions, popped nails, and cracks. Fix all defects that could interfere with the adhesive, backerboard, or tile installation. Install a waterproofing membrane over the floor if necessary.

2 Mark floor joist locations on the walls. Cut the pieces of backerboard so the edges will be centered on the joists. Starting on a wall away from the door, trowel a section of thinset, lay the board, and fasten with screws. Continue the process, working toward the doorway.

3 Starting again at a wall away from the door, tape each backerboard joint with 2-inch pregummed mesh tape. Use 4-inch tape at the corners if the backerboard goes up the wall. Trowel a thin coat of thinset over the tape.

Fix All Defects
Level high and low spots

1 Work in sections and use a 4-foot level. Place the level on the floor and rotate it within a section, noting and marking defects with a carpenter's pencil. (If working on a slab, chip out and fill major cracks.)

Although the floor shown here is a wood floor, the techniques are essentially the same for fixing defects on a cement slab.

2 Pour self-leveling compound or trowel thinset into depressions and feather the edges level with the floor. Use a belt sander to remove high spots on a wood floor. Use a right-angle grinder with a carbide abrasive wheel on a slab. Dewax surfaces and clean.

What If...
You're tiling a kitchen or bathroom?

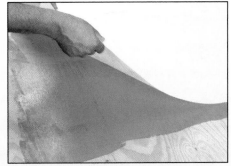

In wet areas such as bathroom floors, apply adhesive with a roller, then lay down the membrane. Trowel on more adhesive. Working in sections start on a wall away from a door and cover the entire floor. Spread the adhesive all the way to the edge of the floor. See page 75 for more details.

INSTALLING CEMENT BACKERBOARD

Cement backerboard is made expressly as a substrate for ceramic and stone tile. Installed over plywood or other underlayment on floors, it provides a solid, stable surface that is unaffected by moisture or temperature changes.

Center the backerboard edges on joists and studs. Mark the joist and stud locations before you start. Because you won't be able to see marks after you have troweled on the thinset, mark joist locations on the walls.

Offset the joints by half a sheet where possible. Leave at least a ⅛-inch gap at the walls (about the diameter of a pencil).

Scoop thinset from the bucket with a margin trowel. Spread with the notched trowel recommended by the adhesive manufacturer.

PRESTART CHECKLIST

☐ **TIME**
About 30–45 minutes per square foot of surface

☐ **TOOLS**
Tarp, tape measure, drywall square, carbide scriber, utility knife, rasp, cordless drill, carbide hole saw, compass, hammer for large holes, notched trowel, margin trowel

☐ **SKILLS**
Precise measuring and cutting, driving fasteners with cordless drill, troweling

☐ **PREP**
Prepare, vacuum, and damp-clean surfaces; install waterproofing membrane in wet locations

☐ **MATERIALS**
Backerboard, thinset, 1¼- and 2-inch backerboard screws, 2-inch gummed fiber mesh tape

Cutting backerboard sections

1 Protect finished floors with a tarp. Backerboard particles will scratch a floor. Mark the line to be cut and position a drywall square or metal T-square on the line. Using a carbide backerboard scriber and firm pressure, scribe the cut-line. Make several passes.

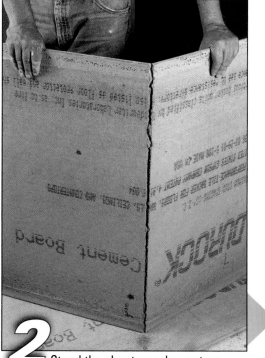

2 Stand the sheet on edge or turn it over. Working from the side opposite the scored line, brace the board with your knee on the line and snap the board.

Cutting small holes

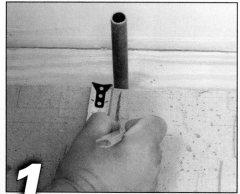

1 Set the board against the pipe or other obstruction. Mark the diameter of the hole to be cut. Use a tape measure to locate the center of the hole. For faucets measure the location of each faucet hole from the wall and from the tub or floor.

2 Use a cordless drill and carbide-tipped hole saw or coring saw to cut small holes in backerboard. Place the drill point of the saw on the mark you made and use light pressure and high speed to cut through the backerboard.

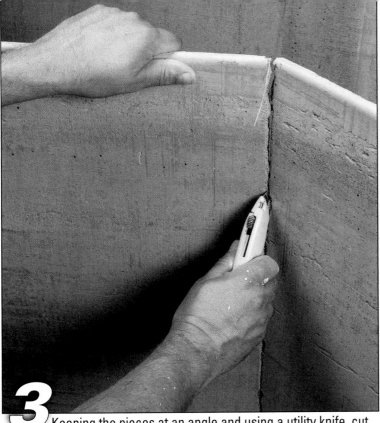

3 Keeping the pieces at an angle and using a utility knife, cut through the board to separate the two pieces. Depending on how deeply you made your first cut, you may have to make several passes with the knife to separate the pieces.

4 Backerboard cuts are rough, whether made with a carbide scriber or a utility knife. Places being joined should have as smooth an edge as possible. Use a contour plane with a serrated blade, a rasp, or a masonry stone to smooth out the edge. Keep the tool perpendicular to the edge of the board and pass over the board several times until its surface is flat.

Cutting large holes

1 When the diameter of a hole to be cut exceeds the size of available hole saws, measure the obstruction and use a compass to mark its location on the backerboard. With a utility knife or carbide scriber, score completely through the backerboard mesh.

2 Support the cutout with the palm of one hand if necessary. Tap the scored edge with a hammer until the surface around the circumference crumbles. Alternatively drill a series of small holes around the circumference.

3 Using a utility knife cut through the mesh on the opposite side of the board. Push the cutout through and smooth the edges with a rasp, serrated contour plane, or masonry stone.

Installing cement backerboard

1 Mix and pour thinset. Hold the smooth side of a notched trowel at a 30-degree angle and spread the mortar in a thick, even coat, forcing it into the subfloor. Work the mortar into ridges, keeping the notched side of the trowel in contact with the floor and at a 45- to 75-degree angle.

2 While the mortar is wet, tip the board on a long edge and hinge it toward the floor. Line up the first board on a joist and keep a gap of ⅛ inch between boards, ¼ inch at walls. Manufacturers' directions vary, but typically you should stagger the joints. Walk on the board to set it in the mortar.

3 Using a cordless drill and phillips bit, drive backerboard screws through the board and into the subfloor at about 8-inch intervals. Use 2-inch backerboard screws at the joists and 1¼-inch screws in the field. Set the screws so they are flush with the surface of the board.

THINSET

Although not impervious to water, thinset exhibits highly water-resistant properties. Thinset mixed with water, however, may crack when cured. To improve its flexibility mix it with a latex additive, following the manufacturer's directions. (Latex-modified thinset is also available.) Latex improves the bond strength of the thinset.

Thinset comes in premixed or mix-it-yourself varieties—a choice that comes down to preference and cost.

Premixed brands cost more, and mixing your own allows you to adjust the mixture to weather conditions, making it wetter in hot and dry climates or stiffer in cold and humid conditions. You can also alter its consistency to provide optimal adhesion over many kinds of substrates and tiles.

Dry-mixed thinset mortar

Organic mastic

Epoxy thinset

Premixed thinset mortar

4 Apply 2-inch pregummed fiberglass mesh tape over each joint, pressing the tape firmly on the backerboard. The tape cuts easily with a utility knife. Use 4-inch tape (if available) for increased strength. Alternatively you can embed ungummed tape in a thin coat of mortar applied to the joints. Use this method where stronger joints are required—in stone tile installations for example.

5 Whether you have ungummed or pregummed tape, finish the joint by applying a thin coat of thinset mortar over the tape. Use a margin trowel to scoop mortar from the bucket. Apply the mortar so it levels the recess in the joint from side to side. Feather the edges to avoid creating high spots under the tiled surface.

SAFETY FIRST
Handling adhesives

Thinset and other adhesives contain caustic ingredients. Solvent-based adhesives are potentially explosive and are harmful when inhaled. Wear gloves and a respirator when mixing all adhesives and keep the area well ventilated.

STANLEY. PRO TIP: **Fix backerboard screw snaps**

Backerboard fasteners, unlike drywall screws, are made to withstand the rigors of tile installations. Occasionally, however, one will snap off. Check the torque setting of your cordless drill to make sure the clutch slips when the screw just dimples the board. If a backerboard screw snaps, remove the loose piece and drive another about 1 inch away from the first one.

Using existing floor tile as substrate for ceramic tile

If the existing ceramic tile floor is in good condition and firmly bonded to the subfloor, you may be able to lay tile directly over it.

1 With a quality hammer or small sledgehammer and cold chisel, break out damaged tile, working from the center of the tile to the edges. **Wear eye protection.** Pull out the broken chips and scrape off remaining adhesive. Vacuum the area.

2 Using a margin trowel or wide putty knife, apply adhesive in the recess and backbutter a replacement tile. Push the tile into the recess until the adhesive oozes up from the grout joints. Make sure the tile is level with the rest of the floor, wipe off the excess thinset, and let cure.

3 Use a sanding block and a coarse grit of abrasive paper to roughen the entire surface of the tile. This will give the tile a "tooth" for the adhesive and strengthen its bond with the floor.

Removing floor tile set in thinset

1 Create a starting point in a central area of the floor by cracking one tile with a small sledgehammer and cold chisel. Grip the chisel firmly and strike it with a sharp blow of the small sledgehammer. **Wear eye protection.**

2 Break out the remaining area of the tile with the sledgehammer and brush the loose pieces out of the recess. Chip out the grout along the edge of an adjacent tile.

3 Tap a wide chisel at an angle under the edge of the adjoining tile and pop off the tile. Repeat the process for each tile until you have removed the entire floor. Dispose of the tile and scrape off remaining adhesive.

INSTALLING NEW UNDERLAYMENT

No matter how you finish your floor, it will only be as good as its underlayment—the supporting layer fastened to the joists. Underlayment provides a smooth, stable surface for the finished floor.

You can lay ceramic tile over hardwood and ceramic floors—if the surface and subfloor are stable and in good condition. The same is true for uncushioned resilient tile or sheet materials on a wood frame floor. But new ceramic tile over an existing floor will raise the surface by at least ¾ inch. Removing the existing floor will minimize any change in floor levels and reveal any hidden faults that need repair.

If your underlayment shows signs of rot or is not thick enough to support the finished floor, or if you're working in new construction, you'll have to install new underlayment, typically ¾-inch exterior plywood. Bring the plywood into the room a few days before installation to acclimate it, which will reduce shrinkage or expansion.

PRESTART CHECKLIST

☐ **TIME**
From 30–45 minutes per square yard

☐ **TOOLS**
Tape measure, chalkline, circular saw, cordless drill, screwdriver bit

☐ **SKILLS**
Measuring and marking, cutting with circular saw, driving fasteners with cordless drill

☐ **PREP**
Remove existing flooring as necessary

☐ **MATERIALS**
¾-inch exterior grade plywood, construction adhesive (optional), galvanized screws

1 Set up 2×4s as a work surface—in an area where they won't be in the way. Start with a full sheet in a corner, squaring it with the room and centering its edges on the joists. When cutting pieces measure from the edge of the board to the center of the joist and snap a chalkline for the cut.

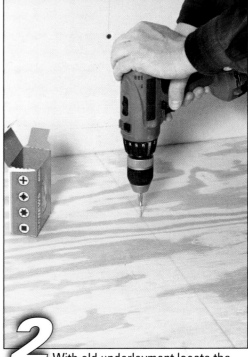

2 With old underlayment locate the joists and mark their positions on the wall. Lay the new sheet down and snap perpendicular joist lines to guide the placement of fasteners. Apply a bead of construction adhesive (optional) and drive in screws that are long enough to penetrate the joists.

3 Set half sheets next to full sheets so the joints are offset. Leave at least a ⅛-inch gap between the sheets (an 8d nail makes a good spacer) and ¼ inch at the walls.

Removing a hardwood floor

To remove hardwood or parquet flooring, start by making several plunge cuts in one or two strips or planks. Chisel out the cut area. Tap a pry bar under the flooring and pry the material up. Insert the bar fully under the strip or plank, not the tongue.

REMOVING MOLDING AND BASEBOARDS

In rooms without appliances preparation of a floor begins with removing moldings and baseboards. (For any room with appliances or fixtures, see pages 66–70.)

Most rooms with wooden baseboards also have a shoe molding (often called quarter round) that covers the gap at the floor. Shoe moldings come off first, then the baseboards—but take the baseboard off only if you plan to finish the room with vinyl or tile. A reinstalled or new wood baseboard will produce voids where it meets the tile. Those gaps are unsightly and difficult to clean, especially in kitchens and baths. So leave the baseboard in place if it is in good repair or if you're not adding a new one. When you lay the new floor, install it up to the baseboard.

If you plan to reuse the shoe molding, number the pieces as you remove them and mark the corner where you started. Shoe molding sections must go back in their original order.

PRESTART CHECKLIST

☐ **TIME**
10 minutes per lineal foot to remove shoe molding and wood baseboard, slightly more for cove molding and tile removal. Nail removal and adhesive cleanup can be time consuming and vary with the length of nails and type of adhesive used.

☐ **TOOLS**
Utility knife, putty knife, pry bar, hammer, scrap wood, nippers or side cutters, handsaw or backsaw—tools vary with type of molding removed

☐ **SKILLS**
Cutting precisely with utility knife, using a hammer and pry bar; threshold removal requires using a handsaw

Removing vinyl cove molding

1 Insert a wide-blade putty knife at the top corner of a joint in the molding. Push down on the knife and lift the molding off the surface of the wall. Slide the full width of the blade under the molding and strip it off, keeping the knife handle parallel to the floor.

2 When you have removed all the molding, use a putty knife to scrape off the remaining adhesive. Keep the knife at an angle that will remove the adhesive without gouging the wall surface. Light pressure and repeated passes work better than trying to remove the adhesive all at once.

STANLEY PRO TIP: **Score the paint line**

Paint that has adhered to the wall and a wood baseboard, vinyl cove molding, or ceramic tile base may pull off the wall when you remove the molding, leaving unsightly chips that require repainting. Repainting is time consuming and new paint often doesn't match the old.

To avoid pulling the paint off the wall when removing a base molding, score the paint line with a sharp utility knife.

Insert the knife in the joint between the wall and the molding and draw the knife toward you at an angle that follows the joint. Use enough pressure to cut through the paint. Paint can be stubborn—use two hands if necessary to cut through several coats. Make several repeated passes; the job will actually go faster, and you'll avoid broken blades and skinned knuckles.

Removing wood shoe molding and baseboards

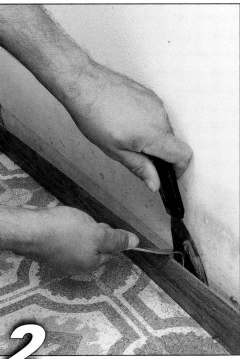

1 Starting at a corner slide a small pry bar behind the shoe. Loosen the shoe until you can insert the pry bar next to a nail. Pry the nail out a little at a time. To avoid splits loosen at least two nails before pulling the molding completely off the wall.

2 Begin at a corner or at a mitered joint, working a wide putty knife behind the baseboard. Loosen each nail with a pry bar. Keep the putty knife behind the bar or use a thin piece of scrap as a shim to avoid marring the surface of the wall. Loosen all nails before removing a baseboard section.

3 If you plan to reuse the shoe molding or baseboard, pull out the nails from the back. Use nippers to grab the nail at the base and lever it partly out. Repeat the process until the nail pops loose.

Removing ceramic tile

Tap a pry bar into the joint. Pop each tile loose. If necessary protect the wall with scrap behind the bar. Scrape off adhesive.

Removing thresholds

1 Use a handsaw or backsaw to cut the threshold in half all the way to the surface of the floor. Cut carefully to avoid damaging other surfaces.

2 Pry up each piece with a pry bar and remove it. If the threshold is screwed down, remove the screws and slide it from under the door trim.

REMOVING APPLIANCES

New flooring must extend under appliances, so cleaning liquids or spills and leaks won't drain over the flooring edge and damage the subfloor.

Remove appliances early in the preparation stage so they won't be in the way when you perform the rest of the demolition, preparation, and repair work.

The space under appliances provides an excellent opportunity to use slightly flawed flooring or pieces of flooring that have been cut inaccurately.

Before moving appliances check to see if they will fit their enclosures after you've laid the new flooring. New flooring may increase the height of the floor, so measure each appliance and add the thickness of the floor and adhesive you might use. To make room you may have to cut the cabinet frame above the refrigerator or shim up a countertop to accommodate a dishwasher.

Plan ahead for proper reconnection of water, gas, or electrical lines.

PRESTART CHECKLIST

☐ **TIME**
15 minutes for a refrigerator, 15–20 minutes for gas appliances and plug-in electric units, more for direct-wired

☐ **TOOLS**
Groove-joint pliers, adjustable wrench, straight and phillips screwdrivers, cordless drill and bits, appliance dolly

☐ **SKILLS**
Removing screws with screwdrivers or cordless drill, removing nuts with wrenches, moving large appliances

☐ **PREP**
Shut off water supply valves

☐ **MATERIALS**
Duct tape and wire nuts

Removing a dishwasher

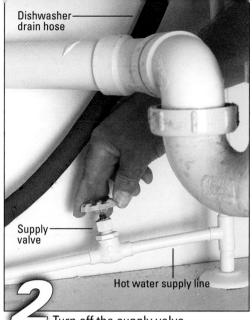

Dishwasher plug

1 Unplug the dishwasher cord from the receptacle under the sink. If you don't see a power plug on the cord, the dishwasher is wired directly into the circuit. The wiring itself must be disconnected. In such installations **shut off the power before proceeding.**

Dishwasher drain hose

Supply valve

Hot water supply line

2 Turn off the supply valve. Disconnect the supply line and drain hose with a wrench. Remove the bottom dishwasher panel for access, tug on the lines to locate their connections, and disconnect them.

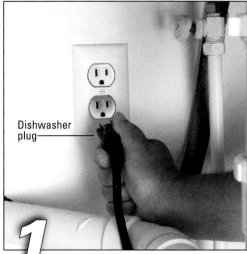

3 The dishwasher is held in the cabinet with screws fastened in the side (and on some models the top and bottom) flanges. Open the dishwasher door for access to the screws and remove them with the appropriate screwdriver or cordless drill.

4 Close the door of the dishwasher and lock it. Grasp the dishwasher by the sides of the door and/or the door handle and slide it forward. Lift up slightly and if it sticks rock the unit from side to side. If necessary have a helper thread supply and drain lines through the cabinet holes as you pull.

Removing a countertop range

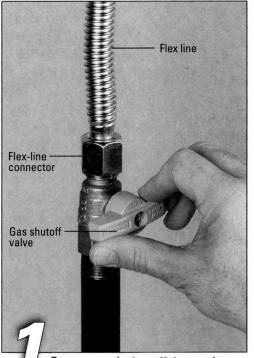

1 For a gas unit **shut off the gas** by turning the handle on the shutoff valve. Using groove-joint pliers loosen the flex-line connector (or pipe) and disconnect the line from the valve. For an electric range **unplug the 220-volt power plug** under the cabinet.

Flex line

Flex-line connector

Gas shutoff valve

2 Your range may be anchored by clips or retainers similar to those used to anchor a countertop sink. Remove any clips or retainers and push up on the unit from below with one hand to create a space for lifting. Lift the unit up and out. Do not kink the flex line, as this may put holes in it.

Removing a stove

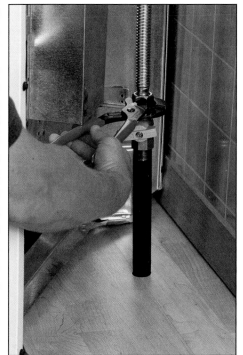

Pull the stove away from the wall far enough to reach the power plug or gas valve. **Unplug the power cord or turn off the gas valve.** Using groove-joint pliers loosen the flex-line connector. Bend the flex line gently and tape it out of the way. Dolly the stove to a different room.

WHAT IF...
An electric appliance is wired directly to the circuit?

If you don't see a plug on the power cord of an appliance, the unit is wired directly to a circuit. **Turn off the circuit breaker** and tape a note to it so someone doesn't turn it on accidentally. Find the junction box to which the appliance is connected; remove the cover plate. Use a voltage tester to check the wires for power.

Wire nut

If they are dead disconnect the wires, noting how they are attached. Loosen the cord clamp on the side of the box and pull out the appliance cord. Screw wire nuts tightly onto the circuit wires and tuck them into the box. Attach the cover plate. **If in doubt call a professional electrician.**

SAFETY FIRST
Use an appliance dolly

An appliance dolly safely moves heavy items. Slide the dolly plate under the unit, tighten the strap, tip the unit back slightly, and roll it away. Enlist a helper to move large appliances.

REMOVING FIXTURES

Although you can leave toilets and sinks in place and floor around them, removing them makes the job easier. With the fixtures out of the way, you'll have more working room, substantially fewer cuts to make, and fewer seams or joints to maintain. You'll spend less time removing fixtures than cutting tiles or other flooring materials, and the result will be more attractive and professional looking.

Over time fixture anchor bolts often rust, bend, and otherwise undergo alterations that make their removal difficult. A few techniques will solve these problems.

PRESTART CHECKLIST

☐ **TIME**
About 30–45 minutes each for toilet and pedestal sink (more if anchor bolts prove stubborn)

☐ **TOOLS**
Plumber's plunger, groove-joint pliers, locking pliers (optional), adjustable wrench, straight and Phillips screwdrivers, allen wrenches, narrow putty knife, hacksaw, mini hacksaw (optional), pipe wrench, tape measure, bucket

☐ **SKILLS**
Removing fasteners with wrenches, removing screws with screwdrivers

☐ **PREP**
Turn off water supply valve(s) for each fixture removed

☐ **MATERIALS**
Bleach, rags, plastic bag, penetrating oil, wood shims, flange extension, new closet flange and bolts, duct tape

Removing a toilet

1 Pour a quart of bleach into the tank, flush, and let it refill. Close the supply valve and reflush, holding the handle down until the tank empties. Push the water out of the trap with a plunger and stuff the bowl with rags. Disconnect the supply line with a wrench or groove-joint pliers.

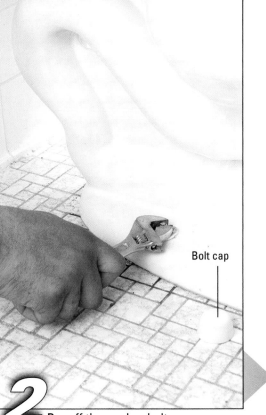

Bolt cap

2 Pry off the anchor bolt caps. Remove the anchor bolts with an adjustable wrench or groove-joint pliers. If the bolts spin, snap, or won't come off, try one of the solutions listed opposite. Even if you have to cut the bolts, you can still remove the toilet and replace the bolts when you reinstall it.

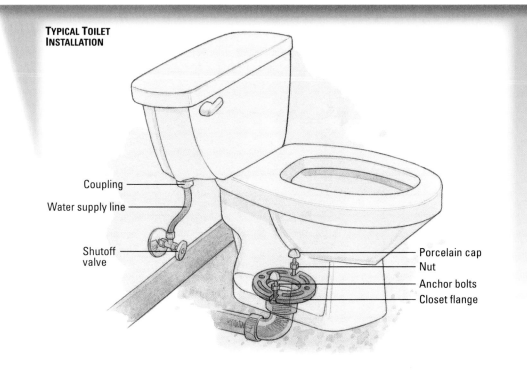

TYPICAL TOILET INSTALLATION

Coupling
Water supply line
Shutoff valve
Porcelain cap
Nut
Anchor bolts
Closet flange

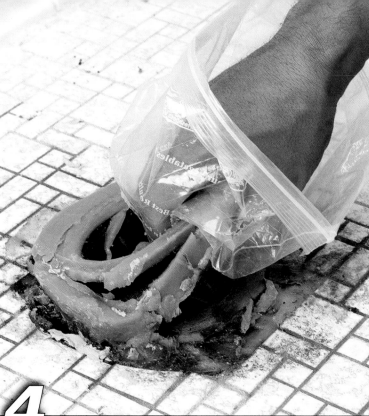

3 The bottom of the toilet trap fits snugly over a wax ring that seals it against the closet flange in the floor (see illustration). To break the seal of the wax ring, rock the toilet gently back and forth as you lift it off the floor. Newer, low-capacity toilets may be light enough for you to lift by yourself, but older toilets can weigh up to 60 pounds. Get help to avoid risk of injury. Lift the toilet off the floor and carry it to another room.

4 With one hand in a plastic bag, grab the inside bottom edge of the ring. Pull it out, pulling the bag over the ring with your other hand. Dispose of the ring. With a putty knife scrape residue from the flange. Stuff a large rag into the drain to keep out debris. Measure from the flange to the height of the new flooring plus backerboard if any. Purchase a flange extension, if necessary, to bring the flange about ¼ inch above the new floor.

WHAT IF...
Toilet bolts spin, snap, or won't come off?

If the bolts snap when you try to remove the nut, pull out the broken piece, remove the toilet, and see if the pieces remaining in the flange will come loose with locking pliers. If they won't you can install a repair flange before you begin laying the new flooring.

If a bolt spins drive a wood shim under the toilet on both sides of the bolt. The resulting upward pressure may keep it from spinning so you can unscrew the nut.

Stubborn nuts may loosen with a squirt of penetrating oil. Let the oil set for about 10 minutes before trying again to loosen the nuts.

If a nut still won't budge, or if the wood shims didn't stop the bolt from spinning, saw the bolt with a hacksaw. Insert the hacksaw blade under the nut and cut through the bolt. If there isn't enough working room for a full-size saw, use a mini hacksaw (as shown).

STANLEY PRO TIP

Install a flange extension

The combined thickness of new flooring materials—cement backerboard, thinset, and tile, for example—may raise the floor by as much as 1 inch. Raise the height of the flange with an extender.

Available at most hardware stores, an extender consists of rings that are stacked over the floor flange and sealed with silicone caulk. Add enough rings to bring the flange at least flush with and preferably about ¼ inch higher than the new floor.

Removing a pedestal sink

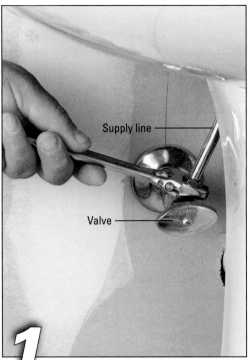

1 Shut off both the hot and cold water valves and loosen the compression nuts on both supply lines with a wrench or groove-joint pliers. Pull the supply line out of the valve. If the sink has fixed-length supply lines, remove the nut and push the lines gently out of the way.

Supply line

Valve

2 Place a pile of rags under the trap to catch any water released as you remove the pipe. Loosen the slip-nut fitting (on both ends of the trap if possible) with groove-joint pliers or a pipe wrench and pull the trap off. Pour the trap water in a bucket.

Water line connection removed

Slip-nut fitting

3 Remove any bolts attaching the top to the pedestal. Lift the top off. If the sink is hung on wall brackets, grasp it near the wall and pull up. Unbolt the pedestal from the floor and lift it off. If the sink is a one-piece unit, unbolt it from the wall and floor. Remove the wall brackets if you plan to tile the wall.

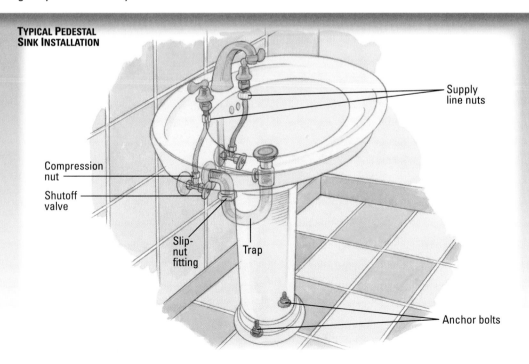

TYPICAL PEDESTAL SINK INSTALLATION

Supply line nuts

Compression nut

Shutoff valve

Slip-nut fitting

Trap

Anchor bolts

Tiling around floor pipes

Many steam and hot water heating systems that use baseboard elements and floor standing radiators have delivery pipes that come up through the floor. When you lay new flooring around these pipes, lay the material within ¼ inch of the pipes and fill the gap with silicone caulk. The caulk will let the pipes move in the hole without making noise.

Remove floor radiators for flooring installations. Shut off the heat supply and disconnect the unit at the outflow side of the valve. Steam and hot water system fittings can be stubborn. Use a pipe wrench or enlist the services of a professional.

Removing resilient tile

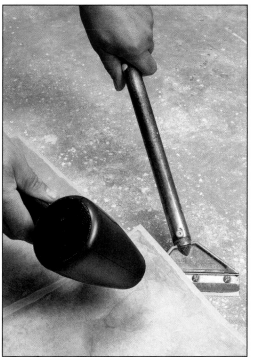

Warm the adhesive with a heat gun. If you don't have a heat gun, use a hair dryer set on high heat. Warm a corner first, insert a floor scraper or wide putty knife, and with the heat on lift up the tile. Scrape the adhesive from the floor with a floor scraper.

Removing resilient sheet flooring

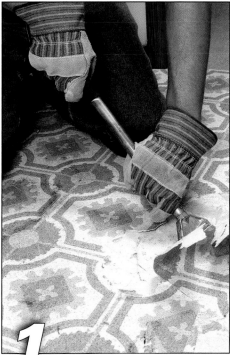

1 Start at a corner or at a bubbled seam. Insert a floor scraper or wide putty knife under the sheet flooring and pry it up. Work down each strip of the material, rolling the strip as you go. If the material is unbacked, use a hair dryer or heat gun to soften the adhesive as you go.

2 Once you have removed the sheet flooring, spray the surface in sections with adhesive remover. Let the remover work according to the manufacturer's instructions, then use a wide scraper or putty knife to peel the residue from the floor.

Repairing resilient surfaces

If you are flooring over a resilient surface on a wood subfloor and the resilient material is damaged in only a few sections, repair it rather than remove it completely.

Using a utility knife cut through the damaged area to the subfloor. Remove the damaged tile(s) or section(s) of sheet material with a wide putty knife or scraper. Scrape the remaining adhesive from the floor within the area.

Using a mason's trowel or a margin trowel, smear the recess with thinset mortar and level it. Let this thinset dry before applying backerboard.

Use this patching method only on resilient material installed over a wood frame floor. Always remove resilients from a concrete slab before laying new flooring.

STANLEY PRO TIP
Cut flooring into strips

Stripping and removing room-size sections of resilient sheet flooring or carpet is time-consuming and heavy work. To make the job easier, cut resilient sheet flooring or carpet into 12-inch strips before you pull or scrape it up.

Asbestos warning

Before you remove any resilient material, check with a professional to determine if it contains asbestos.

Asbestos was used as a binder in most resilient flooring materials prior to 1985, and its fibers have since been found to be a carcinogen, especially dangerous when inhaled. Virtually no material installed prior to 1985 is guaranteed asbestos-free. Asbestos was used in asphalt tile, linoleum, vinyl-asbestos tile and sheet flooring, and asphalt adhesives.

If possible leave asbestos flooring in place and install underlayment or backerboard over it. Never sand, dry-scrape, or dry-sweep any materials with asbestos content. Contact a profession for removal of asbestos flooring. Look in the phone directory under "Asbestos Removal."

Removing conventional carpet

1 Pry up all metal edgings at doorways. Cut the carpet in strips with a utility knife. If the carpet is not tacked or glued to the floor, grab the corner with groove-joint pliers and pull each strip of carpet off the tack strip. Once you get started the carpet should tear easily.

2 If you didn't cut through the pad when you cut the carpet in strips, cut the pad with a utility knife. Then grab each section of pad with both hands and pull it from the floor. Roll the pad as you go and dispose of the rolls. Remove pad tacks or staples.

3 Starting at a joint in the tack strip, work the end of a pry bar under the strip at a nail and pry the nail loose. Wear gloves when carrying the strips to a refuse pile or garbage bin—the points of the tacks are sharp.

WHAT IF...
The carpet or pad is tacked or stapled?

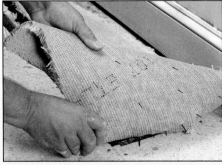

To remove tacked carpet pry up a few tacks with a screwdriver or cat's paw and try to pull the carpet up. If that doesn't work pull up each tack or staple separately. Remove pad staples and any remaining tufts of pad with a screwdriver or cat's paw.

WHAT IF...
The carpet is glued down?

1 Starting at a corner or along one edge of a cut strip, drive a wide putty knife or scraper between the backing and the floor to break the adhesive bond. Roll up the carpet as you go.

2 Once you have removed and disposed of the carpet, go back and scrape up the remaining tufts of pad and adhesive residue with a floor scraper.

Patching damaged hardwood for resurfacing

1 Use a framing square and carpenter's pencil to outline the edge of the damaged area. Set a circular saw to the depth of the hardwood flooring, start the saw with only the front edge of the saw plate resting on the floor, and lower the blade into the cut. Repeat along each line.

2 Chisel out enough flooring to let you insert a pry bar under the flooring. Tap the pry bar under the strips at a nail and pry up. Dispose of the removed flooring. Measure the cleared area and cut a piece of ¾-inch plywood to size. Fit the plywood into the recess and secure with screws. Countersink the screws slightly. If your hardwood floor has been refinished, the patch might be thicker than the floor. Use a belt sander to sand the patch until it's level with the flooring.

WHAT IF...
Flooring is parquet?

Tap the blade of a wide chisel under the edge of one parquet tile and pry the tile loose. Repeat for each tile and scrape up the adhesive with a wide putty knife.

Securing loose planks or strips

Floor tile requires a level, firm surface. Securely anchor any loose hardwood flooring. Walk the floor and mark areas that feel spongy or loose. Fasten loose boards at their edges with ringshank or spiral shank nails, or use a cordless drill and drive 1⅜-inch coated screws through the hardwood and into the subfloor. Predrill the holes to avoid splitting the material.

PREPARING A WOOD SUBFLOOR

After you have removed or repaired the existing surface of the floor, turn your attention to the subfloor. Ceramics and stone must be kept from cracking, and all subfloors must not squeak or sag. Inspect the subfloor and make repairs that will ensure it proves a solid, stable bed.

Dimension lumber—1×4 or 2×6 planking—is not suitable as a bed for some types of flooring, especially tile. Planks expand and contract with changes in temperature and humidity, as does tile but at different rates. The result is cracked tile, broken grout joints, or split seams. Install plywood or backerboard on plank. If the resulting floor will be too high for smooth transitions to adjacent floors, remove the planking and install ¾-inch exterior-grade plywood, followed by backerboard for ceramic or stone flooring.

PRESTART CHECKLIST

☐ **TIME**
30 minutes to check defects; repair time will vary with size and condition of floor

☐ **TOOLS**
4-foot level, cordless drill/bits, hammer, circular saw, trowel, belt sander, nail set, roller

☐ **SKILLS**
Nailing, troweling, belt sanding, sawing, removing fasteners

☐ **PREP**
Remove/repair finished flooring

☐ **MATERIALS**
Subfloor: 2×4 lumber, 8d nails, wood shims, 2½-inch coated screws
Surface: thinset mortar
Installing membrane: membrane and adhesive

1 Divide the floor into imaginary 6-foot sections and within each section rotate a 4-foot level. Use a carpenter's pencil or chalk marker to outline sags, low spots, high spots, and other defects. Walk the floor to test for squeaks and weak spots. Mark these areas.

2 If the entire subfloor is weak, cut 2×4 bridges to fit between the floor joists. Measure the joist spacing across the floor and if the dimensions are equal, cut all the bridges at one time. If the spacing varies cut the pieces to fit. Nail the bridges in place, offsetting each by 24 inches.

LOW SPOTS AND HIGH SPOTS
Level the subfloor

1 Use a mason's trowel or margin trowel to feather the edges of the repair so it is level with the floor. After it dries sand the edges of the repair if necessary.

2 Before you level any high spots on the floor, make sure the heads of all nails and fasteners are set below the surface. Level high spots on the floor with a belt sander. Keep the sander moving while it is in contact with the floor.

3 Shore up broken or sagging joists by nailing a 2×4 cleat against the subfloor. Force the cleat snugly against the subfloor with a 2×4 prop, nail the cleat in place with 8d nails, and knock the prop out to remove it.

4 Fill minor sags and separations between the subfloor and joists by driving shims or shingles into the gap. Tap the shim gently until it's snug—forcing it may cause the flooring above to bow.

5 Fasten loose subflooring material securely by screwing it to the joists. Drive screws into any repairs you have made with shims. You can use ringshank or spiral shank nails as an alternative, setting the nailhead below the surface with a hammer and nail set.

STANLEY PRO TIP

Support the stone

Because stone tiles are more brittle than ceramic tile, they won't forgive unstable subfloors or surfaces that aren't flat. Stone installations require subfloor support that is solid and free from defect. Substrates also must be smooth and level.

When preparing a subfloor for stone tile, be thorough and precise when marking defects such as high spots or depressions. Finish the edges of thinset repairs with care and make sure you have removed all structural defects in the joists and subfloor.

Stone is substantially heavier than tile, and current flooring, especially in large rooms, may not be strong enough to support it. Check with a structural engineer if you are in doubt.

Waterproofing membrane

Although many flooring tiles are water resistant or impervious to water, virtually no flooring installation is completely waterproof without a waterproofing membrane.

Water that penetrates flooring weakens the adhesive (if any), promotes rot, and nourishes organisms destructive to the wood subfloor. Bathrooms, kitchens, and surfaces that require frequent cleaning are especially vulnerable.

One of the easiest membranes to apply uses an adhesive that spreads with a roller. To install start at a wall opposite a doorway and apply the adhesive in sections with a roller (top right). Let the adhesive cure, spread the fiber membrane over it (middle right), and trowel the membrane into the adhesive (bottom right).

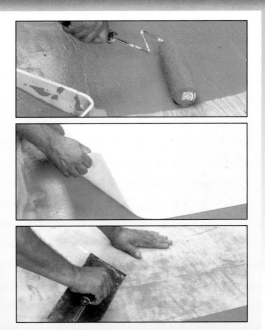

INSTALLING ELECTRIC RADIANT HEAT

If you are planning to install an interior floor of tile, brick, or stone, consider adding the warming influence of electric radiant heat. Installed directly over the substrate (cement board, plywood, a mortar bed, or a concrete slab), this system uses a plastic mat with interwoven heater cable. The mat is embedded in thinset before the final flooring material is installed. Controlled by a wallmounted thermostat or timer, the heater cable radiates warmth at a preset temperature.

The 120-volt circuit or power source for the radiant heat mats must be GFCI protected. Mats are available in a variety of lengths. Check the manufacturer's specifications for the wattage your situation requires. It increases with the room size.

PRESTART CHECKLIST

☐ **TIME**
8 hours to install mat, wire, and tile for an average bathroom

☐ **TOOLS**
Digital ohmmeter, drill, ½-inch bit, drywall saw, fish tape, chisel, hot-glue gun, ⅜-inch trowel, screwdriver, stripper, long-nose pliers, lineman's pliers, tools for laying flooring

☐ **SKILLS**
Stripping, splicing, and connecting wires; installing boxes; running cable

☐ **PREP**
Rough-in plumbing; install the subfloor

☐ **MATERIALS**
12/2 cable, mat, box, armored power cable, thermostat/timer, thinset, flooring, mortar or grout

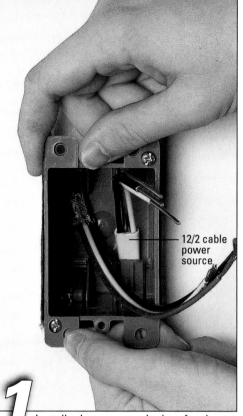

1 Install a large-capacity box for the thermostat 60 inches above the floor. Using 12/2 cable add a new circuit or extend an existing circuit but do not connect the power source. Pull it to the cable box provided with the mat.

Labels: 12/2 cable power source

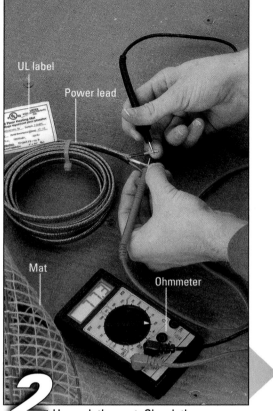

2 Unpack the mat. Check the resistance using an ohmmeter. The reading should be within 10 percent of the rating shown on the UL label. This will be your benchmark for confirming that the heat cable has not been nicked during installation. Write the reading on a piece of paper.

Labels: UL label, Power lead, Mat, Ohmmeter

INSTALLING UNDER-FLOOR ELECTRIC RADIANT HEATING

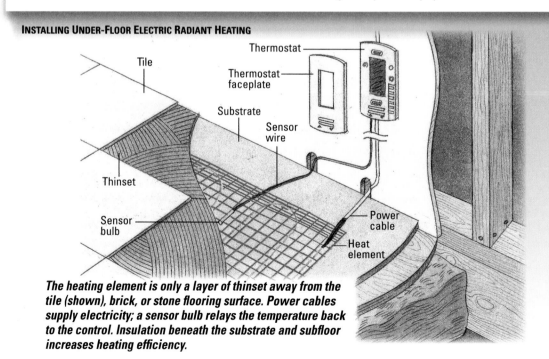

Labels: Tile, Thermostat, Thermostat faceplate, Substrate, Sensor wire, Thinset, Sensor bulb, Power cable, Heat element

The heating element is only a layer of thinset away from the tile (shown), brick, or stone flooring surface. Power cables supply electricity; a sensor bulb relays the temperature back to the control. Insulation beneath the substrate and subfloor increases heating efficiency.

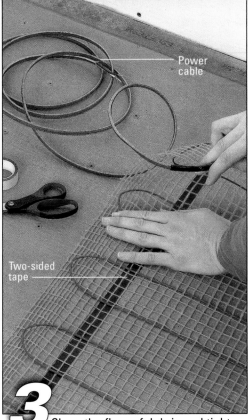

Power cable

Two-sided tape

Channel for power cable connection

Cold chisel

Power cable

Hot-glue gun

3 Clean the floor of debris and tighten any protruding screws or nailheads. Roll the mat so it's no closer than 3 to 6 inches to walls and fixtures. Staple the mat to the floor with ½-inch staples or fasten with double-sided tape every 12–24 inches.

4 If the power lead is thicker than the mat (some are manufactured with ribbon leads), sink it into the substrate if you've used backerboard. Use a cold chisel to cut a channel for it. If you don't recess the power lead, make sure it's adequately covered by mortar.

5 Hot-glue the power cable to the substrate. Mark along the power cable and slide it to one side. Working a few feet at a time, run a continuous bead of hot glue. Press the lead into the bead of hot glue. Make sure the lead wires don't cross each other or run perpendicular to a heater wire.

Strategies for running cable through walls

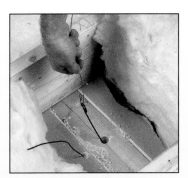

Go downstairs for power by drilling a finder hole directly in front of the wall through which you want to run the cable. Use a wire to mark the spot. Drill a ¾-inch hole and use a fish tape to pull the cable to where it's needed.

By cutting away drywall (save the piece for replacing and taping later), you can run cable horizontally. This allows you to tap into a receptacle (check that the circuit can bear the additional load) in the same room.

If you have attic space above, drop power down to the room where you need it. Drill a finder hole to locate the wall plate. Drill an access hole, run fish tape, then pull the cable to extend a circuit or to create a new circuit.

WHAT IF…
There's a toilet or vanity?

Mats can run under a toilet but must be 3 inches from the toilet ring. In addition a mat can run beneath the kick plate of a vanity. Never overlap mats, never cut a mat to fit, and never attempt to repair a cut or nicked heating wire. If the wire is damaged, the entire mat must be replaced.

Installing electric radiant heat

continued

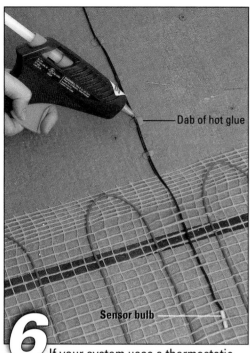

Dab of hot glue

Sensor bulb

6 If your system uses a thermostatic sensor, weave the sensor bulb between two heating elements. Adhere the bulb wire with dots of hot glue. Now check the mat resistance with an ohmmeter. If the reading falls outside the manufacturer's tolerance, find the damaged mat and replace it.

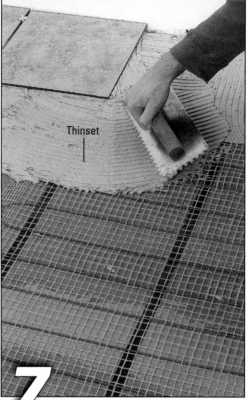

Thinset

7 With the flat side of a ⅜-inch notched trowel, apply thinset over an area of the mat. Then turn the trowel over and rake the thinset to ¼-inch uniform depth. Be careful not to snag the mat. Don't clean the trowel by banging it on the mat. Tile the area of the floor covered with thinset.

Ohmmeter

8 Check mat resistance a second time with the ohmmeter. If the ohm reading drops to zero or infinity, the heating element has been damaged. The tile must be removed and the mat replaced.

Radiant heat for most floors

You can install almost any finished flooring over radiant heat, but the key to the system's performance is how well the flooring materials conduct heat.

Ceramic tile and stone are the best conductors and will allow the system to run more efficiently than other materials. Parquet and laminate are also good conductors. Carpet tile is thinner than broadloom carpet, but still acts as insulation and won't distribute heat as well as solid materials. As vinyl tile has almost no R-value, it's a good choice but should not be heated above 85 degrees F.

No matter which flooring material you install, put separate thermostats in each room to customize the heat for maximum comfort and efficiency.

Plan ahead for wiring

Carefully sketch the system wiring on a dimensional plan. Note the location of the thermostat and any other electrical switches or outlets in the room. Measure the location of the switch/thermostat from a reference point such as an adjoining wall and transfer this measurement to the subfloor in the room below.

If possible locate the thermostat on an interior wall; this will make drilling through the floor plate easier. Place the thermostat as close to the power source as possible. Long lead wires from the power source can reduce the efficiency of the system.

Bathroom heating plan

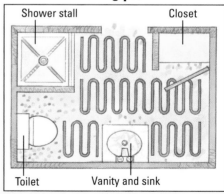

Shower stall

Closet

Toilet

Vanity and sink

Before you purchase a radiant system, sketch the room it will be heating. Mats or piping are not required under closets, major appliances, and vanities. In bathrooms about 50 percent of the total floor area should be heated; in kitchens and living areas about 60 percent.

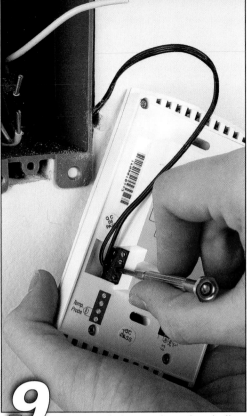

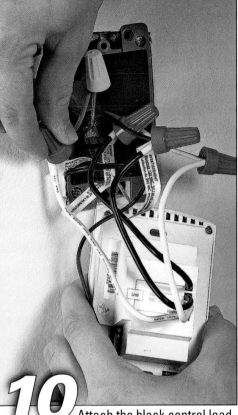

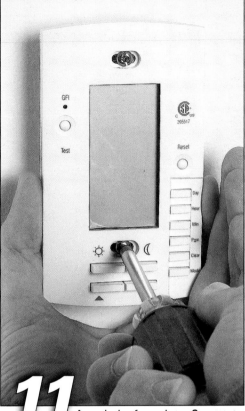

9 The control shown above has built-in GFCI protection. Using a jeweler's screwdriver, attach the two sensor wires to the screw terminals on one side of the control. Connect the ground from the mat power lead directly to the house ground.

10 Attach the black control lead marked "LINE" to the incoming black wire. Connect the white control lead "LINE" to the incoming white wire. Attach the black and white control leads marked "LOAD" to the black and white wires connecting to the mat. Fold the wires into the box.

11 Attach the faceplate. Connect to the power source or connect the line to a new breaker. Turn on the power and follow the manufacturer's instructions for setting the temperature and timer.

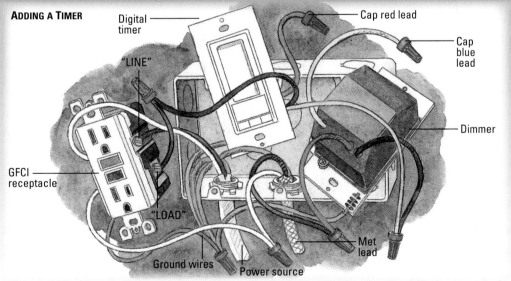

ADDING A TIMER

Digital timer · Cap red lead · Cap blue lead · "LINE" · Dimmer · GFCI receptacle · "LOAD" · Met lead · Ground wires · Power source

This configuration draws power from a GFCI receptacle and combines a timer and dimmer to control the heat level. The result: A warm bathroom floor greets morning bathers. A sensor bulb and line is not needed with this approach.

SAFETY FIRST
Don't overload circuit or components

Checking the amperage demanded by a new installation will let you know if an existing circuit can carry the load or if you'll have to install a new circuit.

Each square foot of electric radiant heating mat draws 0.1 amp. That means adding radiant heating mats to the work area of an average-size bath will add only 5 or 6 amps to the circuit (50–60 square feet of mat). But each component included in the system also has to be up to that amperage. Check dimmers and timers to make sure they are rated to take the amperage.

Installing an underfloor hydronic system

1 Plan a hydronic system so you can locate the holes for the PEX tubing as close as possible to the subfloor and to the ends of the joists. Using a drill and hole saw or Forstner bit ¼ inch larger than the tubing (a spade bit will wear out quickly), drill all holes in the joists before you begin threading the tubing.

2 Lay a coil of tubing on the floor at one end of the room. Walk the end of the tubing down the length of the room and thread the tubing through the first joist. Have a helper unwind the tubing from the coil and push the tubing through the holes as you walk it down the bays between the joists. Untwist the tubing from the roll so it does not kink as you thread it through the holes.

PLAN A HYDRONIC SYSTEM
A job for the pros

Success lies in the planning. Plan your system room by room, using grid paper to draw the tube spacing and the location of the manifold stations (the place where each circuit begins). Have a professional design the layout based on your plans.

PEX tubing comes in different diameters. Make sure the flow of water through the pipes is sufficient for the room you're heating. For example ½-inch tubing needs a manifold station every 300 feet, ⅝-inch tubing needs one every 450 feet.

Space the tubing lines closer together along exterior walls. This increases the output of heat in the coldest areas of the room. Provide access panels to manifold stations so you can make repairs easily.

HYDRONIC THIN-SLAB INSTALLATIONS

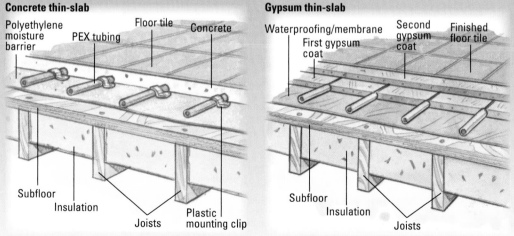

Concrete thin-slab — Polyethylene moisture barrier, PEX tubing, Floor tile, Concrete, Subfloor, Insulation, Joists, Plastic mounting clip

Gypsum thin-slab — Waterproofing/membrane, First gypsum coat, Second gypsum coat, Finished floor tile, Subfloor, Insulation, Joists

Burying a hydronic system in 2 inches of concrete results in a heavier load than most wood-frame floors can handle. Even thin-slabs, which are perfect for adding radiant heat in an addition to your home, may not be suitable in existing construction. They add 15 to 18 pounds per square foot. Thin-slabs also raise the floor level, which requires raising base cabinets and toilet flanges, and shortens the floor-to-sill distances of windows.

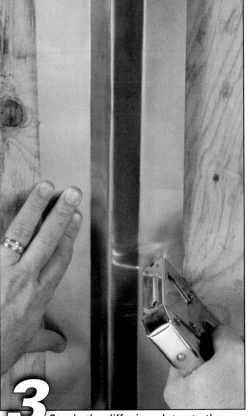

3 Staple the diffusion plates to the subfloor, spacing the plates and tubing as directed by the manufacturer. One-coil systems are generally centered between the joists. If you're working with a system that has a return line, label the inflow and outflow lines and connect the lines to a boiler.

Installing an above-floor hydronic system

Cut ¾-inch plywood or 1× sleepers to a width that will space the tubing consistent with the manufacturer's specifications. Make sure the ends of the tubing will bend without crimping. Mark the locations of the sleepers on the subfloor and fasten the first two with 1½-inch decking screws. Dry-lay a run of tubing to make sure it won't crimp, then fasten the remaining sleepers. If using a diffusion-plate system, snap and fasten the plates between the sleepers. Then press the tubing into the recesses of the plates. Cover the installation with plywood or thinset as recommended by the manufacturer.

CONNECT THE LINES TO A BOILER
Supplying hot water to hydronic systems

Although building codes in some localities may allow water heaters to be used for small hydronic systems, most systems require a hot water boiler or geothermal heat pump. Boiler manufacturers generally make models for home use with and without a self-contained water heater. When planning a hydronic system, make sure the output of the boiler or heat pump meets the room's heat load requirements.

Using precut underlayment

Avoid having to cut and fasten sleepers by using plywood underlayment with channels precut in its surface. Fasten the panels to the subfloor, snap in the diffusion plates (if required), and press the tubing into the channels. Cover the installation with the proper substrate.

INSTALLING CERAMIC & STONE TILE

You'll find that setting the tile is less tedious and more rewarding than preparing a floor for tiling. This is when you begin to see the results of your planning. If you have several tile flooring projects planned, start with the least complicated. That way you can build your skills and gain experience.

Mixing mortar and thinset

Before you mix adhesives read the manufacturer's directions carefully. Always mix mortar and grout in a clean container. Any residue in the bucket may cause the material to cure prematurely and ruin the batch. Thoroughly clean buckets and utensils after each mixing to save time and avoid problems down the line.

Carefully heed the "working" time—how long it takes the material to set up. Once the setting up has started, tile will not adhere. Grout that has exceeded its working time will not work properly into the joints and will pop out when dry. If either material starts to set up before you finish working with it, scrape it off the surface, remix, and reapply.

It takes some practice to discover how much material will cover an area before it sets up. Installation of large tiles will go more quickly than small tiles. Start with a small batch and work up to larger areas.

Heat and humidity affect mortar and grout. You may need to mix a wetter consistency in hot or dry conditions. However do not add water to mortar that has begun to set up in the heat; doing so weakens its strength. Discard the mixture and start over.

Working with mastics

Mastic ingredients may settle in the can, leaving an oily-looking liquid on top. Stir until the consistency is smooth.

If you open a can of mastic and it has begun to harden, throw it out and purchase fresh stock.

Application techniques remain essentially the same no matter what room you are tiling.

CHAPTER PREVIEW

Installing ceramic tile
page 84

Cutting ceramic tile
page 90

Grouting, caulking, and sealing
page 92

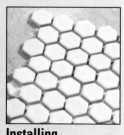

Installing mosaic tile
page 96

Slate makes an excellent floor for all rooms, especially entryways. Its neutral surface acts as a background for any design scheme, and its naturally rough surface provides a built-in nonslip safety feature. Slate is also durable. Hard slates are easy to maintain; softer Indian slates require sealer.

Installing stone tile
page 98

INSTALLING CERAMIC TILE

Prepare the surface using the methods discussed in Chapter 3, Preparing the Room, as well as the strategies shown here for determining the layout. Slab floors in nonwet areas may not require the installation of backerboard. Install backerboard on wood surfaces that will get wet, such as bathrooms or entryways.

Before you trowel on the mortar, sweep the floor clean. Calculate how many tiles you need in each layout grid and stack them around the room closest to each section. That way you won't have to go back and forth for new tiles when you start laying each grid.

Sort through all the tile boxes to make sure the dye lots match and separate out any chipped tiles. Use these for cut pieces.

If you are installing saltillo or handmade tile, its color may be consistent within each carton but vary from box to box. Sort through the tiles; at each layout grid mix some from each box. Doing so spreads the colors evenly in the room and keeps them from occurring in patches.

PRESTART CHECKLIST

☐ **TIME**
About an hour to trowel and set 4 to 6 square feet (varies with tile size)

☐ **TOOLS**
Mortar mixing paddle, ½-inch electric drill, notched trowel, 4-foot level, beater block, hammer or rubber mallet, utility knife, sponge

☐ **SKILLS**
Mixing with power drill, troweling

☐ **PREP**
Install backerboard, clean surface, snap layout lines

☐ **MATERIALS**
Five-gallon bucket, thinset, tile, spacers, ¾-inch plywood squares

Determine the layout

CHECKING A FLOOR FOR SQUARE

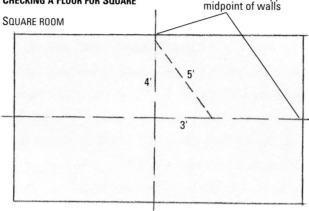

SQUARE ROOM

Chalklines snapped at midpoint of walls

4'   5'

3'

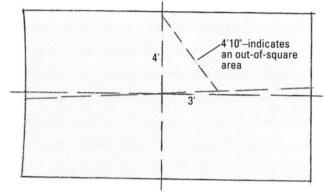

OUT-OF-SQUARE ROOM

4'

4'10"—indicates an out-of-square area

3'

One of the most common problems in planning a tiled floor is out-of-square walls. Walls seldom define a room squarely, but you need some perpendicular reference to square your tile layout with the room. To determine if a floor is square, use a 3-4-5 triangle.

Snap a chalkline on the floor at the midpoints of opposite walls. From the intersection measure out one line a distance of 3 feet. Tape the chalkline at that point and measure and tape a distance of 4 feet on the other line. Now measure the distance between the tapes. If it's 5 feet exactly, the floor is square. Adjust the lines, if necessary, until they are perpendicular.

Make a sketch of the layout of the tile on your floor. Even a rough drawing will help you organize.

Wavy walls can mean you will need to cut some of the edge tiles at different widths. Check the walls with a 4-foot level and mark wavy sections on the drawing as accurately as possible.

LAYING OUT A TILE FLOOR

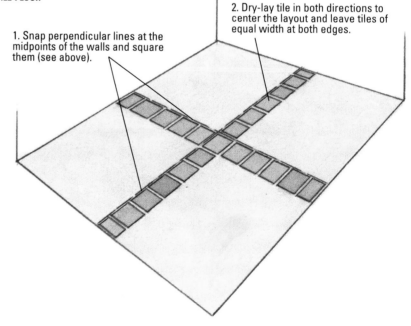

2. Dry-lay tile in both directions to center the layout and leave tiles of equal width at both edges.

1. Snap perpendicular lines at the midpoints of the walls and square them (see above).

Mark the layout lines on the floor

1 Dry-lay your tile with spacers on each axis (see "Laying Out a Tile Floor," opposite bottom). When the layout is square and even, mark the floor at several junctures of the grout lines. Take up the tile and snap a chalkline at the centermost pair of marks.

2 Continue to snap chalklines across the surface of the floor at points that represent the edges of the tile. These layout lines will serve as guides to help you keep each course straight and square with the room.

HOW TO LAY OUT DIFFERENT ROOM CONFIGURATIONS

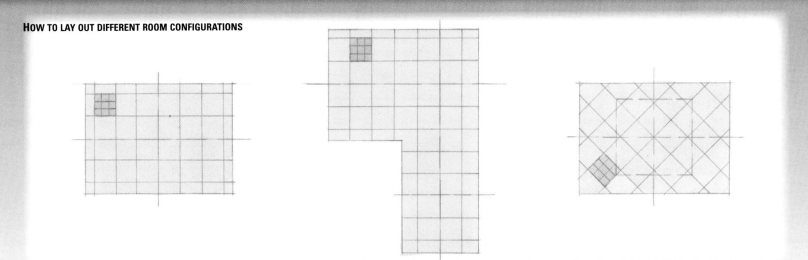

The room's configuration also dictates your approach to layout lines and grids. For small square or rectangular rooms, the number of lines will be minimal, and it is unlikely that you'll need a line at the edges to mark the location of cut tiles. In a large room with large handmade pavers, add lines marking the location of the edge tiles and snap 3-foot grids to help keep it straight. In an L-shape room, position the lines along the longest walls so they fall in both sections. In all cases snap the first pair of reference lines where a grout line will fall.

Setting the tile

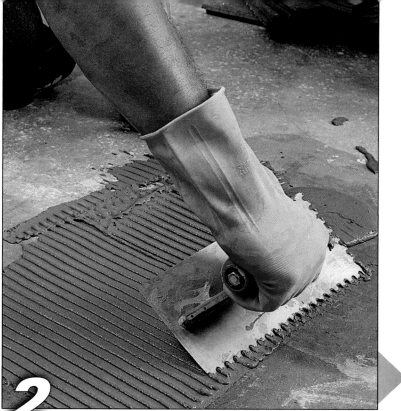

1 Pour the water into a bucket, then add about half the dry thinset. Mix the thinset with a ½-inch drill and a mortar paddle. Keep the speed below 300 rpm to avoid introducing air. Add thinset a little at a time. When the thinset is evenly mixed, let it set for 10 minutes before applying.

2 Dump mortar at the edge of a section of the room. Holding the straight edge of a trowel at about a 30-degree angle, spread the mortar evenly as thick as the depth of a trowel notch. Spread the mortar to the layout line; comb it with the notched edge at about a 45- to 75-degree angle.

MIX THE THINSET

Whether you have chosen thinset or organic mastic, bring it into the room to acclimate it to normal room temperatures—ideally between 65 degrees and 75 degrees F. Mix thinset with water that is clean enough to drink and clean out the bucket after each mix; mortar and adhesive residue can cause a new batch to cure prematurely.

Adding the powder to the water a little at a time reduces airborne mortar dust and makes mixing easier. Let the mixture set for 10 minutes so the water will penetrate any remaining lumps. Then mix again to remove lumps. To test the consistency load a trowel with mortar and hold it upside down. If the mortar falls off the trowel easily, add more dry powder and remix. The ideal consistency is as thick as peanut butter. Clean the subfloor before applying thinset adhesive.

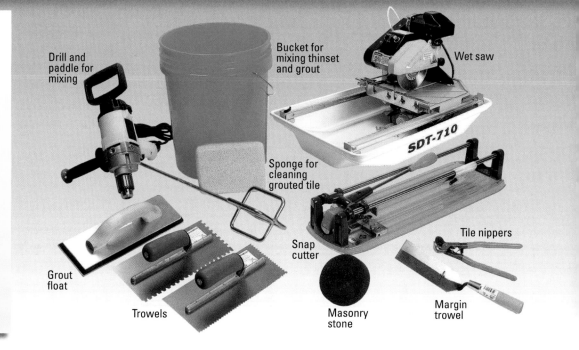

Drill and paddle for mixing

Bucket for mixing thinset and grout

Wet saw

Sponge for cleaning grouted tile

Snap cutter

Tile nippers

Grout float

Trowels

Masonry stone

Margin trowel

3 Starting in the center of the room, set the first full tile at the intersection of your layout lines, positioning it with a slight twist as you embed it in the mortar. Do not slide the tile—sliding can thin out the thinset and push mortar into the joints. Keep the edges of the tile on the layout lines.

4 Using the layout pattern you have chosen, lay the next tile in place with the same twisting motion, keeping the tile aligned on your layout line. Insert spacers between the tiles and adjust the tiles to fit.

5 Following the method outlined in step 4, continue setting tiles in a straight line. Trowel on only as much thinset as you'll cover with each row of tile.

Choose the right trowel

The size of the notches in the trowel you use will depend on the thickness of the tile. The depth of the notch, and therefore the ridge it forms in the adhesive, should be about two-thirds the tile thickness.

For 6- to 8-inch floor tiles, use a ¼- to ⅜-inch square-notched trowel; for large tiles (more than 12 inches), use a deep (½-inch) square-notched trowel.

Combing adhesive so it forms the right-size ridges requires that you hold the trowel at about a 30-degree angle and keep the edges in constant contact with the substrate. If you have trouble making ¼-inch ridges with a ¼-inch trowel, switch to a ⅜-inch notch and hold the trowel at a slightly lower angle.

Testing the mixture

Properly applied thinset forms ridges that compress to cover the entire back of the tile when it is embedded. If thinset is applied too wet, it will not hold these ridges. A dry thinset application will not compress and will result in the tile adhering only to the top of the ridges.

Test a thinset mixture occasionally by pulling up a tile and examining the back. If the thinset completely covers the surface, the mixture is correct, as shown here.

6 Periodically check to make sure the tile conforms to the layout lines in both directions. Lay a long metal straightedge or 4-foot level on the edge of the tile. This edge should align itself with the layout lines. Each joint within the pattern should also be straight. Scrape off any excess thinset that may have spread over a layout line. Adjust the tiles to straighten the joints if necessary.

7 Continue laying the tiles according to your chosen pattern, spacing and checking them as you go. Don't kneel or walk on set tiles. If you need to straighten a tile that is out of reach, lay down a 2-foot square of ¾-inch plywood to distribute your weight evenly and avoid disturbing the tile. Cut at least two pieces of plywood to use, so you can position one while kneeling on the other.

Setting spacers

When laying loose tiles (not sheet-mounted), use plastic spacers to keep the tiles the proper width apart.

Insert spacers vertically in the joint after you set each successive tile. That way the tile will move into the correct placement after it is embedded in the mortar. Once you reach a point where tiles form corners, flip the spacer down into the corner. Pull the spacers before grouting, even if the manufacturer's instructions indicate that you can leave them in place. Spacers may show through the grout.

The tiles have uneven edges?

Tiles with irregular edges, such as saltillo and handmade pavers, may be difficult to keep straight, and spacers will not align the uneven edges. To keep such tiles aligned, make your layout grids small—a nine-tile (three-by-three) layout works well.

Trowel adhesive one grid at a time and set the tiles in place. Adjust the tiles until the appearance of the joints is consistent and expect to make a few compromises.

Leveling the tile

1 When you have finished laying one section or grid of tile, place a long metal straightedge or a 4-foot carpenter's level on the surface and check for any tiles that are higher or lower than the overall surface. Make a beater block out of a 12- to 15-inch 2×4 covered with scrap carpet. Tap high tiles in place using the beater block and a hammer or rubber mallet.

2 If you discover tiles that are lower than the rest, pry them up with the point of a utility knife and spread additional adhesive on the back of the tile. Set the tile back in place and level it with the beater block. Clean excess mortar from the joints while the mortar is still wet. Run the blade of a utility knife in the joint, flicking out the excess as it accumulates on the blade. Pick up loose bits of mortar with a damp sponge. Let the thinset cure at least overnight.

STANLEY PRO TIP: **Tile a hearth**

1 Hearths take a beating, so lay a double thickness of backerboard first. Spread heat-resistant mortar on the existing hearth or subfloor and set one piece of backerboard in it. Embed the board in the mortar. Spread mortar on the top of the backerboard and lay metal lath on it. Then apply mortar to the second piece of backerboard and lay it mortared side down on the metal lath. Embed and realign this piece so the corners of both boards are flush with each other. Clean the excess and let the mortar set for 48 hours.

2 Frame the hearth with wood trim that matches other trim in the room. Spread and comb heat-resistant mortar on the backerboard bed and, starting along an edge with full tiles, set the tiles in place. Be sure to leave a ¼-inch gap along the wood trim. If your hearth design includes insets, set them as you go—don't wait until you've set all the field tiles.

3 After the mortar has cured (at least overnight), grout the joints with unsanded grout, cleaning the tiles thoroughly to remove the excess grout and haze. Caulk the joint along the trimmed edge and seal the tiles with a penetrating sealer. Apply the sealer liberally. It will keep the hearth clean.

CUTTING CERAMIC TILE

Cutting tile requires a little skill and patience—save yourself installation time by practicing a few cuts first.

If the cut tiles in your project will be the same width, cut all of them at once, trowel on the adhesive, and lay the tiles. If the tiles will not be uniform, cut each one separately. Do not let adhesive set longer than its working time while you're making the cuts.

Tile cutting is accomplished with a variety of tools. For one or two cuts you need only a tile nippers or a rod saw with a carbide blade.

Rent a wet saw to cut thicker tiles. If you have several tiles to cut, the wet saw will prove well worth its cost. Water is used to cool wet-saw blades. It comes from an outlet or from water in a trough below it. Do not use the wet saw without water.

Cut tile edges are rough. Either hide them under toe-kicks or smooth them with a masonry stone.

PRESTART CHECKLIST

☐ **TIME**
Less than 5 minutes to mark and cut each tile

☐ **TOOLS**
Felt-tip or china marker, tape measure, snap cutter, wet saw, tile nippers, masonry stone

☐ **SKILLS**
Measuring and marking tile precisely; cutting tile with nippers, snap cutter, or power saw

☐ **PREP**
Install backerboard and field tile

☐ **MATERIALS**
Tile

Sizing the cut

Straight cut: For the last row of partial tiles place the tile to be cut on top of the installed tile closest to the wall. Place another tile over the tile to be cut with its edge against the wall. Trace the edge with a marker. Draw the cutting line parallel to the mark but shorter by the width of two grout lines.

L-shape cut: Place the tile to be trimmed first on one corner, then the other, marking the cutlines with a full tile as you would for a single straight cut. Cut each side shorter than the mark by the width of two grout lines.

STANLEY PRO TIP

Don't wash away the line

The blade of a wet saw is cooled with water, which will wash away a cutline made with a felt-tip marker. When marking tiles that will be cut with a wet saw, use a china marker so the line won't wash away.

Protect your eyes when cutting

Cutting tile with a snap cutter is not especially dangerous, but you should wear eye protection to guard against any fine chips, especially from glazed tile.

A wet saw can discharge chips and larger pieces of tile at high speed, so wearing eye protection is a must. Wear ear protection as well to guard against damage from the noise of the saw.

Wear safety glasses when cutting tile with nippers.

Save on rental costs

Cut all your edge tiles in one day. That way you only pay one day's rental for a wet saw.

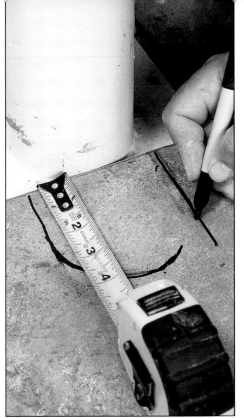

Curved cuts: Set the tile to be cut against the obstruction, lining up its edges with tile already laid. Mark the width of the cut by setting a tape measure on each edge of the obstruction. Move the tile to one side of the obstruction and use the tape to mark the depth of the cut.

Making straight cuts

Snap cutter: Insert the tile in the cutter, aligning the scoring wheel on the cutline. Pull or push the scoring wheel across the cutline, using firm pressure throughout the stroke. Score the tile in one pass. Hold the tile firmly in place and strike the handle with the heel of your hand.

Wet saw: Set the tile securely against the fence with the cutline at the blade. Turn on the saw and feed the tile into the blade with light pressure. Increase the pressure as the saw cuts the tile and ease off as the blade approaches the rear of the cut. Keep the tile on the table at all times.

Making curved cuts

1 Using a wet saw make several relief cuts from the edge of the tile to the curved cutline. Relief cuts do not have to be exactly parallel to each other, but make sure they stop just short of the curved line.

2 Place the jaws of tile nippers about an inch away from the curved line and carefully snap out the waste at the relief cuts.

3 Working the nippers on the cutline, snap away the remaining excess. Don't try to "bite" through the tile with the nippers. Instead grasp the tile tightly with the tool and use a prying motion.

GROUTING, CAULKING, AND SEALING

Grouting, caulking, and sealing are not difficult tasks, but they do take time. Don't rush these steps—they affect both the final appearance of your tiling project and its longevity.

Bring all materials into the room to acclimate them to its temperature, preferably between 65 and 75 degrees F. Prepare the surface by removing spacers and cleaning excess mortar from the joints and surface. Lightly mist the edges of nonvitreous tile with water so they won't absorb too much moisture from the grout. Vitreous tiles don't require misting.

Use a margin trowel to mix grout in clean containers, following the manufacturer's instructions and adding powder to liquid a little at a time. Let it set for 10 minutes and stir again to loosen its texture. Grout should be wet enough to spread but not runny.

PRESTART CHECKLIST

☐ **TIME**
From 15 to 30 minutes to mix, float, and clean a 4-foot-square section (varies with tile size). About 5 minutes to caulk a 10-foot joint, 45 minutes to seal a 15×20-foot floor, longer if applying sealer to joints only

☐ **TOOLS**
Utility or grout knife, nylon scrubber, margin trowel, grout float, grout bag (optional), applicator or mop for sealer, caulk gun

☐ **SKILLS**
Spreading grout with float; using caulk gun

☐ **PREP**
Install all tile; let mortar cure

☐ **MATERIALS**
Grout, bucket and water, sponge, rags, sealer, caulk

Grouting tile

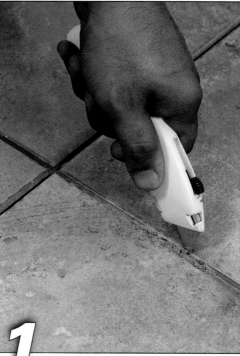

1 Remove the spacers if you haven't already. Inspect the joints for any remaining adhesive and scrape residue with a utility or grout knife. Remove any remaining hardened mortar from the tile surface with a nylon (not metal) scrubber.

2 Mix the grout to the consistency recommended by the manufacturer; dump or scoop out a small pile with a margin trowel. Working in 10-square-foot sections, pack the grout into the joints with a grout float. Hold the float at about a 30- to 45-degree angle; work the grout in both directions.

WHAT IF...
The grout joints are wide?

Irregular tiles look best with wide grout joints, but wide joints may be hard to fill with a grout float. Use a grout bag for these tiles and for rough tiles whose surfaces will be difficult to clean.

Fit a metal spout on the bag equal to the width of the joint. Fill the bag with grout. Working down the length of the joint, squeeze the bag, overfilling the joint slightly. Compact the excess and sweep loose grout with a stiff broom when dry.

STANLEY PRO TIP

Avoid voids when power mixing grout

Power mixing can introduce air bubbles in grout and leave voids in it. Mix grout by hand with a margin trowel, adding the powder to the water. Let the mix set for 10 minutes, then remix before applying.

Tips for grouting stone

Use the grout recommended by the manufacturer. Nonsanded grout tends to recede when curing, so you may need to apply it twice if the joints in your stone installation are set at 1/16 inch. Seal stone before grouting to ease cleaning and again after grouting.

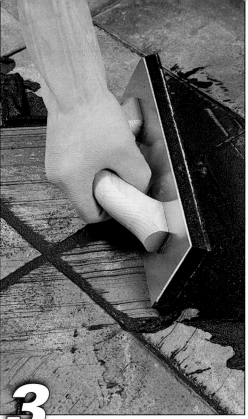

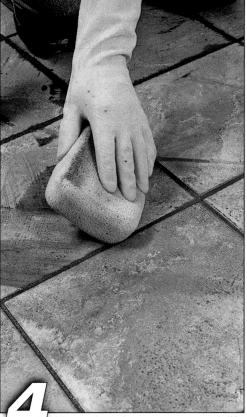

3 Once you have grouted a section, hold the float almost perpendicular to the tile and scrape the excess from the tile surface. Work the float diagonally to the joints to avoid lifting the grout. If you remove grout replace it in the joint and reclean the surface. Let the grout set.

4 When a just-damp sponge won't lift grout from the joint, start cleaning. Wring out all excess water from a damp sponge and rub the surface in a circular motion. Rinse and wring out the sponge often. Repeat parallel to the joints to make them neat and once more to finish cleaning.

5 Let the surface dry about 15 minutes, then remove the grout haze from the surface with a dry, clean rag. Avoid terry-cloth material as it tends to lift out uncured grout. Tile with a matte finish might require another cleaning with fresh water and a clean sponge.

Sealing grout and tiles

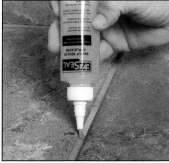

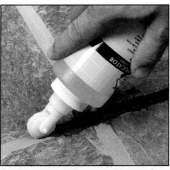

Although latex or polymer-modified grouts resist staining, you'll get the best protection from stains by sealing the grout.

On glazed and other impervious tiles apply the sealer only to the joint, using an applicator designed for this purpose.

To protect saltillo and other soft-bodied tiles, seal the entire surface with a mop or applicator as recommended by the manufacturer.

Different sealers can leave stone in its natural color or enhance its richness.

Caulking the joints

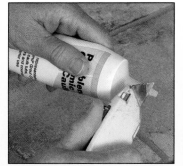

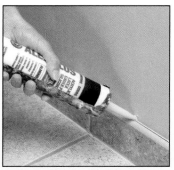

Use a utility knife to cut the nozzle to the width of the joint and at a 45-degree angle. Cut through the nozzle in one pass. Before you apply the caulk, practice the techniques on scrap.

Starting in one corner squeeze the handle of the caulk gun gently

and apply the caulk to the joint. Keep the caulk gun moving as you squeeze so the caulk won't overrun the joint. Finish the surface of the caulk with a wet finger or sponge. Light pressure will avoid gouging.

Adding a tile base

1 Out-of-level floors force you to adjust the base tiles to make their top edges level. You'll make up the difference in the joint at the floor. Lay the bullnose tile against the wall with spacers. Adjust the tile heights with plastic wedges until the top edges of all tiles are level. Make sure the joint at the floor is as even as possible from one end to the other. Continue the layout on adjacent walls. Mark the wall at the top edge of the final layout.

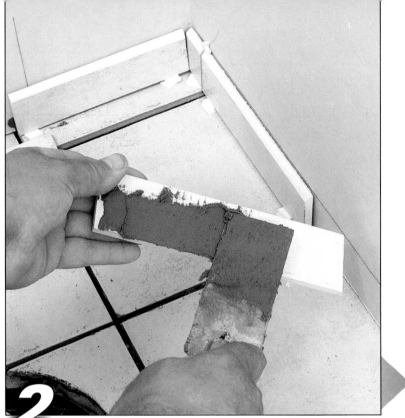

2 Remove the tiles and snap a level chalkline at the mark you made. Mark all the walls with chalklines in a similar fashion. Mix up enough thinset to cover the area in which you'll be working. Backbutter each tile and set in place.

WHAT IF…
Bullnose is not available for your tile?

If bullnose trim is not available in the style you need, cut trim tile from the same stock you laid on the floor. Determine the height of the edging you want and cut enough tiles to run the entire length of the wall. Cut each piece of the tile only once. Even if you can get more than one piece from a large floor tile, you'll want a factory edge on top. Install the cut tile and, if the factory edge is not finished to your liking, grout the top edge.

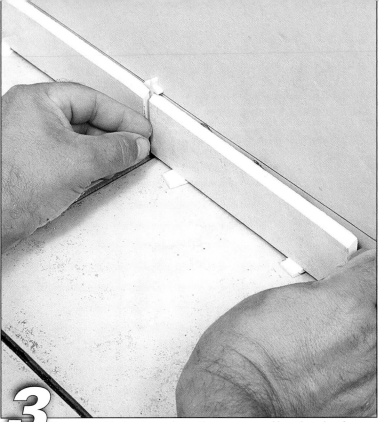

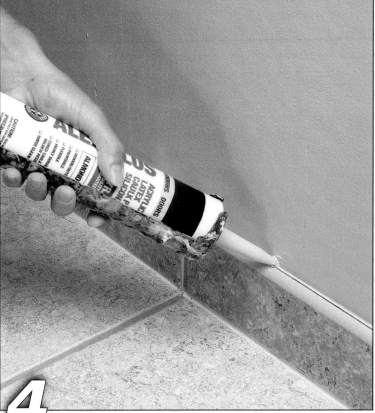

3 Press the tile in place, inserting spacers. Use the plastic wedges to keep the top edge in line. About every 3 feet use a 4-foot level to make sure the top edge is level. Adjust the tile if necessary by gently pushing or pulling on the wedges as needed. Gently remove excess mortar from the joints with a utility knife. Clean the surface. Set and clean corner tiles. Let the mortar cure overnight before grouting.

4 As a final step grout the trim tiles and caulk the joints at the floor and top edge. Force grout into the vertical joints with a grout float. When the grout has partially cured, remove the excess from the joint at the floor with a utility knife and from the surface with a damp sponge. Sponge-clean the surface at least twice. Wipe off the haze with a clean rag. Caulk the joint at the floor and along the top edge of the trim. Smooth the caulk with a wet finger or sponge.

Wrap the corners

Double-bullnose tile has two rounded edges—one on top and another on the side. It is made especially to provide a smooth way to finish outside corners. The vertical rounded edge covers the square edge of the adjoining tile.

Easing the transitions

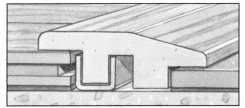

A reducer strip eases the transition from a thicker to thinner floor, from wood to ceramic tile for example.

A universal threshold is used when wood flooring butts up against a carpeted floor.

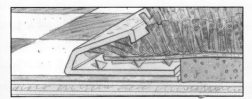

Carpet edging is an inexpensive transition between carpet and another floor material.

T-molding is used as a transition between floors of the same height.

INSTALLING MOSAIC TILE

Not long ago setting mosaic tile meant embedding each small piece in a mortar bed. Later, sheets of mosaic held together by paper facing helped reduce installation time. These early face-mounted sheets, however, were difficult to line up.

Modern mosaics are bonded to a sheet with plastic dots or on a plastic mesh, paper, or threaded backing.

You'll find mosaics in many colors and in squares, rectangles, random designs, and all forms of geometric figures. Most mosaic tiles are glass or high-fired porcelain, so they're impervious to moisture. Porcelains come with glazed surfaces for walls and nonslip surfaces for floors.

If the style you've chosen is available only in dot-mounted sheets, make sure the dots are free of any residual manufacturing oil. This oil interferes with adhesive bonding. Check two or three sheets in each carton, wiping them with a paper towel.

If replacing a carton is not an alternative, either change your design or wash the back of each sheet with a mild detergent.

PRESTART CHECKLIST

☐ **TIME**
About 5 to 6 hours (not including grouting) for an 8×10-foot room

☐ **TOOLS**
Chalkline, power drill, mixing paddle, notched trowel, beater block, rubber mallet, 4-foot metal straightedge

☐ **SKILLS**
Measuring, setting tile

☐ **PREP**
Remove existing flooring; repair or replace underlayment

☐ **MATERIALS**
Epoxy mortar, mosaic sheets

1 Lay out perpendicular lines in the center of the room and snap grid lines at intervals of the same dimensions as the mosaic sheet. Mix the epoxy adhesive and, using a ¼-inch notched trowel, spread and comb the adhesive on a small area, just inside the layout lines.

2 Set the corner of the first sheet just inside the corner of the layout lines. Square the sheet to the lines and embed the tiles firmly into the mortar with a beater block and rubber mallet. Make sure the entire surface of the sheet is level in the mortar—mosaics show depressions dramatically.

Arranging random patterns

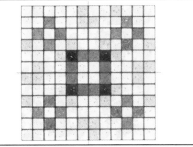 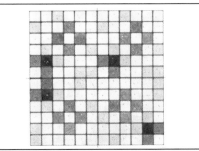

A mosaic pattern that features randomly placed colored tiles is more difficult to set than one that has regular geometric patterns—you have to balance color throughout.

Lay the sheets on the surface in a dry run, changing their positions until you get the arrangement right. Then take up the sheets and number them so you can mortar them in the same order.

Such experimentation produced the balanced pattern (above left), but this pattern with its centered square is not the only balanced design possible with these tiles. Avoid patterns like the one shown (above right). Although it is composed of the same tiles, the pattern appears chaotic.

3 Pull the sheet up and check it for full coverage. If some of the tiles show bare spots, apply more mortar. Lay the sheet facedown on a clean surface and skim more mortar on the back. Recomb the mortar bed with a larger notched trowel and reset the sheet with the beater block.

4 Set the next sheet using the same technique. After four or five sheets, you should have a feel for the proper amount of mortar. As you embed the tiles with the beater block, make sure the edges of each sheet are level with its neighbors, then line up all the joints.

5 Continue setting the tiles using a metal straightedge to keep the joints straight. Wipe excess mortar from the surface of the tile with a damp (not wet) sponge. Make sure you remove all of the excess—dried mortar is very difficult to remove. Let the mortar set, then grout and clean the tiles.

STANLEY PRO TIP

Keep colors consistent

It's impossible to set mosaics without some of the mortar creeping up into the grout joints. To keep your work from looking blotchy when you apply the grout, use the same product for both the mortar bed and the grout—100 percent solid epoxy of the same color. Alternatively you might be able to color the mortar to match the grout, but such attempts often result in noticeably different shades.

Embedding the mosaic sheets into the mortar will inevitably force some mortar onto the surface of the tiles. Before you set the next section, use a synthetic scrubbing pad to clean the tile, then wipe it with a dampened sponge. Don't use too much water—it will wash out the epoxy from the joint and weaken it.

WHAT IF...
Mosaic tiles need to be cut?

One advantage of mosaics is that the small individual tiles can often fit around obstacles without being cut. Use a utility knife to cut the backing in the contour of the obstacle and strip away the tiles.

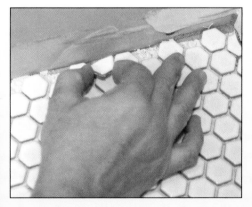

If you need to cut an individual tile, remove it from the backing and cut it with a snap cutter. Backbutter the cut piece and set it into the mortar.

Installing Stone Tile

Stone tile requires the same firm and level setting bed as ceramic tile—only more so. Because stone is brittle and the minerals that make up its pattern are not perfectly "cemented" to each other, it is subject to fracture along the grain lines.

Stone also suffers from the normal physical inconsistencies found in any natural material. Some pieces might not be exactly as wide or thick as the others.

When set the top edges of all tiles should be flush. Backbutter each tile before you set it in the mortar bed and test it to make sure its edges are flush with its neighbors.

Most stone tile comes from the factory with beveled edges, so cutting a tile will leave it with an unbeveled edge. Hone the edge of the cut tile with a rubbing stone or with sandpaper wrapped around a block of wood. To polish a tile to a high sheen, use progressively finer grits of carbide sandpaper (from 120 to 600).

Prestart Checklist

☐ **Time**
About 10 hours for an 8×10-foot room. Allow 3 to 4 hours for grouting and cleanup on the next day.

☐ **Tools**
Sponge, chalkline, power drill with mixing paddle, notched trowel, beater block, rubber mallet, 4-foot metal straightedge, grout float, wet saw, dry-cutting saw

☐ **Skills**
Marking, setting, cutting tile

☐ **Prep**
Remove existing flooring; repair or replace underlayment

☐ **Materials**
Thinset mortar, stone tile, grout

1 Stone tile often has a dusty residue on its back, and this dust weakens the adhesive bond. Wipe your finger across the back of the tile and if it comes up dusty, clean the backs of the tiles with a sponge and water. Let the tiles dry before bedding them.

2 Lay out a dry run so the edge tiles are the same size. Then snap lines as guides. Using white thinset for light-color tiles, trowel thinset on the subfloor and backbutter the tile. Set and level the tiles, adding mortar to the back as needed. Line up the tiles with a straightedge.

What If...
You have to cut a hole in the stone?

Cutting holes for obstacles such as floor vents becomes a relatively easy task with a dry-cutting saw equipped with a diamond blade. The saw allows you to get almost all the way into the corners to make a clean cut.

Mark the outline with a china marker (not a felt-tip, which may bleed). While a helper steadies the tile, lower the saw into the middle of the line, then back to the other corner. Knock out the cut piece with tile nippers and trim the corners square. Don't worry if the cutline is slightly errant; it will be hidden under the vent cover.

3 When the mortar for the field tiles has set sufficiently (usually overnight), cut the edge tiles with a wet saw and lay them in a mortar bed, backbuttering each tile as you go. Measure for each individual edge tile—it's unlikely that the room will be square and all the tiles the same size.

4 Let the mortar for the edge tiles cure for 24 hours. Mix a batch of unsanded grout, enough to cover a small section. To keep the stone tiles from absorbing too much water from the grout, wet them with a spray bottle. Apply the grout with a float. Remove excess grout from the surface of the stone. When the grout has set for about 15 minutes, wipe the haze with a damp sponge. Finish grouting the entire installation, working in sections to clean the excess before it hardens. When the grout has completely cured, seal the tiles as necessary.

WHAT IF...
Edge tiles are not available?

Some manufacturers produce stone bullnose, but if your selection doesn't come with them (and you need them to finish stone-tiled steps or a hearth), make your own by rounding the edges with a rubbing stone. As an alternative start with coarse carbide sandpaper wrapped around a wood block and polish with finer grades.

STANLEY PRO TIP: **Use adhesive alternatives for stone**

If you've laid granite tiles in an entryway or bathroom and have some left over, granite tiles make an attractive substitute for a granite slab on a countertop. If your tiles are cut to a consistent thickness, you can use silicone adhesive instead of thinset. Lay the tiles in a dry run. Lift one at a time, apply silicone to the substrate, and press the tiles in place. Line up the tiles with a straightedge.

For some stone tiles expensive epoxy mortar is the preferred adhesive, but you might be able to save money by sealing the back of the tiles with a nonporous epoxy sealer. Once the coating has cured, set the tiles in regular thinset mortar.

INSTALLING WOOD FLOORS

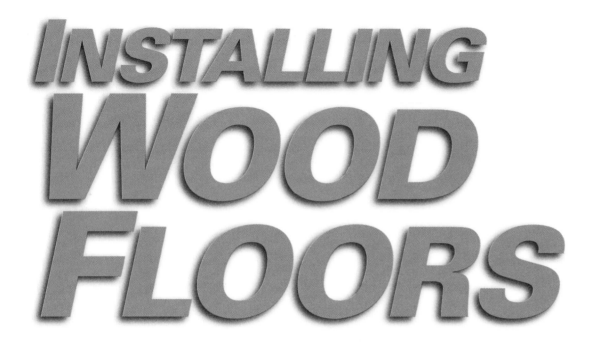

Although wood flooring is generally more expensive to buy and install than carpet or vinyl, it should last for decades. You'll find a number of wood floor options from which to choose.

Beautiful choices

Solid wood flooring is made from one continuous piece of solid wood, typically measuring ¾ inch thick. Wood strips are anywhere from 1½ inches to about 2¼ inches wide. Planks are wider than 2¼ inches. Most strip and plank flooring is milled with tongue-and-groove edges so boards will fit together, but some planks are flat-edged for a more rustic look. Wood strips or planks are generally nailed to the subfloor.

Engineered wood flooring is made from layers of wood stacked and glued together under heat and pressure. There are usually three or five layers stacked with grains running perpendicular to each other. All wood expands and contracts with heat and humidity, but engineered wood is more dimensionally stable because the layers keep the movement in balance. Because it is less inclined to swell and shrink, engineered wood can be laid in areas where solid wood cannot, such as over concrete or in high-moisture areas. Engineered wood flooring comes in types that are nailed or glued to the subfloor or glued edge-to-edge (tongue-and-groove). Engineered wood floors are also available that simply click together.

Parquet floors are made from custom-crafted wood tiles that are used to create a patterned floor. Parquet tiles are generally glued down to install.

Features to consider

A factory finish—usually four or more coats of ultraviolet-cured urethane resins—is one that the manufacturer applies at the plant. Because the finish is applied under strict environmental controls, manufacturers say it is more consistent and durable. Factory-finished floors can be installed right out of

---

Wood floors are a smart investment. This classic flooring will never go out of style.

CHAPTER PREVIEW

Installing wood strips or planks
page 102

Engineered wood floors
page 112

Installing wood stairs
page 122

Installing parquet tile
page 124

No matter what decorating style you select for a room, hardwood floors introduce timeless beauty.

the box, making them stress-free when you are living in a house as the floors are being replaced. There are many different stain colors and finishes from which to choose.

Onsite finishing allows the builder to custom-fit and finish your floor to the space. Many flooring professionals maintain that the smoothest finish can be achieved by sanding and finishing a floor onsite. Custom finishing gives more versatility in colors too. You do have to put up with the messy and time-consuming tasks of repeated sandings and finish applications.

Installing cork tile
page 128

INSTALLING WOOD STRIPS OR PLANKS

Hardwood lasts longer than other flooring options and can be refinished several times (solid hardwoods can be refinished an unlimited number of times)—or even restained to change the appearance. Today's polyurethane finishes allow installations in kitchens and half baths, as long as you take precautions to minimize water spills. Engineered woods are considered more stable for kitchen and bath applications.

Unfinished flooring gives you almost unlimited color stain options. The drawback: Unfinished flooring must be sanded and finished after installation, which typically requires the expertise of a professional and puts the room out of service for several days.

Prefinished flooring features a factory-applied finish that homeowners sometimes favor because it eliminates sawdust and finish vapors, and the room can be used within 24 hours after installation. The color options for prefinished flooring are not as varied as for unfinished flooring. Most engineered wood flooring is prefinished.

Stack and acclimate the wood planks or strips in a part of the room that you plan to floor last so the stack isn't in the way as you work. A bay window served as an out-of-the-way spot to store this supply of wood strips. For more on acclimating the materials, see below.

PRESTART CHECKLIST

☐ **TIME**
One day for a 10×10-foot room

☐ **TOOLS**
Measuring tape, pencil, hammer, chalkline, backsaw, pneumatic staple gun

☐ **SKILLS**
Measuring, sawing, nailing

☐ **PREP**
Prepare the subfloor as suggested in Chapter 3

☐ **MATERIALS**
15-pound tar paper, wood flooring, flooring nails, wood filler

STACK AND ACCLIMATE

Because wood expands and contracts, it is important to let the flooring planks or strips acclimate to the temperature and moisture conditions in your house. Have it delivered at least 72 hours in advance and store it in the room where it is to be installed.

For storage upon an on-grade concrete floor, provide a 4-inch airspace beneath the stacks or cartons of wood.

The ideal room temperature for two weeks prior to installation and throughout installation is 60°–75°F with humidity at 35–55 percent.

Matching wood floors

Even if you install the same wood upstairs as you have downstairs and apply the same stain, the two floors will still look different because one has gradually changed appearance with everyday wear and tear. However if you want an aged look on your new floors, you can apply a finish, called ambering, that will create an aged look.

Oil-base finishes give more ambering than water-base finishes. In fact some finishes are described as nonambering, so these will remain clear and will not lend themselves to the aged look you want.

You can also have the new floors artificially distressed, a look that's achieved by pounding the floors with hammers, chains, and rocks. Or you can simply buy a new floor that is already distressed.

1 Working near one end of the longest wall that's perpendicular to floor joists, drive a nail partially into the floor as a joist locator. (Nails securing subflooring offer clues to joist locations.) Use a measuring tape to find subsequent joists, which are usually 16 to 24 inches on center; mark this end of each joist with a protruding nail.

2 Undercut the bottom portion of the casing so planks or strips fit neatly below. Lay a wood plank or strip alongside the casing and rest the backsaw on top. The plank or strip keeps the saw at the correct height as you cut.

Two types of flooring nailer

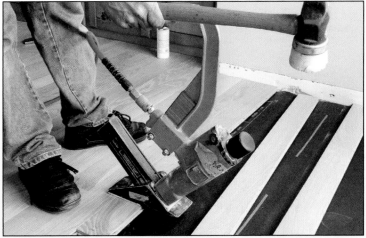

Put away the hammer for this project and rent a pair of pneumatic nail guns to get the job done right. The beauty of using a pneumatic nail gun is consistency—every nail will go in at the same angle and depth. A face nailer works best for the first and last boards you'll install. Use a side nailer for securing tongues to the subfloor. Use barbed flooring nails with the face nailer and cleat nails with the side nailer.

3 Staple one layer of hardwood floor underlayment onto the subfloor, running the lengths perpendicular to joists and overlapping edges by about 4 inches. (Allow the nail markers you've driven into the subfloor to poke through the felt.) This cushioned layer helps prevent squeaks.

4 Working along the opposite wall that runs perpendicular to the floor joists, locate the end of each joist. Mark the location of this end of each joist with a nail. Snap a chalkline between marks.

Wood floor species

Knowing a little about wood species will help you make a wise choice for your home's floors.

Some of the hardest domestic species are hickory, pecan, hard maple, and white oak. Next on the list: white ash, beech, red oak, yellow birch, green ash, and black walnut. Cherry and mahogany are softer but still make gorgeous and durable floors. Pine is a softwood, so it may dent and ding, but for many homeowners that adds to the floor's charm. And, like hardwoods, pine should last the lifetime of your home. Southern yellow pine is the hardest pine and is recommended for higher-traffic areas. Heart pine, from the center section of old-growth Southern longleaf yellow pine, can be difficult to locate and expensive, but some experts say heart pine rivals red oak in hardness. Pine flooring is often sold in widths from 4 to 16 inches to simulate what was used in Colonial-era homes.

Earth-friendly options

Salvaged lumber offers an aged and distressed look. Antique or recycled lumber involves more labor (removal from old buildings, pulling out nails, drying, etc.). But it can be worth the price if you're hoping to lay a floor that matches an old pine one.

When buying recycled lumber make sure it has been kiln-dried. Even 150-year-old lumber can still have a high moisture content. Often flooring planks are cut from old barn beams, and moisture levels can differ in various parts of the beam.

There is no formal grading for antique lumber, but most dealers offer grades depending upon the number of nail holes and other damage. In addition to grade ask how long the boards are. It can be difficult to get long boards in antique woods, and the look of a floor made up of 3-, 4-, and 5-foot lengths is much different than one with boards that are 8 or 16 feet long.

If you are installing primitive planks (and not barnwood flooring with tongues and grooves added) keep in mind that there will be gaps between boards once they are laid—another quality that adds to the appeal. With this type of flooring it's best to vacuum, rather than sweep. Otherwise you're just sweeping dirt into the cracks.

5 To serve as a guide for laying the first course straight, snap a chalkline perpendicular to the joist lines and near your starting wall. (See page 32 to learn how to establish square.) The first course in the installation shown here abuts an existing wood floor. (See page 102 for information on matching new wood to old.) Start the first course with the groove side facing the wall or existing flooring.

6 First and last courses must be nailed through the face of the planks or strips, 1 inch out from the wall. Predrilling $\frac{1}{16}$-inch pilot holes through the board face prevents nails from splitting the board.

SNAP A CHALKLINE

1 Use a measuring tape or ruled straightedge to locate the first mark. At the opposite end of the surface, make a second mark.

2 Position one end of the chalkline on the first mark.

3 Draw the string and stretch it across the second mark. Hold the string taut over the marks.

4 Pull upward on the string and release. The string will snap onto the surface and leave behind a chalk guideline.

Installing wood strips or planks continued

7 Lay the first board so it parallels the guidelines you established for square. Use spacers supplied (or suggested) by the manufacturer to position the course the prescribed distance from the wall. (This gap—usually ¾ inch—allows for expansion of the wood.) Use a hammer or a pneumatic face nailer to secure the first board.

8 Follow your guideline as you lay subsequent boards, abutting planks or strips end to end, drilling pilot holes, and securing the flooring with face-driven nails. The end of the last board should be cut to leave a ¾-inch gap between it and the wall.

How to cut hardwood flooring

Prevent splitting by rip-cutting hardwood planks facedown. Cut the piece ¼ inch narrower than the available space so there's room for the board to expand. Snap a chalkline between your cut marks for a clear guideline.

Rest the foot of the circular saw on a second piece of flooring placed beside the one you are cutting. Use a clamp to secure the pieces if necessary.

9 Because strips or planks tend to look the same within a bundle, unwrap several bundles of flooring and lay the pieces out (a process called racking). Mix them up for a balanced appearance and stagger joints across the entire floor.

10 To install the next row, cut the board so these end joints are offset from the previous row by at least 6 inches. Snug the boards tight end to end and row to row. These rows are still close enough to the wall that you need to use the face nailer or a hammer. Drill pilot holes and nail through the tongues for best results.

When using a power mitersaw to crosscut hardwood planks, lay the pieces faceup to avoid splits.

A jigsaw or coping saw works best for cutting curves or notches in hardwood. Clamp the piece you're cutting. Cut the plank facedown when using a jigsaw.

Installing wood strips or planks continued

11 After the third row or so you should be able to use the side nailer. (The nailer requires about 6 inches of space to operate.) Position the nailer so the lip fits over the edge of the plank. Strike the knob with a rubber mallet to release the nail and air pressure, which drives the nail through the tongue at the correct angle and into the subfloor. Drive nails 4 inches from each end and space subsequent nails about 8 inches apart.

12 Continue laying the flooring row by row, working your way across the room. The nailer should be driving nails to about $1/16$ inch below the surface of the flooring tongue. If the nail isn't sunk to the desired depth, adjust the air pressure accordingly.

WHAT IF...
You need to reverse direction?

There are instances, such as when you are flooring multiple rooms, when you need to change the direction of the planks. Changing direction means you will have to join the first row of planks groove to groove—usually within doorways.

One option is to install a T transition strip, which does result in a slight rise in the floor within the door opening.

A smoother alternative is to transform the groove side of the plank into a tongue edge. To do this, cut a wood spline (a long, thin strip of wood) to length. Run a bead of wood glue along one edge of the spline and slip it into the groove of the plank that is in place. Slip the groove of the next board over the new spline and nail the plank in place as usual.

13 Avoid using bowed planks if you can. However if you're running low on material and must use one, screw a piece of lumber to the subfloor about 1 inch from the plank. Use the lumber as a brace while you drive a wedge of lumber into the space between the lumber and the bowed board. Once the plank is straight and in position, nail it in place.

14 When you need to apply flooring around an obstacle, such as a built-in cabinet or fireplace hearth, frame around the base. You may need to miter the ends of the boards to <u>get a snug fit</u>. If the tongue will abut the cabinet or other obstacle, slice it off. Since you are working close to an obstacle, face nail these planks.

GET A SNUG FIT

Load the power flooring nailer with nails recommended for your type of floor. Experiment with depth settings; the nailheads should just barely sink below the wood surface. Fit the nailer to a tongue, make sure it rests flat, and hit it with the mallet.

To keep the courses parallel, tap the boards together before nailing. Use a wood scrap as a driving block to protect the flooring. Or use the neoprene head of the power nailer mallet.

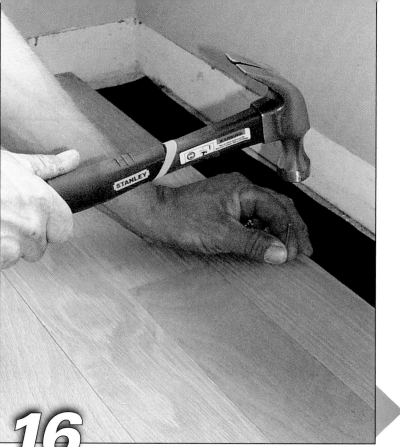

15 Where a plank will meet a corner, position the end of the board against the wall and mark where the corner meets the board. Cut the necessary notch using a jigsaw, allowing a ½-inch gap for expansion.

16 Lay all of the planks for the last row before nailing them into place. Because these are too close for using the side nailer, you'll have to drill pilot holes and face-nail.

Transitions

Gaps between rooms, from floor to floor, and at thresholds will need some type of transition piece to give the room a professionally finished appearance. If the new wood floor is higher than an adjoining existing floor, plan to use a reducer strip for a smooth transition. A reducer strip features a beveled or rounded surface that will descend from the thicker flooring to the thinner material. Cut the strip to length and fit the groove over the tongue of the wood flooring. (Or install a spline as noted on page 108.) Face-nail the reducer strip as shown, countersinking the nailheads below the surface of the wood. Fill the holes with wood putty.

17 You may need to rip-cut the last course. Protecting the wall with a wood scrap, push the last courses tight with a pry bar. Drill pilot holes and drive flooring nails through the face of the boards. Set the nails and fill with wood filler.

18 Conceal the gap between the last row and the wall with baseboard and shoe molding. Align the bottom edge of the baseboard so it is flush with the top of the wood floor; secure the baseboard to the wall. Secure the shoe (or quarter-round) molding to the baseboard slightly above the wood planks.

T-molding
Shaped like the letter from the alphabet when viewed from the edge, T-molding spans the gap between flooring materials of equal height. Typically plan to glue a piece of T-molding into place.

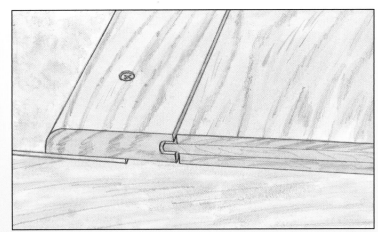

Reducer strip
When floors between rooms make a level change, a wood reducer strip offers an attractive transition—even between differing materials.

ENGINEERED WOOD FLOORS

Engineered wood floors are made with different installation techniques in mind, including nail-down, glue-down, glued-edge, and click-together varieties.

Thinner planks (3/8 inch) are nailed down (on a wood subfloor) for stability. One of the drawbacks of a nail-down installation is that it is more prone to squeaks and pops. To minimize noise make sure the subfloor is clear of debris and level.

A 1/2-inch-thick engineered wood floor can be nailed or glued down. Gluing is a viable technique over concrete.

Engineered wood planks that measure 5/8 inch thick can be installed as a "floating" application. Edges are joined (glued or clicked together) but the planks themselves are not secured to the subfloor.

Constructed as a wood veneer over plywood, engineered wood installs over radiant heat and on concrete.

PRESTART CHECKLIST

☐ **TIME**
A 10×10 room takes 6 to 8 hours

☐ **TOOLS**
Measuring tape, chalkline, hammer, pry bar, hammer stapler, pneumatic nail gun (for nail down), power saws, trowel (for glue down)

☐ **SKILLS**
Accurate measuring, using a power saw and a nail gun (for nail-down), hammering, troweling (for glue-down)

☐ **PREP**
Clear subfloor of debris

☐ **MATERIALS**
Manufacturer's underlayment, engineered wood, tapping block, flooring nails, suggested adhesives (for glue-down and floating installations)

Nailing an engineered floor

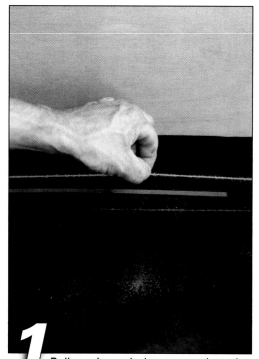

1 Roll out the underlayment and staple to the subfloor. Starting on the longest outside wall (usually the straightest), measure from each end of the wall the width of one plank (including the tongue) plus the expansion gap. Snap a chalkline between marks to serve as a guideline.

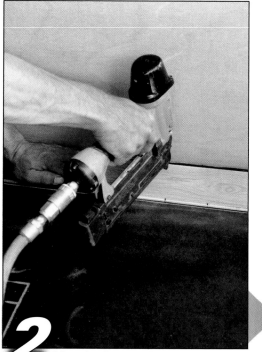

2 Align the first plank, tongue side out, with the chalkline. Use a pneumatic face nailer to secure the plank, driving nails 4 inches from each end and evenly spaced every 10–12 inches.

The side story

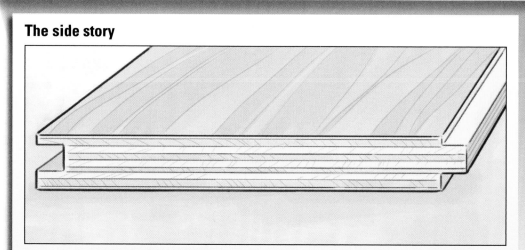

Take a closer look at a cross section of engineered wood, and you can see the bottom layers of wood pressed together. The grains in each layer (usually 3 to 5 plies) run in opposite directions to strengthen the plank. As humidity levels change in a room, solid wood planks expand and contract. An engineered wood plank is more stable, however, because the cross layers counteract one another.

3 After cutting the last board in the row to length (allowing for the gap suggested by the manufacturer), use a pry bar to coax the plank into position. (Be sure to use a piece of wood at the end of the bar to protect the wall as you pry.)

4 Stagger joints in subsequent rows by 6 inches. Use the pneumatic nailer to drive nails through tongues; use a tapping block and a hammer to snug together tongues and grooves, edge to edge and end to end. Be sure to leave the suggested gap between the ends of the rows and the wall.

5 Rip-cut the last row of planks to width; cut to length to leave the suggested gap between the ends of the planks and the wall. Face-nail to secure the last planks to the subfloor.

Frequently asked questions

Q. Where can I install engineered wood?

A. Aboveground-level, ground-level, and belowground-level subfloors are all suited to engineered wood flooring. Plan to lay down a 4- to 6-mil plastic vapor barrier in any areas where there are slightly higher moisture conditions, or seal concrete with a concrete sealer approved by the manufacturer. Always check with your flooring manufacturer to determine if bathroom installations are recommended.

Q. Can I install engineered wood over another flooring material?

A. A floating engineered wood floor installation (glued-edge or click-together) can be installed over other flooring that is stable and level.

Q. Can the surface be refinished in the future?

A. Check the warranty offered by the manufacturer because many of the factory-applied finishes are guaranteed to last from 15 to 30 years. In the event that refinishing is necessary, many engineered wood floors offer a veneer that can be sanded at least once. If the ability to refinish the surface is important to you, check with your manufacturer before purchasing the product. Because the engineered wood veneer layer is substantially thinner than a solid hardwood plank (the veneer usually ranges from $1/16$ to $1/8$ inch thick), consider professional refinishing unless you have experience using a drum sander.

Q. How soon can I use my engineered wood floor?

A. Most nail-down and click-together installations can be used immediately. Glue-together and glue-down floors have a recommended drying/setting period. Check with your manufacturer prior to installation to find out for sure.

Gluing an engineered floor

1 Measure out in two places from the installation wall a distance equal to the width of several planks (include the tongue in the measurement) plus the expansion gap recommended by the manufacturer. Snap a chalkline. If you're concerned about not being able to see the entire chalkline beneath the glue, secure a straight board to the floor and align it between the guideline and the wall.

2 Using a trowel and adhesive recommended by the manufacturer, spread adhesive on the floor. Apply only enough to an area that you can surface with flooring in about 15 to 20 minutes.

STANLEY PRO TIP: **Ensuring a glue-down success**

Some special concerns to keep in mind when gluing down engineered wood planks include the importance of properly preparing the subfloor before applying adhesive. For example adhesive will not stick well to concrete floors that have been previously sealed or painted and have not been properly prepared. Or if you suspect that the moisture content of your concrete floor may be somewhat high, select a glue that's formulated to double as a vapor barrier.

It's crucial that the concrete floor is flat, with high spots ground down and low spots filled with an approved leveling compound. Poor preparation such as using glue not recommended by the manufacturer or not using enough adhesive can result in popping noises or

loose planks in the future. Following the manufacturer's guidelines (for the flooring as well as for the adhesive) results in a long-lasting installation.

Check the instructions that come with your flooring to determine what type of trowel to use when applying adhesive to the subfloor. The spacing of the notches determines how much adhesive is laid down. One way to check if you are putting down the correct amount of adhesive is to immediately lift up a plank that you have just installed. If at least 80 percent of the back of the board is coated with adhesive, the plank should adhere nicely.

Read the adhesive manufacturer's directions and follow them closely. Some adhesives must

cure for a brief time (called "flash time") before laying the planks. Others require that you lay the planks immediately after spreading the adhesive onto the subfloor.

During installation try to avoid sliding the backs of planks through the adhesive so that boards aren't inadvertently pulled out of position as the glue dries.

Plan to wait 24 hours before walking on the surface or returning furniture to a glue-down engineered wood floor.

For best appearance install the flooring parallel to the longest, straightest wall (generally an outside wall). However the flooring should be laid perpendicular to floor joists to prevent sagging.

3 Facing the tongue of the plank toward the guide board, slip the first plank into position. Snug the end of the next plank into the end of the first plank and lay it down into the adhesive, making sure the groove is against the guide board. Continue working your way down the row in this manner. Cut the last plank to length, leaving the recommended expansion gap.

4 For the second and subsequent rows, stagger end joints as suggested by the manufacturer. In some cases you may be able to use the leftover length from a preceding row as the first piece in the new row.

USING A TROWEL
Holding the trowel at 45°

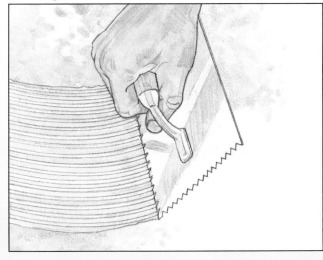

When applying adhesive hold the trowel at a 45-degree angle to the floor as shown. This will allow you to cover 40 to 60 square feet of subfloor per gallon.

Keep in mind that the notches will leave very little adhesive between the ridges, allowing chalklines to remain visible so you can lay boards straight.

Otherwise plan to install a temporary guide board as a dimensional marker indicating the location of the chalkline.

SAFETY FIRST
Knees and more

Read the safety guidelines on the adhesive you plan to use. In all cases provide adequate ventilation for the space you will work in (although today's adhesives do produce less odor than their predecessors). It's also a good idea to operate a fan in the room to help circulate fresh air.

Preserve your knees by wearing comfortable padded-cloth knee pads (the plastic type might scratch your new floor). Safety goggles should be worn to protect your eyes from glue spatters. Also keep in mind that gluing down a floor is messy work. Wear old clothes that you don't mind ruining.

One final thought: Keep children and pets far away from the adhesive.

Gluing an engineered floor *continued*

5 Snug boards end to end first, then slip the tongue into the groove of the preceding row. Once you cut the last board in the row to fit (allowing for the recommended expansion gap), snug it into place using a pry bar. Place a scrap of wood between the end of the bar and the wall to avoid damage.

6 Continue laying rows of engineered wood planks across the room, kneeling only on portions of the unsurfaced subfloor. (Or use a kneeler board to distribute your weight.) Stagger end seams as suggested by the manufacturer.

STANLEY PRO TIP

A trick with tape

You can prevent planks from pulling apart as the adhesive dries by spanning the seams with blue quick-release painter's tape as shown. Don't leave the tape on for more than 24 hours as it could leave a residue or mar the finish.

STANLEY PRO TIP: **Clean adhesive from surface**

Whether you are gluing planks to the subfloor or edge to edge, wipe the surface frequently to remove excess glue. Use a cleaner recommended by the flooring and adhesive manufacturers. To prevent a difficult-to-remove residue haze from forming on your new flooring, switch to a clean towel as needed. Never apply blue painter's tape to the plank surface before wiping away the adhesive residue as the tape may be difficult to remove later.

7 As you reach the last row on the opposite wall, if you must be on the flooring you just laid, distribute your weight on a kneeler board. Rip-cut the planks for the last row if needed, allowing for the recommended expansion gap.

8 After 24 hours (or using a kneeler board), return to the wall where you started the installation and remove the guide board. Rip-cut the planks for the last row as needed.

9 Use a piece of scrap wood to protect the wall as you use the pry bar to snug the last row into place.

WHAT IF…
You glue your fingers?

Read the can label before using the adhesive to be sure you have the recommended solvent on hand. Use a rag to wipe the surface and your fingers as soon as stray adhesive appears. Try to minimize glue forced into seams so that the tongues and grooves maintain a tight fit. As much of the glue as possible should remain "below deck."

STANLEY PRO TIP: **Rolling the floor**

Never strike the flooring with a rubber mallet because it may damage the plank surface. Instead use a foam-covered roller (if recommended by the manufacturer) to bond the planks to the subfloor and ensure more uniform adhesion. Check with the adhesive manufacturer to see what weight roller to use—100 pounds is common. Wait the recommended amount of time before rolling the floor but don't wait too long. If the glue is too dry, the rolling process will be ineffective.

Floating an engineered floor

1 Roll out the foam underlayment in the same direction that you plan to install the flooring. Extend the underlayment a few inches up the wall and trim the excess before installing moldings. Tape the seams with the tape provided. Or overlap the precut seams and adhere with the double-sided tape provided.

2 Measure a distance equal to the width of two planks (include the tongue in the measurement) from two places on the installation wall plus the expansion gap recommended by the manufacturer. Snap a chalkline. Temporarily secure a straight board to the floor and align it between the chalkline and the wall. Use this board as a guide for laying the flooring.

STANLEY PRO TIP

Checking for low spots

Using a straight, long piece of lumber, rotate it on the floor to find low and high spots. Draw a circle around problem areas. Use several layers of roofing felt to build up depressions less than ¼ inch deep. Fill deeper depressions with self-leveling compound. Grind down high spots.

FLOATING A FLOOR ON CONCRETE

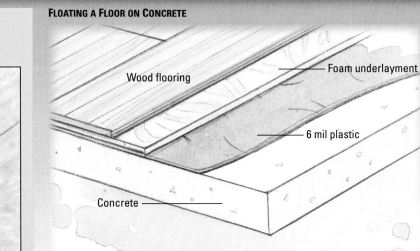

Wood flooring

Foam underlayment

6 mil plastic

Concrete

A floating engineered wood floor can be laid directly onto concrete after it has cured for at least 30 days. (Check with your flooring manufacturer regarding the recommended curing time.) Lay down 6 mil plastic, then the foam underlayment as shown prior to laying down the floating floor.

3 Apply a bead of recommended glue to the tongue on the end of the plank. Position the plank against the guide board with the groove facing the guide board. Snug the end of the next plank over the glued tongue on the end of the first board. Secure the two lengths with a tapping block.

4 Continue this first row, gluing the planks end to end. Use the pull bar to snug the last board—cut to length—into position.

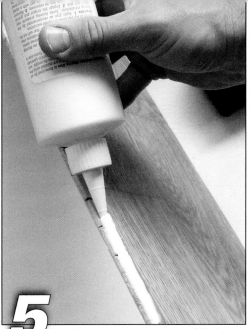

5 For the second row start with the leftover length from the last board in the first row. Or cut another board to length so the joint is staggered. Apply a thin bead of glue to the tongue of the plank in the first row. Snug the groove of the second row onto the glued tongue, using the tapping block.

6 Continue installing subsequent rows in the same manner, snugging long sides together first with the tapping block, then using the tapping block to position the lengths end to end. Be sure to leave the suggested expansion gaps where planks meet the wall.

7 Rip-cut the last row of planks to the desired width, allowing for the suggested expansion gap. For uneven walls scribe the board for an accurate fit.

8 Pull up the guide board to lay the last rows. Rip-cut the planks to fit, scribing where necessary for an accurate fit. Stay off the floating floor for the time recommended by the manufacturer. Finish the floor by covering perimeter gaps with baseboard and quarter-round moldings.

Installing a click-together engineered wood floor

1 Roll out the underlayment in the same direction that you plan to install the flooring. Abut edges or overlap as directed by the manufacturer. Seal the edges as recommended.

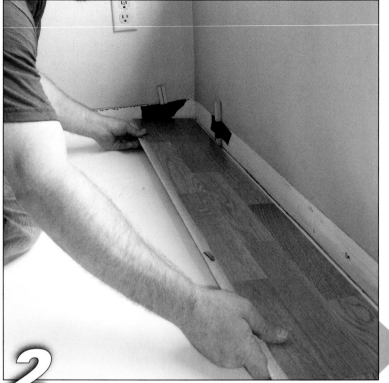

2 Select the longest plank available; start from the right and position the first plank with the groove toward the wall. Use ½-inch wood scraps at the wall to maintain the required expansion gap. Continue working down the first row, clicking together the planks end to end. Cut the end plank to fit as needed.

CLICKING TOGETHER
Angle and click

To install the second and subsequent rows, first interlock the plank end to end, then interlock the long sides. You will have to angle the edge to properly fit the tongue and groove together, then push down. Use the tapping block to complete the seat or click the lengths together.

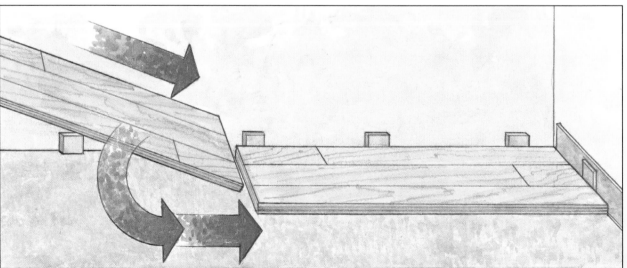

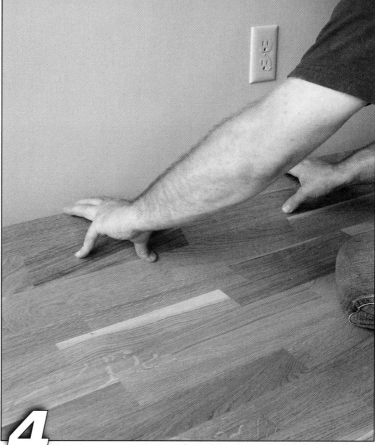

3 Start the second row using the leftover length from the last piece in the first row—provided the piece is at least 8 inches long and 6 inches away from an end joint. Otherwise cut another piece to the desired length. Use the tapping block to seat the tongue and groove together.

4 Use the same technique (see "Angle and click," opposite, bottom) to complete all the rows. You may need to rip-cut the last row to fit, allowing for the recommended expansion gap. If necessary use a pry bar to seat the last row.

Shave off the lip to install under doorjambs

To fit click-together engineered wood planks under door casing, reduce the height of the groove lip. This avoids a visible gap. Using a small plane or a utility knife, shave off about 75 percent of the groove ledge as shown. Remove the board and slip it into place beneath the casing; snug with the pry bar if needed. Run a thin bead of glue along the top edge of the tongue on the next plank and snug into place, using a pry bar if needed. Use blue painter's tape to hold the boards secure until the glue dries.

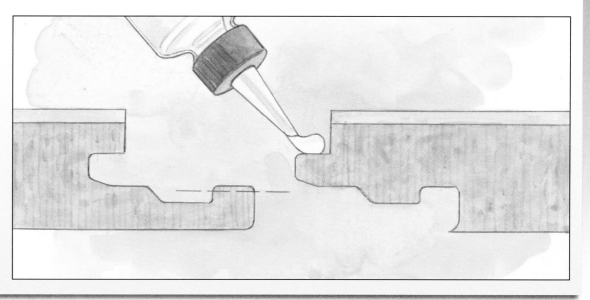

Installing Wood Stairs

You can refresh your old staircase with new treads and risers. Wood replacement treads are available that can be secured directly over the existing "subfloor" treads and risers. The "body" of these replacement treads is ½ inch thick so that your steps will remain a consistent height. The nose on the replacement tread is 1 inch thick to retain the illusion of a standard tread.

You can also opt to remove the old stair surfaces and begin anew as shown here. Select a wood type for the new treads and risers that will complement flooring and moldings in the rooms the stairs adjoin. Standard stair treads come with a rounded (bullnose) front edge and measure 1 inch thick and 11¼ inches deep. Plan to measure the width of each stair because each one will vary slightly in width.

Stairs that are enclosed on both sides (with no balusters) are a job you can do yourself. For anything more complicated plan to hire a finish carpenter to do the job.

Prestart Checklist

☐ **Time**
About 1 hour per step

☐ **Tools**
Measuring tape, power saw, compass, pneumatic nailer

☐ **Skills**
Measuring, scribing, and using a power saw and pneumatic nailer

☐ **Prep**
Remove old stair surfaces if desired

☐ **Materials**
Stair treads, risers, wood putty

1 Rip-cut the individual risers to the desired height. Measure the width of the riser and add ¾ inch. Cut the riser to length. Temporarily tack the board in place.

2 With the riser in place, separate the legs of a compass to ⅜ inch. Draw the compass down the wall as shown, scribing a line onto the riser. Cut off the excess using the scribe as a guide and repeat the process on the opposite end of the riser. Scribe and cut the remaining risers in the same manner.

PARTS OF A STAIRCASE

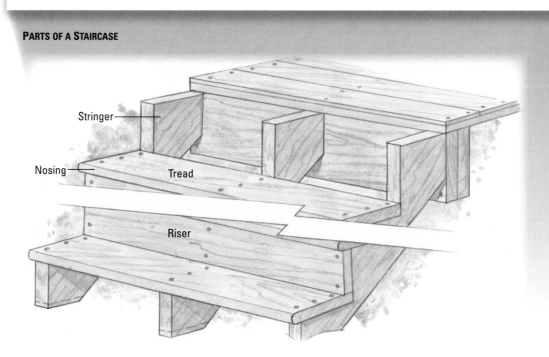

Stringer

Nosing

Tread

Riser

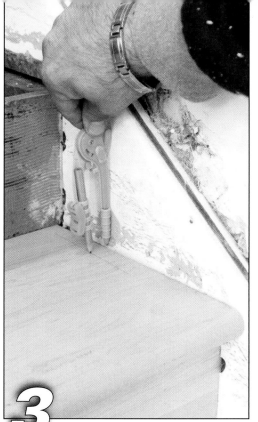

3 Cut stair treads so they will overhang risers by 1 inch. Measure the width of each tread (which is the length of the board) and add ¾ inch. Cut the tread to length. Scribe the end of the tread, following the same scribing procedure as described in Step 2.

4 Cut off the excess, following the scribed guidelines. Scribe the other end of the tread, following the same procedure as before, and cut off the excess tread.

5 Position treads on the stairs and secure each one with a pneumatic face nailer. Fill nail holes with wood putty.

STANLEY PRO TIP

Installing engineered wood on stairs

You may also opt to use the same engineered wood you used on the floor to refresh a staircase.

Start by adding a layer of plywood over the top of each existing riser so the riser is now flush with the front edge of the existing tread. Cover the plywood with engineered flooring. (Measure the riser in two places before cutting.) If necessary scribe the riser as described in Step 2, opposite.

Test fit the riser in place. Cut a piece of bullnose tread to fit the front of the stair. Snug it in place over the test-fitted riser. Measure the remaining space and cut flooring to fit.

As you cover the stairs with engineered wood, use the same adhesive that you used on the floor to secure the pieces. It's also a good idea to mark the pieces as "riser" or "tread" so you don't confuse the two after test fitting.

When you're ready to install the pieces, start with the bottom step and install the riser first, then the nose on the step above, and finally the tread. Repeat this order for each step.

STANLEY PRO TIP

Ordering treads and risers

When you are ready to shop for hardwood treads and risers, here's what is commonly available:

Stair treads are typically 1-inch thick and 11¼ inches deep and are available in widths starting at 36 inches and increasing in 6-inch increments to 72 inches. (Note that you can usually special order stair treads in any thickness, depth, or width.)

You may also discover that your stairs need "returns." These are attached to the side of the exposed tread, giving it a finished appearance. To determine whether you need a right-hand return or a left-hand return, stand at the bottom of the stairs and look up. If the right side is exposed, you need a right-hand (RH) tread. If the left side is exposed, then order a left-hand (LH) tread. If both sides are exposed, you need double return treads.

INSTALLING PARQUET TILE

Most parquet tiles are cut with tongues and grooves, which makes installation easy. In the long run it pays to purchase the highest quality tile you can afford. A higher quality finish offers greater longevity and quicker installation time. The tongues and grooves of less expensive tiles may not fit together smoothly.

To seat the tiles against each other, tap them with a hammer and a block of wood. Avoid sliding the tiles and kneel on sheets of plywood as you get deeper into the project. Be sure there is no adhesive between the knee boards and the tiles. Otherwise you'll pull up the tile when you move the board.

Take special care in laying your first 10 to 12 tiles—these determine how well the joints on the rest of the floor line up. If any adhesive gets on the tiles, clean it immediately with a rag soaked in solvent. Never apply the solvent directly to the tiles—it could mar the finish. Don't forget to leave a ½-inch gap between the edge tiles and the walls.

PRESTART CHECKLIST

☐ **TIME**
About 12–15 hours for an 8×10-foot floor

☐ **TOOLS**
Pencil, hammer, extension cord, shop vacuum, fan(s), jigsaw or circular saw, chalkline, tape measure, notched trowel, carpenter's square, 100-pound floor roller, trim saw

☐ **SKILLS**
Measuring and cutting

☐ **PREP**
Repair floor as necessary

☐ **MATERIALS**
Cork strips, mastic or adhesive, parquet tiles, adhesive solvent, rags

1 Prepare the subfloor, then snap chalklines between the midpoints of opposite walls. If the shape of the room is irregular or features protrusions, snap the lines on the largest rectangular portion of the floor. That way your installation will be centered on the primary focal point of the floor. Square the lines with a 3-4-5 triangle and adjust the lines if necessary. Dry-lay the tiles so you have edge tiles of the same width and adjust the lines again if necessary. Set a cork expansion strip along the wall when you're dry-laying the tile.

PREPARE THE SUBFLOOR

You can apply parquet over several different subfloors. Each calls for slightly different preparation.

■ **Wood:** In new construction install ¾-inch plywood. On an existing wood floor, remove the finish and repair. On planks wider than 4 inches, install ⅜-inch underlayment. Fill all nail holes and depressions and sand smooth.

■ **Concrete:** You can lay parquet on concrete at and above grade. Check for moisture by taping plastic sheets to the slab every 2 feet. If moisture beads under plastic after a couple of days, don't install tile. Remedy the moisture problem if possible. If moisture is still present, choose another finished flooring material. Clean and roughen the surface slightly to aid the adhesive bond.

■ **Vinyl tile or sheet goods:** If existing material is cushioned, remove and prepare subfloor. If tile is installed on a wood floor and is loose, waxed, or glossy, sand or strip the finish and repair.

■ **Ceramic tile:** Level the tiled surface with self-leveling compound. Remove damaged tile and repair.

■ **Carpet:** Remove carpet and repair wood or concrete subfloor. Install lauan plywood over the plywood subfloor.

Spreading the adhesive

Spreading the right amount of adhesive takes practice. Comb out the adhesive so the ridges measure about ⅛ inch tall.

2 Scoop a small amount of adhesive onto the floor. Holding the trowel at a 45-degree angle, comb out the adhesive with the notched side of the trowel. Spread the adhesive up to but not on top of the chalklines. Allow the adhesive to become tacky according to manufacturer recommendations.

3 Set the first tile in the adhesive exactly at the intersection of the layout lines. Use the edge of the tile, not the edge of the tongue or inside surface of the groove, to line it up. Position the tile with some precision. Avoid sliding the tile, as this will push up the adhesive.

4 Hold the second tile at a slight angle to the first. With the tongue engaged in the groove of the first tile, push the tile simultaneously down and toward the first tile. Continue in a pyramid pattern. Tap the tiles together with a rubber mallet.

WHAT IF...
You need to remove baseboards?

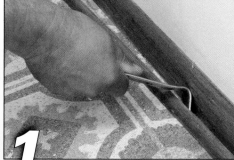

1 Starting at a corner slide a small pry bar behind the shoe. Loosen the shoe until you can insert the pry bar next to a nail. Pry the nail out a little at a time. To avoid splits loosen at least two nails before pulling the molding from the wall.

2 Begin at a corner or a mitered joint, working a wide putty knife behind the baseboard. Loosen each nail with a pry bar. Keep the putty knife behind the bar or use a thin piece of scrap as a shim to avoid marring the wall. Loosen all nails before removing baseboard sections.

Undercut the door casing

After installing underlayment set a tile on the subfloor at a doorway and use a trim saw to undercut the door jambs and molding by the thickness of the tile. This allows you to slip tiles under the trim instead of having to make intricate cuts in pieces of tile.

Installing parquet tile *continued*

5 Using the same techniques continue laying the parquet in the remainder of the first quadrant. When you reach a point where you have to work from the surface of the newly laid tile, spread your weight evenly over a 2×2-foot plywood sheet. When you reach the walls, mark the tile for <u>cutting the border or edge tiles.</u> Mark and cut each tile individually—don't cut them all to the same width unless you're absolutely sure the room is square.

6 Once you've completed the first quadrant, use the same methods to install the tiles in the remaining quadrants. Always start at the intersection of the layout lines. If you're installing the parquet in sections, roll each section with a rented 100-pound floor roller to set the tiles firmly in the adhesive. After applying adhesive roll the floor within the time suggested by the manufacturer. Install cork expansion strips, usually provided by the manufacturer, along the edges.

SAFETY FIRST
Ventilate the workspace

Many adhesives used in the installation of parquet are petroleum based and contain chemicals that evaporate rapidly. These chemicals and others, called "driers," are volatile and sometimes toxic.

When installing a parquet floor, be sure to provide plenty of ventilation—open windows to create cross drafts, exhaust the fumes to the outside with a window fan, and extinguish any pilot lights on gas-fired appliances. Wear a respirator and gloves.

CUTTING THE BORDER OR EDGE TILES

1 To mark tiles for cutting, set a loose tile bottom side up exactly on top of the last tile, then a marker tile on top of that one. Run a pencil down the edge of the marker tile to mark the cut.

2 Clamp the tile to a supporting surface and cut it with a jigsaw equipped with a fine-tooth blade. Cut the tile facedown if using a regular blade or circular saw, faceup with a reverse-cutting blade.

Installing parquet on the diagonal

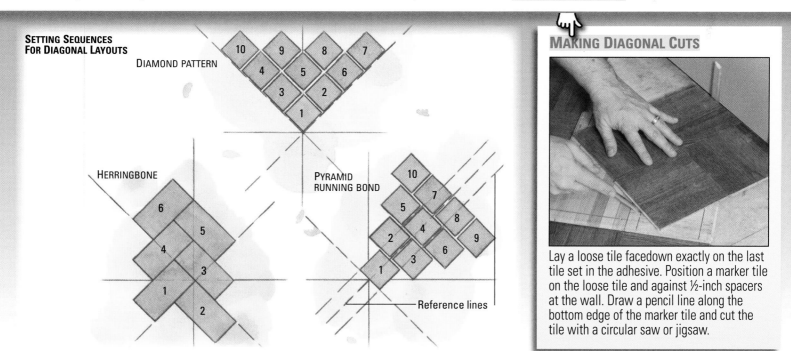

1 Begin your diagonal layout in the same fashion as a perpendicular installation—snap chalklines at the midpoints of opposite walls and square the lines with a 3-4-5 triangle. From the center point, mark an equal distance on all four lines and connect the marks. Snap chalklines from the corners through the midpoints on the connecting lines (below). Dry-lay the tiles along the diagonal so you'll achieve edge tiles of equal width.

2 Starting at the intersection of the layout lines, spread and comb mortar along one of the diagonal quadrants. Lay the first tile square against the intersection of the lines, using the edge of the tile (not the tongue or groove) as your reference plane. With the second tile slightly raised, engage the tongue in the groove of the first and press down and in. Continue setting tiles using this technique, one quadrant at a time, making diagonal cuts at the walls.

SETTING SEQUENCES FOR DIAGONAL LAYOUTS

DIAMOND PATTERN

10 9 8 7
4 5 6
3 2
1

HERRINGBONE

6
5
4
3
1
2

PYRAMID RUNNING BOND

10
7
5 8
2 4 9
3 6
1

Reference lines

MAKING DIAGONAL CUTS

Lay a loose tile facedown exactly on the last tile set in the adhesive. Position a marker tile on the loose tile and against ½-inch spacers at the wall. Draw a pencil line along the bottom edge of the marker tile and cut the tile with a circular saw or jigsaw.

INSTALLING CORK TILE

Because cork tile is so porous, it requires a longer acclimation period (three to four days) than many manufactured materials. That means if you normally run the air-conditioner in the summer and you're setting the tile in July, you should turn the air-conditioner on during the acclimation period. The same goes for the furnace in cooler seasons.

Like vinyl tile the resilience of cork tile dramatically reveals subfloor defects. Some manufacturers require priming the subfloor (no matter what kind it is) before applying one part of a two-part adhesive (the second part is already on the cork tile). Other brands don't require a primer.

One thing is consistent throughout the industry: The mastic used is a reciprocal adhesive. That means it's a contact cement and sticks only to itself. Although it allows you some minor movement to line up the tiles, once you apply pressure with your hand, a roller, or a mallet, you will not be able to move the tile. If you've misaligned a tile, you will have to cut it out and replace it.

Mix up the tiles from several boxes before you lay them to spread any variations randomly across the floor.

1 Locate the center of the room or its largest rectangular surface by snapping chalklines at the midpoints of opposite walls. Don't worry that the adhesive will obscure the lines; it will dry clear. Adjust the lines so the layout has edge tiles of even width.

2 Using a brush so you don't splash adhesive on the wall, start applying adhesive along the walls of one quadrant only. Then work from this line back toward the center of the room, applying the adhesive with a paint roller. Let the adhesive become tacky (45 minutes to an hour).

PRESTART CHECKLIST

☐ **TIME**
20 minutes per square yard, not including subfloor preparation

☐ **TOOLS**
Fans, utility knife, tape measure, metal straightedge, chalkline, roller, pan, putty knife, mallet, beater block

☐ **SKILLS**
Measuring, laying, cutting tile

☐ **PREP**
Repair and level subfloor

☐ **MATERIALS**
Primer (required by some manufacturers), adhesive, cork tile, cork tile finish

Preparing the subfloor

■ **Wood:** In new construction install ¾-inch plywood. On an existing wood floor, remove the finish and repair. On planks wider than 4 inches, install ⅜-inch underlayment. Fill depressions and sand smooth.

■ **Concrete:** Check for moisture by taping plastic sheets to the slab every 2 feet. If moisture beads under plastic, don't install tile. Remedy the moisture problem if possible. Clean and roughen the surface slightly to give the adhesive a "tooth." Don't install cork tile below grade.

■ **Vinyl tile or sheet goods:** Remove material and repair subfloor.

■ **Ceramic tile:** Level the surface with self-leveling compound. Remove damaged tile and repair.

■ **Carpet:** Remove carpet and prepare/repair wood or concrete subfloor as above.

STANLEY PRO TIP
Alternate colors of layout lines

Cork tile is one of the few materials that looks better when its joints are offset from row to row. Getting the offset tiles on the same plane isn't possible without an offset layout line.

Once you've snapped your center layout lines, measure to their right (not their left—you won't have adhesive there) a distance equal to half the width of a tile. Mark each end of the room, then snap a new line with different colored chalk. Then spread the adhesive in that quadrant as above.

3 Set the first tile with its edges lined up with the intersecting layout lines. Hold the second tile with its edges next to the first and lower it into place, keeping the bottom edge on the layout line. Tap the entire surface of the tiles with a rubber mallet to secure them in the adhesive.

4 Using the same techniques apply the remaining tiles in the row, tapping them with a mallet and a carpet-covered beater block (page 89). Start the next row on the offset lines and proceed across the quadrant. Always work from installed tile to the corner—don't worry about kneeling on the tile—you won't dislodge it. However kneeling or placing anything on the bare adhesive will weaken its bond. After you've laid the field tile, mark, cut, and install the edges.

WHAT IF...
A tile is misaligned when setting?

Every now and then you'll probably set a tile imprecisely on the layout lines. To remove a mislaid tile, use a wide putty knife inserted under a fresh corner. Slice the adhesive by moving the putty knife from side to side and prying it up at the same time. Reapply the adhesive to the floor and to the tile if it survives the removal process.

Protect the floor

Cork tile is not a "set and forget" product. Most tiles require the application of a finish after you have laid them. Before you apply the finish, vacuum the surface thoroughly and remove the residual dust with a very dry mop. Let the tile dry and apply the finish with a roller. Wait two weeks before washing the floor.

If adhesive gets on the walls

Adhesive made for most cork products is water soluble. If you happen to get adhesive on the wall, wipe it away with a disposable moist towel or rag.

  If the adhesive dries where you don't want it, you can rub it off with a dry rag.

INSTALLING LAMINATE FLOORING

Where a beautiful visual effect is paramount and practicality is important, laminate flooring fits the bill. Many single-tile patterns are made to look like wood, but you'll find an increasing number of granite, marble, and stone look-alikes, as well as abstract designs and ceramic patterns. You can choose from individual laminate tiles or planks with tile "visuals"—individual tiles printed on a plank, complete with grout lines.

Durable and affordable

Laminate flooring provides exceptional durability at a moderate cost—the material costs more than resilient tile but less than solid wood flooring. It's quick to install and easy to clean. A tough-wearing melamine top coat gives laminate staying power. This top layer borrows technology from the manufacture of laminate countertops but is much more durable. It resists the impact of high-heeled shoes and damage from burns and stains.

The next layer is printed to look like the material of choice—wood, stone, or ceramic tile. Below that are several layers that provide strength—these layers are typically made from wood composites.

Easy to install

For many years the primary method of installing laminate flooring was to clamp and glue the pieces together, but recent innovations include glueless snap-together systems that install much faster and more easily. Both glued and glueless laminate floors float—they aren't nailed or glued to the subfloor. They lay on a foam underlayment (which make them comfortable underfoot) and are held in place by their own weight.

Unlike solid wood planks, laminate can be installed either perpendicular or parallel to the floor joists.

Laminates offer a range of design and installation options that fit most budgets and skill levels.

CHAPTER PREVIEW

Installing snap-together tiles
page 132

Installing snap-together planks
page 136

Installing glued laminate tiles
page 140

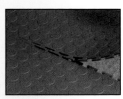

Installing snap-together garage floors and play surfaces
page 144

Laminate's extremely durable melamine top coat makes it an excellent flooring choice in rooms with lots of foot traffic.

INSTALLING SNAP-TOGETHER TILES

Locking laminate tiles snap together and like their glued counterparts, float on a foam underlayment. The underlayment allows the floor to expand and contract as a unit and makes it feel comfortable underfoot. Assembly varies by manufacturer. Some styles use a tongue-and-groove configuration. Others employ locking strips. Some brands require that you angle the units as you engage the tongue and groove. Others snap together with the aid of a tapping block and hammer. The tilt-and-engage style is the most common. Installing the first three rows of tiles works best if you connect the tiles a few feet away from the wall, and then slide them as a unit in place. Then you'll be able to work on top of the tile that you've installed. Acclimate the tiles by leaving them for 48 hours in the room where you are installing them. If you will be using laminate baseboards, extend the underlayment 2 inches up each wall.

PRESTART CHECKLIST

☐ **TIME**
About 5 to 6 hours for an 8×10-foot floor, not including subfloor preparation

☐ **TOOLS**
Tape measure, metal straightedge, jigsaw, circular saw or tablesaw, trim saw, utility knife, hammer, tapping block, pull bar, pencil

☐ **SKILLS**
Measuring, setting, and cutting laminate

☐ **PREP**
Repair and/or replace subfloor

☐ **MATERIALS**
Underlayment, laminate planks, masking tape, caulk

A. Preparing the layout

1 Roll out the underlayment, butting or overlapping the joints as instructed by the manufacturer. Tape the joints as instructed. Measure the room and divide the result by the width of the tiles. Add the remainder to the width of a tile and divide by 2. This is the width of your first and last border row.

2 Open three cartons and mix the planks so color variations spread throughout the room. Use your computations from Step 1 to mark the width of the tile for the border row. Rip enough border tiles for your starting wall. When using a circular saw, place the finish side down.

Preparing the subfloor

■ **Wood:** In new construction install ¾-inch plywood. On an existing floor remove the finish and repair. Install ⅜-inch underlayment on tiles wider than 4 inches. Fill all depressions and sand.

■ **Concrete:** Check for moisture by taping plastic sheets to the slab every 2 feet. If moisture appears under the plastic after a few days, don't install the tiles. Remedy the moisture issue.

■ **Vinyl tile or sheet goods:** If the existing floor is cushioned, remove it and repair the subfloor. If resilient flooring is installed on a wood floor and is loose or glossy, sand or strip.

■ **Ceramic tile:** Level the surface with self-leveling compound. Remove any damaged tile.

■ **Carpet:** Remove carpet and repair the wood or concrete subfloor as described above.

Choosing single laminate tiles

Laminate flooring is also available in individual square tiles, which offer more design options than planks. However you may have a hard time finding them and because production costs are higher for individual pieces, these tiles are slightly more expensive than their plank equivalents. On the other hand using planked products results in increased waste because they require more end cuts to fit, so the cost difference may even out in the long run.

3 Starting in the center of the wall, snap the border tiles together. When you no longer have space for a full tile, center the row, leaving an equal space at each end. Measure from the edge of the tile face (not the tongue) to the wall and subtract ¼ inch (to allow for spacers).

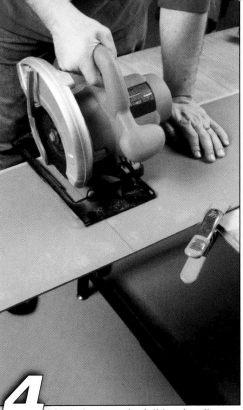

4 Mark the top of a full border tile, using the length from Step 3 and measuring from the edge of the face. Transfer the mark to the back of the tile with a combination square; cut the tile with a circular saw. Cut the left and right ends from separate tiles to maintain the pattern.

5 Lock the left and right ends of the border row in place. Then push the border row against the wall, inserting ¼-inch spacers every foot or so. Number the order of the tiles on small pieces of masking tape.

Laying out the grout lines

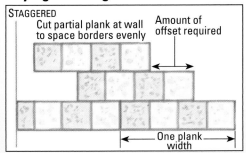

STAGGERED
Cut partial plank at wall to space borders evenly
Amount of offset required
One plank width

How you design the pattern formed by the grout lines of planked tile depends on the size of the visual and how much the manufacturer requires the joints between the planks to be offset. Some planks can only be laid in a straight grout pattern. Others are sized with visuals that may permit more flexibility. Each will require some experimentation in planning the borders.

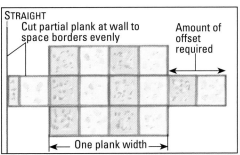

STRAIGHT
Cut partial plank at wall to space borders evenly
Amount of offset required
One plank width

Both staggered and straight patterns will produce evenly spaced tiles at the walls but require cutting partial planks and result in more waste than an offset plank pattern. An offset plank pattern produces grout joints spaced randomly from row to row. Some manufacturers recommend the offset shown here. Others specify different lengths for each starting plank.

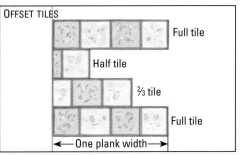

OFFSET TILES
Full tile
Half tile
⅔ tile
Full tile
One plank width

Because different grout patterns create dramatic differences in the appearance of a room, decide on the pattern in the planning stage and purchase a product that will produce the look you want. Bring your design to a tile retailer to get help in choosing the style that will meet your needs and be sure to get detailed instructions on how to lay the tile in the pattern of your choice.

B. Marking and cutting contours

1 Variations in the wall can affect the layout, so the first row should follow the contour of the wall. Draw a compass along the tiles, skipping the spacers. (Read the instructions; some recommend doing this after laying three rows.) Snap the second row together and cut the end tiles.

2 Disassemble the border tiles and use a jigsaw with a fine-tooth blade to cut the scribed line. With a reverse-cutting blade, set the good side up to avoid chipping the tile. If using a regular blade, keep the good side down.

C. Installing the tiles

1 Working away from the starting wall, reassemble the border-row tiles in their original order. Maintain the offset directed by the manufacturer and snap the end tile of the second row to the first row. Tilt the tile and pull the tongue into the groove. Prop the tile on a piece of scrap.

STANLEY PRO TIP

Moistureproof concrete slabs

Most laminate products require a moisture barrier when laid on a concrete slab. Polyethylene sheets usually serve this purpose, but check with your retailer if the manufacturer's instructions don't address this aspect of installation.

Using a pull bar

When you reach the end of a row, you won't be able to lift the tile to snap it in place. In this case use a pull bar to assemble the units. Slide one end of the bar over the far end of the tile and tap the other end until the tile snaps into place.

Closing the gaps

From time to time even your best efforts will leave a gap between tiles. Close up these gaps as you go, using a tapping block and a hammer.

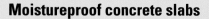

2 Tilt the second tile and push the tongue into the groove of the first one. Depending on the instructions you can either pull each tile toward you and into the first row as you go or wait until you have assembled the entire row. Regardless of the method lower the tile until it snaps in place.

3 Continue using the same methods to fit the tiles together. When you have completed the first three rows, slide the assembly toward the starting wall, stopping short by a little more than the thickness of the spacers. Insert the spacers against the wall and snug the rows against them.

4 Continue snapping the tiles together, working toward the other wall, closing gaps as necessary with a tapping block and trimming the final row to fit. Tilt the final row and pull it into place, using a pull bar to snug the tiles together. Trim the underlayment flush with the tiles as necessary.

Undercut the door trim

Like any other tile laminate units raise the height of the floor. To avoid notching tiles around the door trim, set a tile on the subfloor at a doorway and use a trim saw to undercut the doorjambs by the thickness of the tile. If it's necessary to trim the doors as well, use a circular saw to trim from the bottom.

Sealing the edges

Most manufacturers recommend sealing all exposed edges of laminate tile. This is especially important in bathroom and kitchen installations to avoid water (or moisture) getting under the tiles.

Some manufacturers recommend painting the edges with glue. But the safest way to protect an installation is to caulk the edges with mildew-resistant silicone caulk. In bathrooms caulk around the toilet, tub, and vanity. In kitchens caulk in front of the dishwasher, icemaker, exterior doorways, and opening to the laundry room.

TRIMMING THE FINAL ROW

Despite your best efforts to make the last row of tiles come out exactly the same width as the beginning row, it won't—and that is why you don't cut all the edge tiles at once. Cut each tile in the last row separately, setting in the spacers first and marking loose tiles with a guide tile. Set the cut tiles in place, snapping them to each other and to the field tiles with the pull bar and tapping block.

INSTALLING SNAP-TOGETHER PLANKS

Like laminate tiles, laminate planks snap together. And like their glued counterparts, they float on a foam underlayment. This allows the floor to expand and contract as a unit and makes it feel comfortable underfoot. Assembly varies by manufacturer. Some styles use a tongue and groove configuration. Others employ locking strips. Some brands require that you angle the units as you engage the tongue-and-groove. Others snap together with the aid of a tapping block and hammer. The tilt-and-engage style is the most common. Installing the first three rows of planks works best if you connect the planks a few feet away from the wall and then slide them in place as a unit. Then you'll be able to work on top of the planks that you've installed. Acclimate the planks by leaving them for 48 hours in the room where they will be installed. If you will be using laminate baseboards, extend the underlayment 2 inches up each wall.

PRESTART CHECKLIST

☐ **TIME**
About 5 to 6 hours for an 8×10-foot floor, not including subfloor preparation

☐ **TOOLS**
Tape measure, metal straightedge, jigsaw, circular saw or table saw, trim saw, utility knife, hammer, tapping block, pull bar, pencil

☐ **SKILLS**
Measuring, setting, and cutting laminate

☐ **PREP**
Repair and/or replace subfloor

☐ **MATERIALS**
Underlayment, laminate planks, masking tape, caulk

A. Prepare the layout

1 Roll out the underlayment, butting or overlapping the joints as instructed by the manufacturer. Tape the joints as instructed. Measure the room and divide the result by the width of the planks. Add the remainder to the width of a plank and divide by 2. This is the width of your first and last border rows.

2 Open the cartons and mix the planks so color variations spread throughout the room. Use your computations from Step 1 to mark the width of the plank for the border row. Rip enough border planks for your starting wall. When using a circular saw, place the finish side down.

Preparing the subfloor

■ **Wood:** In new construction install ¾-inch plywood. On an existing floor remove the finish and repair. Install ⅜-inch underlayments on planks wider than 4 inches. Fill all the depressions and sand.

■ **Concrete:** Check for moisture by taping plastic sheets to the slab every few feet. If moisture appears under the plastic after a couple of days (page 204), don't install the laminate planks. Remedy the moisture problem if possible. Clean the concrete thoroughly and let dry.

■ **Vinyl tile or sheet goods:** If the existing material is cushioned, remove it and repair the subfloor. If the resilient material is installed on a wood floor and is partially loose, waxed, or glossy, strip the material or sand it down to create more tack.

■ **Ceramic tile:** Remove any damaged tiles and level the surface with self-leveling compound.

■ **Carpet:** Remove the carpet and pad and repair the wood or concrete subfloor as described above.

3 Starting in the center of the wall, snap the border planks together. When you no longer have space for a full plank, center the row, leaving an equal space at each end. Measure from the edge of the plank face (not the tongue) to the wall and subtract ¼ inch (to allow for spacers).

4 Mark the top of a full border plank, using the length from Step 3 and measuring from the edge of the face. Transfer the mark to the back of the plank with a combination square; cut the plank with a circular saw. Cut the left and right ends from separate planks to maintain the pattern.

5 Lock the left and right ends of the border row in place. Then push the border row against the wall, inserting ¼-inch spacers every foot or so. Number the order of the planks on small pieces of masking tape.

Installing a moisture barrier

If you are planning to install laminate planks over concrete, you'll probably need to lay down a moisture barrier by lining the floor with polyethylene sheeting. Most manufacturers require sheeting that is 6 mils thick, but follow your manufacturer's guidelines. Overlap the seams by 8 inches or as recommended. Do not install a moisture barrier over a wooden subfloor as this may result in mold and/or mildew and cause the planks to warp.

Note that glued planks are generally approved for use in full baths, but some snap-together laminates are not, as not all snap-together connections are waterproof—which means moisture can seep between the planks.

Undercut the door trim

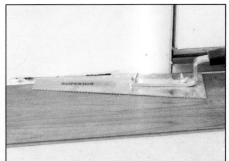

Like many other types of flooring, laminate planks raise the height of the floor. To avoid notching tiles around the door trim, set a tile on the subfloor at a doorway and use a trim saw to undercut the doorjambs by the thickness of the plank. If it's necessary to trim the doors too, use a circular saw to trim the bottoms of the doors.

B. Marking and cutting contours

C. Installing the planks

1 Variations in the wall can affect the floor layout—the first row must follow the contour of the wall. Draw a compass along the planks, skipping the spacers. (Some manufacturers recommend doing this after laying the first three rows.) Snap the second row together and cut the end planks.

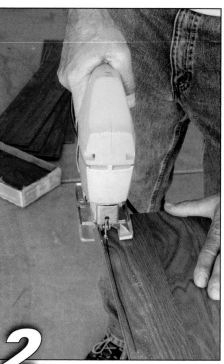

2 Disassemble the border planks and use a jigsaw with a fine-tooth blade to cut the scribed line. With a reverse-cutting blade, set the good side up to avoid chipping the plank. If using a regular blade, keep the good side down.

1 Working away from the starting wall, reassemble the border-row planks in their original order. Maintain the offset directed by the manufacturer and snap the end plank of the second row to the first row. Tilt the plank and pull the tongue into the groove. Prop the plank on a piece of scrap.

Using a pull bar

When you reach the end of a row, you won't be able to lift the plank to snap it in place. In this case use a pull bar to assemble the units. Slide one end of the bar over the far end of the plank and tap the other end until the plank snaps into place.

Closing the gaps

From time to time even your best efforts will leave a gap between planks. Use a tap block and hammer to close up these gaps before laying the next plank.

2 Tilt the second plank and push the tongue into the groove of the first one. Depending on the instructions you can either pull each plank toward you and into the first row as you go or wait until you have assembled the entire row. Regardless of the method lower the plank until it snaps in place.

3 Continue using the same methods to fit the planks together. When you have completed the first three rows, slide the assembly toward the starting wall, stopping short by a little more than the thickness of the spacers. Insert the spacers against the wall and snug the rows against them.

4 Continue snapping the planks together, working toward the other wall, closing up gaps as necessary with a tapping block and trimming the final row to fit. Tilt the final row and pull it into place, using a pull bar to snug the planks together. Trim underlayment flush with the planks as necessary.

Sealing the edges

Most manufacturers recommend sealing the exposed edges of the end planks. This is especially important in bath and kitchen installations so that moisture doesn't get under the planks.

Some manufacturers recommend covering the edges with glue; others recommend caulking the edges with mildew-resistant silicone caulk.

In bathrooms you'll need to caulk around the toilet, tub, and vanity. In the kitchen, caulk around the front of the dishwasher, refrigerator, icemaker, and any exterior doorways. In the laundry room caulk around the washer and dryer and the laundry tub.

TRIMMING THE FINAL ROW

Despite your best efforts to make the last row of planks come out exactly the same width as the beginning row, it won't—and that is why you don't cut all the edge planks at once. Cut each plank in the last row separately, setting in the spacers first and marking loose planks with a guide plank. Set the cut planks in place, snapping them to each other and to the field planks with the pull bar and tapping block.

INSTALLING GLUED LAMINATE TILES

When you're shopping for glued laminate tiles or tiled planks, you'll find as many varieties of edge construction as you would for a glueless floor. Some manufacturers sell planks that install with or without glue. Which is best? Glued joints are stronger than most unglued installations. Use them in rec rooms, children's playrooms, and in environments where activity might disrupt the joints, and in kitchens and baths where the glue will keep moisture out of the joints. If you're considering laminate planks for a bathroom or kitchen, however, make sure the manufacturer's warranties apply to installation of the material in these rooms. The joints of some products swell for a few months after installation. Swelling is normal and disappears when the glue cures. Before installing the tiles mix three boxes together to distribute color variations, then acclimate the tile to the room for 48 hours.

PRESTART CHECKLIST

☐ **TIME**
About 10 to 12 hours for an 8×10-foot floor, not including subfloor prep

☐ **TOOLS**
Tape measure, straightedge, jigsaw, circular saw or tablesaw, trim saw, compass, hammer, tapping block, pull bar, utility knife, pencil

☐ **SKILLS**
Measuring, setting, and cutting laminate

☐ **PREP**
Repair and/or replace subfloor

☐ **MATERIALS**
6-mil polyethylene, foam underlayment, laminate tiles, masking tape, glue

A. Setting up the rows

1 If you're installing the planks on a slab, lay down a 6-mil sheet of polyethylene as a waterproofing membrane. Then roll out the manufacturer's underlayment, following the directions for seaming. Some makers recommend butt joints, others suggest overlapping seams. Some say to tape their seams, some don't. If you're installing laminate baseboards or putting the planks in a bathroom or kitchen, extend the underlayment 2 to 3 inches up the wall and tape the seams with clear waterproof tape (available from a laminate retailer).

How much do you need?

Estimating the amount of materials you'll need for a laminate floor starts with the coverage in a carton. Some tiles are 15½ inches square, others are a foot square. Some planks are just under 4 feet long and a foot wide, others are larger.

Find out the carton coverage from the manufacturer or retailer—most large companies now maintain thorough Internet websites, complete with colors, patterns, and specifications.

When you order tiles add 5 percent to the amount you think you need. When ordering tiled planks add 15 percent. The extra accounts for mistakes and any damaged units.

Generally you can expect one roll of underlayment to cover about 100 square feet of floor. For a room of this size, you'll need two bottles of glue.

Orient the first tile

When you are ready to start laying laminates, make sure you start the first unit with the proper orientation. Most—but not all—laminates are installed by engaging the tongue of the new unit into the groove of the one already in place. Don't assume this is true for your product. Read the manufacturer's instructions before starting. Some laminates require you to remove the tongue from the first row.

2 Follow the directions for laying out a locking tile border (pages 132–135), ripping the border planks in even widths. Then dry-fit the border row, adjusting and cutting the end planks to equal lengths. Dry-lay the border row, working from left to right. Do not apply glue yet.

3 With the border row in place, dry-fit the second row of planks, starting with the end pieces (as required by your layout pattern) and working from left to right. Tilt and engage the tongues into the grooves (or use whatever installation method is required by the manufacturer's instructions).

4 Dry-fit the third row of planks. Stand back and inspect the installation to make sure the joints run parallel to the starting wall. If they don't you may have to trim the edge planks to straighten the installation. Mark the order of the tiles on pieces of masking tape and disassemble the planks.

WHAT IF...
You're laying single tiles?

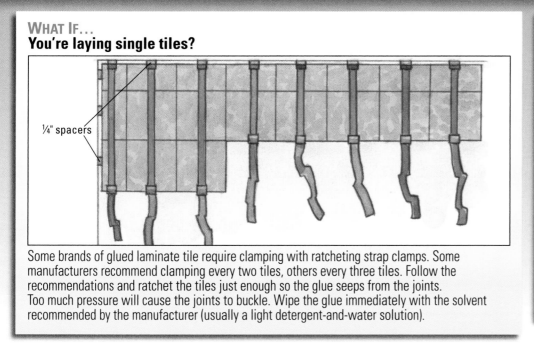

¼" spacers

Some brands of glued laminate tile require clamping with ratcheting strap clamps. Some manufacturers recommend clamping every two tiles, others every three tiles. Follow the recommendations and ratchet the tiles just enough so the glue seeps from the joints. Too much pressure will cause the joints to buckle. Wipe the glue immediately with the solvent recommended by the manufacturer (usually a light detergent-and-water solution).

The larger the floor, the wider the gap

All laminate flooring requires a gap around the edges of the room to give the flooring a space to expand and contract with changes in humidity. Manufacturers' instructions generally call for about ¼ inch; this measurement is the minimum gap required.

Because wood fibers expand in relation to the amount of wood in the floor, the larger the floor area, the wider the gap has to be. In fact the ¼-inch standard holds true for floors only from 100 to 1,000 square feet. From 1,000 to 1,800 square feet, you'll need to expand the gap to ⅜ inch, and for a 3,000-square-foot area, to as much as ⅝ inch. Large installations, generally over 40 linear feet in either direction, require a T-molding between sections (see page 111).

B. Installing the tiles

1 Replace the spacers along the wall if necessary. Set the end tile in the corner and using the method recommended by the manufacturer, apply glue to the second tile—either the tongue, the groove, or both. Engage the tiles with the method recommended by the manufacturer and pull them together. Properly applied glue seeps from the joint in a thin line. Wipe immediately with a damp rag, then wipe the residue again.

2 At this point work across the wall, gluing and locking the entire first row of border tiles. Or set the tiles in a stair-step pattern as recommended by the manufacturer. If clamping is required the clamps should cross the installation every 3 to 4 feet. Pull the clamps moderately tight and let the glue set for 15 to 30 minutes before releasing and resetting the clamps. For products not requiring clamps, tape the joints if required.

STANLEY PRO TIP

Start tile under toe-kick

Before you choose a starting wall, consider any obstacles in the room, especially those that would interfere with putting down the first row. For example a vanity or kitchen cabinet toe-kick will make it difficult to tilt the planks, especially if the last row will be installed there. Start the installation under the toe-kick and work toward the opposite wall.

Close the gaps

Tapping block

As you research laminate products, you may notice that each manufacturer configures the tongues and grooves differently. Most, however, require the use of a tapping block. When you snug tiles together with a tapping block, be careful not to damage the geometry of those edges. You might think you can get by with a scrap tile for a tapping block, but it's better to purchase the one made by the manufacturer. Tap gently to avoid damaging the edges of the tiles.

3 When you reach walls or other obstructions, you may not be able to tilt or tap the tiles together. Make sure you have cut the end tile long enough to fill the space. Insert the short end of a pull bar over the end of the tile and tap the tiles together with a hammer.

4 Continue assembling the tiles, snugging the clamps every row or two and giving the glue ample time to dry before setting the next row.

5 When you reach the last row, scribe the tiles to conform to the surface of the wall. Be sure to include the spacer when you mark the tile for cutting. After cutting remove the spacer so it's easier to fit the tiles together. Use a pull bar to snug the tiles.

Apply the right amount of glue in the right places

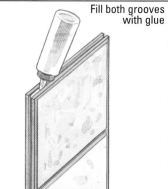

Fill both grooves with glue

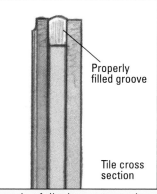

Properly filled groove

Tile cross section

Glue top of tongue only

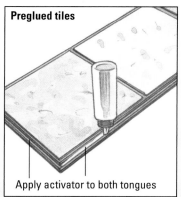

Preglued tiles

Apply activator to both tongues

Different brands of laminate tiles require different gluing methods. Some manufacturers recommend gluing the tongue of the tile, others the groove, and still others, both the tongue and the groove.

One style of tile does not use glue at all—the edges come preglued and require the application of an activator.

One requirement that is consistent among all the products

is the amount of glue you need to apply—and getting it right may take some experimenting. Properly applied glue just barely seeps from between fully closed joints. If you apply too little, the boards won't

stay together; too much and the boards won't stay together tightly.

Be sure to clean the excess off the surface immediately. Dried laminate glue proves difficult to remove.

INSTALLING SNAP-TOGETHER GARAGE FLOORS AND PLAY SURFACES

Snap-together modular flooring systems, also referred to as suspension floors, make garage floors and athletic surfaces more attractive and comfortable underfoot than blacktop or a concrete slab. Most systems simply lay on top of a concrete slab, so they can be taken apart and reassembled. The most common of these surfaces are made from interlocking polypropylene or PVC tiles designed to provide more traction underfoot than concrete. Because the material gives it reduces knee strain. Tiles designed for outdoor use have a wafflelike appearance that allows water to drain off quickly. The garage floor systems typically feature a coin- or diamond-pattern top designed to clean easily and not be damaged or stained by common chemicals.

PRESTART CHECKLIST

☐ **TIME**
About 3 hours for a double garage or a 15×20-foot outdoor surface, not including subfloor preparation

☐ **TOOLS**
Tape measure, utility knife, pencil, electric saw (optional)

☐ **SKILLS**
Measuring, setting, and cutting tiles

☐ **PREP**
Pour and/or clean concrete subfloor

☐ **MATERIALS**
Tiles

1 Start by making sure your subfloor is clean, level, and firm. If you are installing the floor in a garage, start the installation at the center point of the overhead garage door and work your way toward the back wall.

2 Otherwise measure the length and width of the room and divide the dimensions in two. Locate and mark the center of the room. This is the approximate starting point for the installation. Check the number of full tiles and the width of part tiles required to reach the walls in each direction.

Garage floors

This polypropylene garage floor comes in a variety of colors.

3 The tiles are designed to fit tightly together. Use a rubber mallet to hammer the tiles into position. On reaching the walls cut the edge tiles so as to leave a ¼-inch-wide gap between tiles and the wall.

4 Use a sharp blade to cut the edge tiles and use a good nonslip straightedge. Make several light cuts rather than one heavy cut. Use a cutting board to prevent damage as you cut the tiles from the front.

Rubber tile

Most rubber flooring tiles install in a fashion similar to other dry-back resilient tiles and are an excellent surfacing choice for home gyms and playrooms. For proper installation the subfloor must be clean, dry, level, and free of defects.

Other snap-together products

This attractive indoor/outdoor surface floats on top of a concrete slab. If you choose to move the surface, you can add or subtract additional tiles to fit any location. The tiles come in a variety of colors so that you can create a floor to match your high school, college, or professional team's colors. Neutral tones are also available.

INSTALLING RESILIENT FLOORING

Resilient floors offer a wide selection of colors and styles and are available in a variety of forms: tile and sheet, dry-backed, and self-stick.

Resilient tile

Resilient tiles are one of the easiest flooring materials to install and are available in designs that closely mimic other materials: stone, brick, ceramic, and wood. Thanks to computer technology the patterns are so realistic that only the softer feel underfoot gives the material away. Because of this give it is often the flooring of choice for people who spend a great deal of time working on their feet.

Dry-back resilient tile

Dry-backed tiles are typically laid on top of a special adhesive that you must apply with a trowel.

Self-stick

Self-stick tiles, also referred to as peel-and-stick tiles, come with the adhesive already applied to the tile back; you simply peel off the protective paper backing and press the tile onto the subfloor.

Sheet vinyl

Like resilient tiles standard sheet vinyl requires the application of an adhesive to firmly hold the floor in place. Full-spread vinyl requires glue to be spread over the entire floor; perimeter bond requires adhesive to be applied only around the edges. Perimeter-bond sheeting is easier to install and more forgiving of underlayment flaws, but it is also more prone to coming loose.

Cove molding

Cove molding is an easy-to-install baseboard designed to protect the bottom of a wall and creates a nice transition between a vinyl floor and the wall, particulary in utility areas, bathrooms, and laundry rooms.

Loose-lay vinyl

Loose-lay vinyl has a heavy fiberglass backing that causes the sheet to lay flat on the floor without the help of glue. A special double-sided tape holds the material in place at thresholds and other transitions.

Resilient floors are easy to install and provide years of attractive service.

CHAPTER PREVIEW

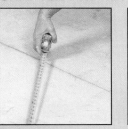

Laying out a resilient tile floor
page 148

Installing dry-backed resilient tiles
page 150

Installing self-stick vinyl tile
page 152

Installing sheet vinyl flooring
page 154

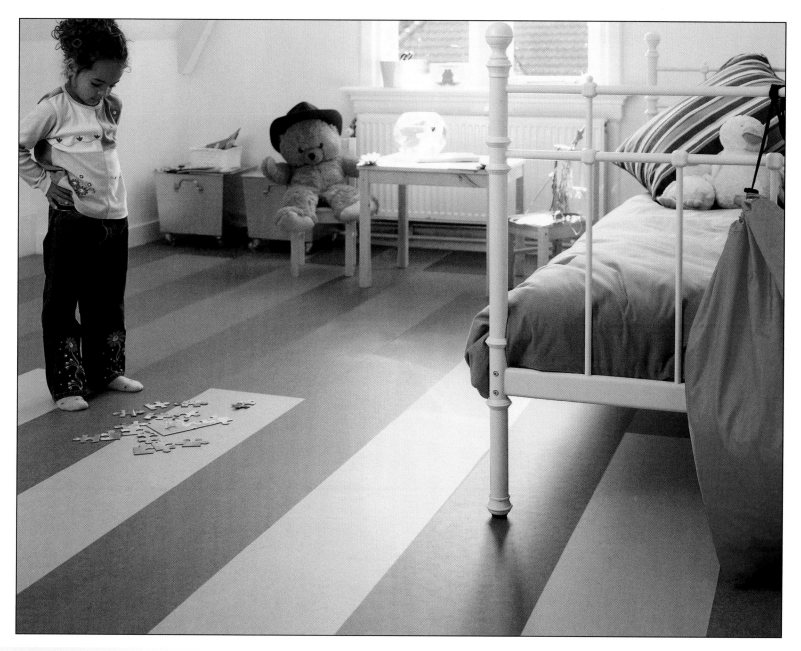

Vinyl flooring is comfortable underfoot and is an excellent choice in rooms where durability and affordability matter.

Installing vinyl cove molding
page 156

Installing loose-lay sheet vinyl
page 158

LAYING OUT A RESILIENT TILE FLOOR

In most situations laying out the room and setting resilient tile in quadrants works best. Starting in the center of the room allows the focal point of the tile pattern to correspond to the focal point of the floor area. More importantly laying out the installation in quadrants results in edge tiles that are the same width on all four sides. The quadrant method, however, requires some experimentation. To get evenly spaced edge tiles you'll have to lay a row of tiles on one chalkline axis at a time and push the row back and forth until the spaces at the ends are the same depth.

Bear in mind that edges look better if they are at least a half-tile wide. If your first trials end up with narrow slivers, take a tile out of the row and recenter the row on the layout line. Repeat the procedure for the other axis. Because carpentry is an inexact science, almost no room is perfectly square. In older homes especially you may find the out-of-square condition so severe that it results in one wall of radically tapered tiles. Try to "fix" your layout so tapered tiles fall in the least conspicuous part of the room—for example on a wall opposite a doorway, in indirect light, or hidden underneath furniture.

1 Prepare the subfloor and mark the center of the room by snapping chalklines between the midpoints of opposite walls. If the shape of the room is irregular or features protrusions that cover the center of a wall, snap the lines on the largest rectangular portion of the floor.

2 Check the lines for square using a 3-4-5 triangle (page 84). Measure and mark 3 feet on one line and 4 feet on the other. If the distance between the two marks is 5 feet, your lines are square. If not you'll have to adjust the lines—use a long 2×4 to mark the diagonal on the floor.

PRESTART CHECKLIST

☐ **TIME**
Two hours for an 8×10-foot area, not counting preparation

☐ **TOOLS**
Tape measure, chalkline, carpenter's pencil

☐ **SKILLS**
Measuring, marking

☐ **PREP**
Remove furniture, appliances, and old flooring

PREPARE THE SUBFLOOR

As its name implies, resilient tile conforms to every imperfection in the surface of the material upon which it's laid. Any light that reflects from that surface will magnify the imperfection and ruin the appearance despite all your hard work, which makes preparing the subfloor properly a must.

Wood. In new construction install ¾-inch plywood and ¼- or ½-inch lauan or OSB for a smooth surface. On existing wood floors install lauan plywood or OSB, staggering the joints and leaving a ¹⁄₃₂-inch gap between them. Fill and sand all nail holes and gaps with a filler that's compatible with your tile adhesive.

Concrete. You can apply vinyl tile to concrete below, at, and above grade. Clean and smooth the surface (pages 52–53). Grind off any protruding imperfections. Check for moisture by taping plastic sheets every 2 feet. If moisture beads under plastic after a couple of days, do not install tile. Remedy the moisture problem

first if possible. If moisture persists choose another finished flooring material.

Vinyl tile or sheet goods. If existing material is cushioned, remove and prepare subfloor as above. If tile is installed over a wood floor that is loose, waxed, or glossy, cover with lauan plywood. On a concrete slab remove gloss and level embossed surface with an embossing leveler.

Ceramic tile. Remove tile and repair wood and concrete subfloors or level the tiled surface with self-leveling compound. Install lauan over plywood subfloor.

Carpet. Remove carpet and repair wood or concrete subfloor as above. Install lauan plywood over plywood subfloor.

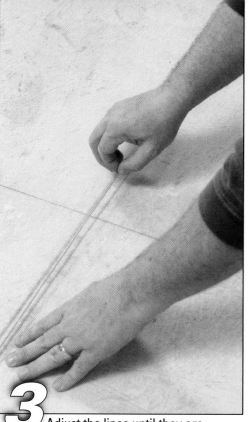

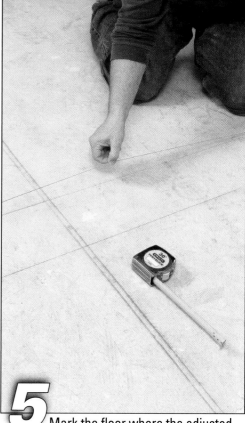

3 Adjust the lines until they are square by moving the chalkline slightly and resnapping the lines. If the diagonal measured more than 5 feet, move the line slightly clockwise with reference to the center point. If it was less than 5 feet, move it counterclockwise.

4 Dry-lay a row of tiles along both axes—from wall to wall. Measure the space for the tiles that will abut the wall. Adjust the line of tiles until the edge tiles are the same width and at least a half-tile wide. Repeat the adjustment on the other axis until you have even borders.

5 Mark the floor where the adjusted lines will fall and pull up the tiles. Resnap a new chalkline on these marks. This will give you a revised "center" point from which you will begin laying the floor. Make sure the adjusted lines are square.

LAYING OUT A RESILIENT FLOOR

STANDARD LAYOUT

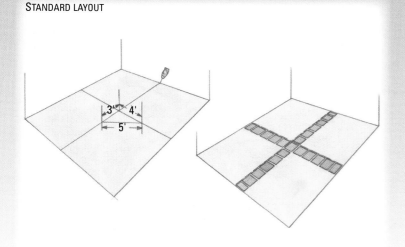

3' 4'
5'

Snap perpendicular lines at the midpoints of the walls and square them. Dry-lay tile in both directions to center the layout and leave tiles of equal width at both edges.

DIAGONAL LAYOUT

1. Establish perpendicular lines at midpoints of walls.

2. Mark equal distances from the intersection and connect the marks.

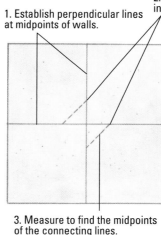

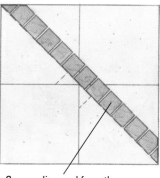

3. Measure to find the midpoints of the connecting lines.

4. Snap a diagonal from the corners through the midpoints of the connecting lines. Dry-lay tiles along the diagonal.

INSTALLING DRY-BACKED RESILIENT TILES

When choosing an adhesive for dry-backed tile, be sure to read labels carefully. Picking an adhesive requires a bit of science—you'll find latex-base solutions, asphalt emulsions, alcohol resins, rubber cements, and epoxies. Ask your supplier to match the qualities of the adhesive to your jobsite.

Most vinyl adhesives are solvent-base, and that means they handle differently from thinset and other cement-base mortars. They tend to "grab" the trowel and are difficult to spread evenly. Practice spreading adhesive on a piece of scrap plywood before applying it to the floor. When you work with solvent-base adhesives, properly ventilate the room: Open the windows and exhaust the fumes with a window fan. Wear a respirator for full protection.

Work as much as possible from the untiled subfloor. To keep from tiling yourself into a corner, kneel on 2×2 squares of plywood at the last rows. Cut two pieces so you can move them alternately as you work across the floor.

1 Starting at an intersection of lines, spread adhesive with the smooth edge of a notched trowel. Lay the adhesive right up to—but not over—the layout lines. Then comb the adhesive with the notched edge of the trowel. Let the adhesive become tacky.

2 Line up the first tile with the intersection of the layout lines and set it on the adhesive. Then set the second tile against the first one and lower it in place. Don't slide the tiles—you'll push mastic up between the joints. Check the grain direction and set the rest of the quadrant.

PRESTART CHECKLIST

☐ **TIME**
About 4 hours for an 8×10-foot floor

☐ **TOOLS**
Trowel, utility knife, hair dryer, chalkline, straightedge, carpenter's pencil, 100-pound floor roller

☐ **SKILLS**
Setting and cutting tile

☐ **PREP**
Repair subfloor and snap layout lines

☐ **MATERIALS**
Tiles, adhesive, solvent

SETTING SEQUENCES (PERPENDICULAR LAYOUTS)

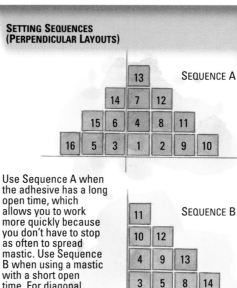

SEQUENCE A

Use Sequence A when the adhesive has a long open time, which allows you to work more quickly because you don't have to stop as often to spread mastic. Use Sequence B when using a mastic with a short open time. For diagonal setting sequences see *page 127.*

SEQUENCE B

CHECK THE GRAIN DIRECTION

Most resilient tiles have a grain that results from the manufacturing process. The grain itself is virtually invisible but it does affect the color and perception of the pattern, depending on the angle of the light falling on the tile. Other tiles, both with and without grain, have a pattern that is directional.

Both grained and patterned tile must be laid in a certain order to achieve the ideal appearance. Look on the back of each tile before you lay it. If it has arrows imprinted on it, use the arrows as a guide. Dry-lay the tile with the arrows going in one direction, then experiment with the pattern, installing the arrows differently. Once you discover a result you like, use it consistently as you set the tile.

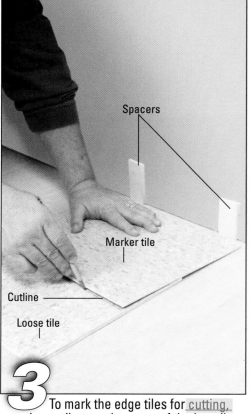

3 To mark the edge tiles for cutting, set a loose tile exactly on top of the last tile in a row. Then set a marker tile on top of that one, positioning it against ¼-inch spacers at the wall. (Resilient tile won't expand much, but the subfloor will.) Run a pencil along the edge of the marker tile to mark the cutline.

Spacers
Marker tile
Cutline
Loose tile

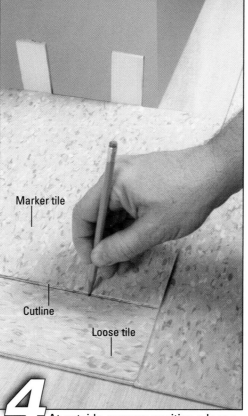

4 At outside corners position a loose tile and a marker tile as if you were cutting an edge tile. Mark the loose tile as you did in Step 3 and reposition the loose tile and marker tile to the other corner. Mark the loose tile for the corner cutout.

Marker tile
Cutline
Loose tile

5 When you have set one quadrant, clean off excess or spilled adhesive with the solvent recommended by the manufacturer (usually detergent and water). Don't wet the floor—excess liquid weakens the adhesive. Set the remaining quadrants. Roll the floor when finished.

CUTTING VINYL TILE

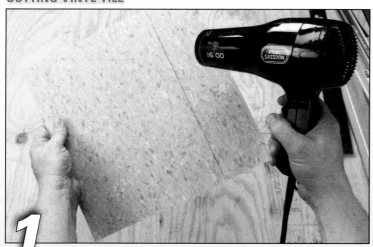

1 Brittle resilient tiles cut more easily if you warm the cutline slightly with a hair dryer. Use a carpenter's pencil to mark the cutline and a utility knife to make the cut.

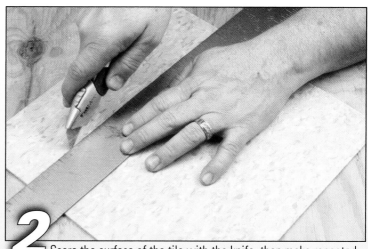

2 Score the surface of the tile with the knife, then make repeated passes until you have cut through the tile. If the cut edge will not be visible, snap the tile after a few passes with the knife instead.

INSTALLING SELF-STICK VINYL TILE

Self-stick vinyl tile (also called peel-and-stick tile) is a do-it-yourselfer's dream material. It requires only basic skills, minimal time, and a few tools. It also requires a precise eye when setting the first tile and those in the first row adjoining it. How straight the remaining installation looks depends in large part on the accuracy of the first row. The steps shown here include the application of a primer. Some manufacturers don't recommend a primer. Others do, but only on porous surfaces such as plywood. Once the tile comes into contact with the floor, the adhesive is unforgiving—you won't be able to adjust the tile's position. If you misalign a tile, you'll probably have to pull it up and replace it. The tile will likely be damaged, but you might be able to find a place for it as a cut tile in a corner. The paper backings on self-stick tile are slippery underfoot. Keep the jobsite safe by placing a wastebasket at your side as you lay the tiles. Don't remove the tile backing until you're ready to set the tile. Dispose of the backing immediately.

PRESTART CHECKLIST

☐ **TIME**
About 2 hours for an 8×10-foot floor

☐ **TOOLS**
Long-handled roller, tape measure, heavy-duty scissors, putty knife, utility knife, chalkline, straightedge, square

☐ **SKILLS**
Laying tile accurately, cutting tile

☐ **PREP**
Repair, clean, and lay out floor

☐ **MATERIALS**
Primer, self-stick tile, cove molding

1 Prime the subfloor, if necessary, with the product recommended by the manufacturer. Most primed surfaces benefit from two applications—the first one thinned and the second full strength. Both coats will go on easily with a long-handled roller.

2 Snap chalklines from the midpoints of opposite walls to locate the center of the room. Square the lines with a 3-4-5 triangle (page 84) and dry-lay the tiles along each axis. Move the layout until you have even tiles at the edges, then resnap the lines.

Cutting self-stick tile

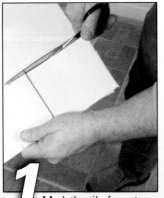

1 Mark the tile for cuts around obstructions but leave the backing on before cutting it. Using heavy-duty household scissors, cut the tile along the lines.

2 Peel off the backing and dispose of it immediately. The backings are slick, and if you step on one you might fall.

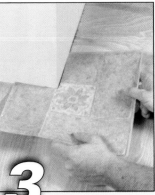

3 Position the tile carefully, placing the leading corner or edge against the neighboring tiles or the obstruction before you press it in place.

3 Arrange the tiles loosely along the layout lines with the arrows (grain) facing in the same or opposite directions (depending on the look you want). Starting at a corner of the tile and working slowly, peel away the paper backing. Don't pull fast—you might tear the backing, and a fresh edge is difficult to raise from the center of the tile. Set the corner of the tile at the intersection of the lines and press it down. Then roll it with a small roller.

4 Using the layout configuration of your choice (page 127), continue setting the tiles, making sure each one butts squarely against its neighbors on two sides. Don't forget to maintain the arrows consistently. If you mistakenly lay a tile with the wrong orientation, warm the tile with a hair dryer to soften the adhesive and pry it up immediately with a wide putty knife. The tile is likely to be damaged.

Installing vinyl cove molding

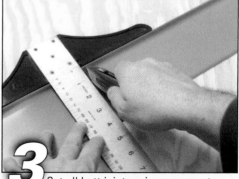

1 To fit an inside corner, score the back of the molding with a utility knife and cut a V-notch in the coved base. If you can't get the molding tightly in the corner, cut the material on your score marks. Cut and install all corners first, then cut and install straight runs to fit between them.

2 To fit an outside corner, warm the molding with a hair dryer before adhering it to the wall. You can increase the flexibility of the molding by paring away a thin layer from the back. Don't cut through the material.

3 Cut all butt joints using a square to guide the knife. After applying the adhesive roll the molding with a J-roller and press the flange against the floor and wall with a piece of 1× scrap.

INSTALLING SHEET VINYL FLOORING

One advantage of sheet vinyl flooring is that it has fewer seams than other materials, making it an excellent choice for kitchens, baths, laundry rooms, and other utility areas. Because it comes in rolls that are 12 feet wide, you can install it in smaller rooms with no seams at all. There are two types of sheet vinyl. Full-spread vinyl has a felt backing and requires an adhesive that spreads over the entire floor surface. That makes installation a little time-consuming; however it rarely comes loose from the floor. It requires an almost flawlessly smooth underlayment—even small particles under the sheet will show up as bumps when the sheet is glued down. Perimeter-bond sheet vinyl is laid with adhesive only around the edges of the room, making it easier and quicker to lay. It is more forgiving of minor underlayment flaws but is more prone to coming loose.

PRESTART CHECKLIST

☐ **TIME**
About 4 hours for full-spread vinyl on a 10×12-foot floor

☐ **TOOLS**
Utility knife, compass, scissors, floor roller, seam roller, straightedge

☐ **SKILLS**
Measuring and cutting accurately, lifting, seaming vinyl

☐ **PREP**
Install or repair underlayment without surface defects; remove all floor trim

☐ **MATERIALS**
Butcher paper or kraft paper, masking tape, duct tape, vinyl sheet goods, adhesive, seaming solvent

1 Cover the perimeter ¼ inch from the walls with butcher or kraft paper. Heavier paper moves less. Cut small triangles and tape the sheet to the floor through the holes. Overlap all edges at least 2 inches and fasten with duct tape. Roll up the template and take it to the room where you'll cut the sheet.

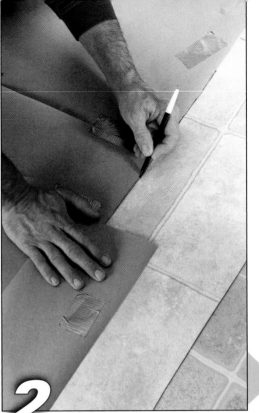

2 Unroll the vinyl sheet faceup. Overlap seam edges by 3 inches and tape the seam. Unroll the paper template on the sheet, lining up the edges of the template with pattern lines. Tape the template to the sheet and mark its edge on the sheet with a washable marker.

Shopping for quality

Vinyl was designed to replace linoleum, which graced many mid-20th-century homes. (Linoleum is still available today.)

All vinyl floor goods, however, are not created equal. The adage "You get what you pay for" applies. The quality and the durability of the material vary widely and depend almost entirely on how much vinyl it contains.

Solid vinyl is tough, longest lasting, and the most expensive option. Its color and pattern are formed by embedded colored vinyl chips in the vinyl base material. Solid vinyl products also boast more choices of colors and patterns. Because the color and pattern go clear through the sheet, they don't wear off easily.

The same goes for **vinyl composition** products, whose pattern and color are ingrained but are composed of both vinyl and nonvinyl ingredients. The reduced vinyl content makes this product less expensive.

Rotogravure vinyl sheets get their pattern from a printing process, and the printed layer has no vinyl content at all. It is protected by a urethane wear layer. Once this layer wears to expose the printed pattern, the design will begin to disappear.

You can tell a lot about the quality of vinyl sheet goods by their thickness. Thicker materials contain more vinyl and will last longer. To determine the right material for your application, consider the room's use. For example it makes sense to install a less expensive sheet in an infrequently used guest bath and a more expensive material in the kitchen.

3 With a straightedge along the marks on the sheet, cut it with a utility knife. Roll up the sheet with the pattern side in and carry it to the floor. Unroll the sheet, sliding it under door casings, and tug and shift it into place.

4 For a full-spread floor, lift up one half of the sheet and fold it back. For perimeter bond, lift up the edges. Spread adhesive from the corners to the center with a ¼-inch notched trowel. Refold the sheet back into place. Adhere the second sheet (or the other half if not seaming the sheet vinyl).

5 Roll the entire surface from the center to the edges with a rented 100-pound floor roller. Use a damp rag to wipe up any adhesive around the edges of the vinyl. Replace the trim, then install baseboards and shoe molding or vinyl cove base. Install thresholds and rehang the doors.

SEAMING THE SHEET VINYL

1 To cut a straight seam, overlap the edges 3 inches and snap a chalkline where you want the seam. Using a straightedge and utility knife, cut through both sheets in one pass. Pull back the edges and apply adhesive under them. Push seam edges down into the adhesive.

2 Roll the seam with a seam roller (called a J-roller). Use moderate pressure to avoid pushing adhesive up through the seam. Wipe off excess adhesive and let it cure. Then apply seaming solvent to fuse the edges.

STANLEY PRO TIP

Easy seams

Place seams on an inconspicuous, low-traffic section of the floor whenever possible. Symmetry is not necessarily your goal— a seam running down the center of the bathroom floor for example is likely to be distracting. Consider placing the seam perpendicular to the room and close to a far wall. Find your best seam location before you start cutting the sheet to fit.

After you've laid your floor, protect it until both adhesive and seams have set.
■ If possible don't walk on the seams for at least 8 hours.
■ Keep the room temperature at 65 degrees or above for 48 hours to help the adhesive cure properly.
■ Don't wash the floor for 5 days.

INSTALLING VINYL COVE MOLDING

Vinyl cove molding is an easy-to-install baseboard designed to protect the bottom of a wall. The material stands up to brooms and wet mops and resists scuffing, so it is a good choice for laundry rooms, utility areas, and bathrooms.

The vinyl molding comes in flexible 4-inch-high strips that are about 1/16 of an inch thick. Two styles are available: One style is flat and packaged in rolls, and the other has a small curve (called a cove) at the bottom. The cove molding creates a cleaner installation because the cove curves out slightly from the wall, covering the expansion gap at the edge of the floor.

PRESTART CHECKLIST

☐ **TIME**
From 1 to 2 hours for every 24 linear feet

☐ **TOOLS**
Utility knife, caulk gun with a special tip designed for cove molding

☐ **MATERIALS**
Cove molding, caulk designed for use with cove molding, chalk marker

 **STANLEY** PRO TIP

Thresholds for resilient flooring

Because vinyl is so thin, to create an attractive transition you can usually install the trim designed for the abutting flooring material right over it.

You can also install specialty moldings as shown on page 157.

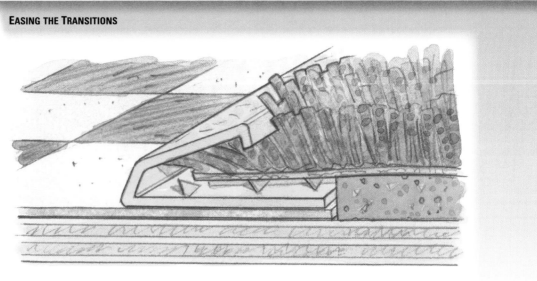

1 Start in the corner of the room. Using a utility knife cut the cove molding to the exact length of the wall. Load the caulk gun with a special cove molding tip and the manufacturer-recommended adhesive. Using the caulk gun carefully apply a thin layer of the adhesive to the backside of the molding. Push the molding against the wall and firmly press along the entire surface to secure it to the wall. If you need more than one length, repeat this step, butting two straight-cut endpieces together.

EASING THE TRANSITIONS

Carpet edging is an inexpensive transition between carpet and another floor material. T-molding is used as a transition between floors of the same height.

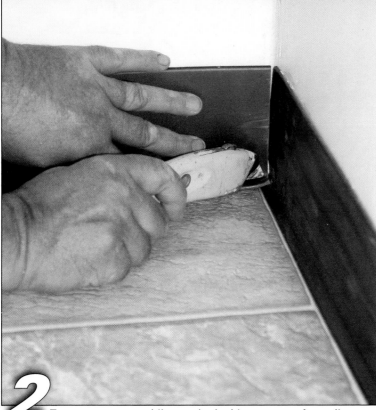

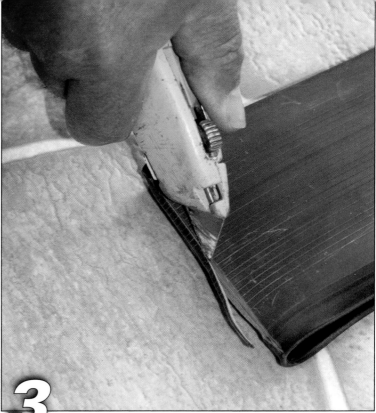

2 To secure cove molding to the inside corners of a wall, adhere the cut molding to the corner edge. Using a utility knife carve away the cove on the next piece of molding so that it nests against the first piece and then glue the second piece in place. Avoid creating seams at outside corners.

3 To secure cove molding to the outside corners of a wall, stand the molding in place against the wall and mark with chalk where the piece will turn the corner. Bend the piece face-to-face at the mark and trim away about half the thickness of the molding as shown. Test fit the molding to make sure the recess fits the corner. Once you are sure of the fit, apply adhesive with a caulk gun to the back of the molding and press the molding in place as in step 1.

Saddle threshold

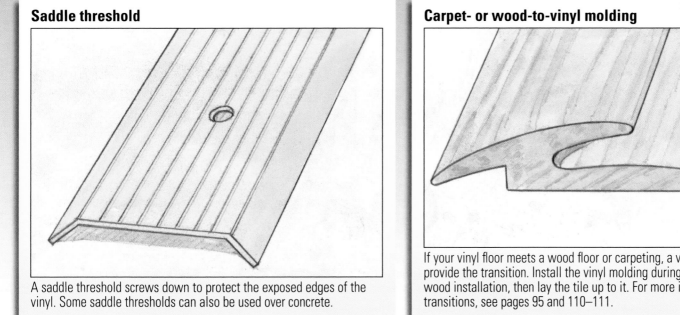

A saddle threshold screws down to protect the exposed edges of the vinyl. Some saddle thresholds can also be used over concrete.

Carpet- or wood-to-vinyl molding

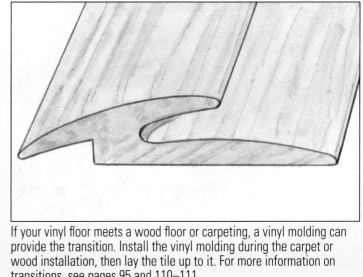

If your vinyl floor meets a wood floor or carpeting, a vinyl molding can provide the transition. Install the vinyl molding during the carpet or wood installation, then lay the tile up to it. For more information on transitions, see pages 95 and 110–111.

INSTALLING LOOSE-LAY SHEET VINYL

Loose-lay sheet vinyl does not require adhesive. Once you cut it to size and put it in place, it's installed. It's an ideal solution for covering surfaces such as painted concrete, to which adhesives don't adhere well. You can also roll it up and move it—something you might want to do if the washer overflows, for example.

Fiberglass backing

Loose-lay vinyl has a heavy fiberglass backing that allows the sheet to lay flat on the floor without glue. You can purchase the flooring at most home centers and flooring stores. Standard sheet vinyl is not heavy enough to be installed in this fashion— it will slip and curl over time.

To prevent loose-lay vinyl from curling up in high traffic areas, secure the material with double-sided tape at the doorways. Before installing this or any floor covering, make sure the subfloor is clean, dry, and smooth.

PRESTART CHECKLIST

☐ **TIME**
About 3 hours for loose-lay vinyl on a 10×12-foot floor

☐ **TOOLS**
Scissors, utility knife

☐ **SKILLS**
Measuring and cutting accurately, lifting

☐ **PREP**
Install or repair underlayment without surface defects; remove all floor trim

☐ **MATERIALS**
Butcher paper or kraft paper, masking tape, duct tape, loose-lay vinyl tape, loose-lay vinyl sheet

1 Lay out and cut a template just as you would for standard sheet vinyl (page 154). Your particular brand of loose-lay vinyl may require a slightly different-size expansion gap, so read the manufacturer's directions carefully. Spread out the vinyl on a clean floor that is larger than the template, tape the template to it, and cut the vinyl to shape. If the vinyl requires a seam, follow the instructions on page 155 for seaming standard sheet vinyl.

STANLEY PRO TIP: **Smooth subfloors**

Like other forms of vinyl, the material is resilient—it springs back when you push on it and conforms to the surface on which you install it. If there are bumps of glue, popped-up nails, or uneven bits of concrete on the subfloor, the vinyl will flow over the spot and create a slighty elevated area. As you walk on the spot, you'll eventually wear through the elevated area and you'll be able to see the spot from the vinyl surface. To ensure a smooth application, sand and clean the subfloor so there are no imperfections that will show through the vinyl.

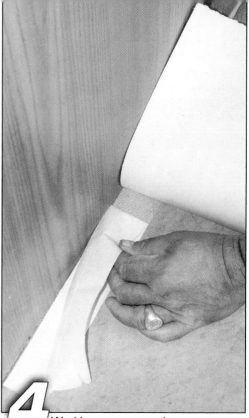

2 To prevent curling use double-sided tape designed for loose-lay vinyl to secure the flooring at thresholds and under appliances and fixtures. Cut the tape to the proper length, remove the protective paper from the side you will be adhering to the subfloor, and press the tape in place.

3 Roll up the vinyl and bring it into the area where you are installing it. Unroll it. Using a clean push broom, smooth the flooring in place. If the floor has a seam, roll back the connecting pieces and apply double-sided tape to the subfloor along the entire length of the seam.

4 Working at one taped area at a time, roll back the vinyl so you can see the double-sided tape. Remove the tape's protective backing, roll the vinyl back over it, and press the flooring in place. Repeat this procedure for each of the taped areas.

Linoleum floor

Linoleum is a durable, all-natural alternative to vinyl flooring. Made from linseed oil, plant resins, wood fiber, and powdered limestone on a jute backing, linoleum is environmentally friendly. Linoleum naturally resists bacteria, making it an excellent choice for bathrooms, kitchens, and children's rooms. However don't use linoleum in basements or other rooms where moisture seeps through concrete, as it can damage the backing. People with chemical sensitivities should note that linoleum has a distinct, yet not unpleasant, odor for several weeks after installation as the linseed oil in the material continues to cure. Linoleum is sold in rolls and tiles and installs in a fashion similar to vinyl flooring but requires the use of a special linoleum-compatible adhesive.

INSTALLING CARPETING

Carpet is the flooring that invites you to walk barefoot and stretch out on the floor. Carpet tiles are an excellent choice for do-it-yourselfers. Installing large pieces of carpet, on the other hand, requires some special tools, skills, and heavy lifting, so it's often left to the professionals. Some rental shops do offer the tools however, and with a little patience, it is possible to install it yourself.

If this is your first installation, choose a plain carpet as opposed to a patterned one as it will be easier to install. Avoid installing berber until you are seasoned at carpet installation as it requires extra skill to install.

Carpet is available in three basic types:

Residential carpet is ⅜ to ½ inch thick, is often made of nylon, and comes in a variety of styles, from friezes to berbers. It's most often installed over a cushion and fastened down with tack strips.

Commerical carpeting features a dense, short nap designed to withstand heavy use. There is little or no cushion, making it less comfortable underfoot. It it an excellent choice for some home applications, such as over concrete or in a home office or hobby space. For added durability commercial carpet requires a glued rather than stretched installation.

Outdoor carpeting is designed to withstand water and sunlight. Most outdoor carpets are made from olefin, a waterproof synthetic fiber. Outdoor carpeting has a special backing made of mildew-resistant fabric and requires a glue-down installation.

Carpet grain

Like many other flooring materials, carpet has a grain that makes the fibers lean in one direction: If you run your hand over the carpet in one direction, the fibers lie down. If you run your hand in the other direction, the carpet fibers stand up.

If you cut a piece of carpet in half and turn one of the pieces 180 degrees, the grain creates the impression that the carpet is not a perfect match. When installing carpet tiles or seaming together carpet pieces, make sure the grain runs in the same direction to avoid noticeable seams.

CHAPTER PREVIEW

There are three ways to install carpeting: stretch it in place, glue it down, or adhere self-stick tiles.

Installing seamless stretched carpet
page 162

Installing seamed and stretched carpet
page 170

Installing glued and seamed carpet
page 174

Installing carpet tile
page 180

**Installing carpet
on steps**
page 182

*There is nothing more comfortable
underfoot than thick, padded
carpeting. It's an excellent flooring
choice in rooms where people may
want to sprawl on the floor.*

INSTALLING SEAMLESS STRETCHED CARPET

Carpet comes in rolls that are 12, 13½, and 15 feet wide. If possible choose a width that will enable you to carpet the entire area without a seam. If a seam is necessary, see pages 170–179. Carpet is sold by either the square foot (a square area in which each side is 1 foot long) or the square yard (a square area in which each side is 3 feet long). To compare prices multiply the price per square foot by 9 to determine the price per square yard, or divide the price per square yard by 9 to determine the price per square foot. To determine how much carpet you need, sketch the shape of the room, including entryways, on paper. Measure the length and the width of the room in feet and inches, then round up to the nearest foot. Round up the width to one that the carpet comes in—12, 13½, or 15 feet. If you are carpeting a room that is 14'1"×17½ feet, you'll need a piece of carpet that is 15 feet wide and at least 18 feet long.

PRESTART CHECKLIST

☐ **TIME**
15 minutes per square yard, not including subfloor preparation

☐ **TOOLS**
Tape measure, carpet knife, straightedge, knee kicker, power stretcher, wall trimmer, hammer, chalkline

☐ **SKILLS**
Measuring, lifting, laying, cutting, and stretching carpet

☐ **PREP**
Repair and level subfloor

☐ **MATERIALS**
Carpet, pad, tack strips, binder bar, transition moldings

1 _Prepare the subfloor,_ then thoroughly clean the existing floor of the room you plan to carpet: Sweep and vacuum the floor and, if necessary, scrape up any paint, joint compound, or putty so that the surface is completely smooth. Make sure the subfloor is completely dry before installing any padding or carpeting.

PREPARE THE SUBFLOOR

■ **Wood:** In new construction install ¾-inch plywood. On an existing wood floor, remove the finish and patch any holes. On planks wider than 4 inches, install ⅜-inch underlayment. Fill depressions and sand smooth.
■ **Concrete:** Check for moisture by taping plastic sheets to the slab every 4 or 5 feet and letting the sheets sit overnight. If moisture beads under the plastic, don't lay the carpet. Remedy the moisture problem first, then thoroughly clean the surface and allow it to dry.
■ **Vinyl:** If the existing material is cushioned, remove it and repair the subfloor. If existing vinyl is installed on a wood floor and is waxed or glossy, sand or strip the finish. Glue down any loose corners.
■ **Ceramic tile:** Remove any damaged tile and level the surface with self-leveling compound.
■ **Carpet:** Remove the old carpet and, if necessary, repair the subfloor as described above.

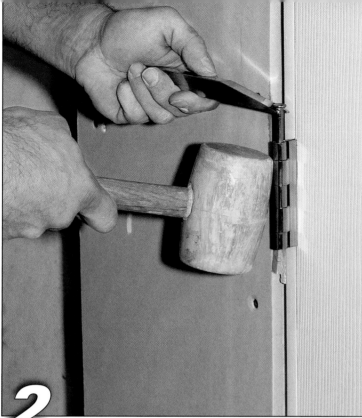

2 If there are doors that open into the room you are carpeting, take them off the hinges so they won't get in your way. Removing the doors will also make it easier for you to cut the doorjambs if necessary. If laying doors on top of each other, place a towel between them so they won't get scratched.

3 Install tack strip around the perimeter of the room, making sure to maintain a ⅜-inch distance between the tackless strip and baseboard. Cut the strips to fit with a strip cutter or heavy snips. Align the strips so that the manufacturer-printed arrows point toward the wall. Nail tackless strips around air vents and other floor openings, with the exception of thresholds and doorways as the tacks on the strips are sharp and may poke through the carpet.

SAFETY FIRST
Using specialty tools

You don't actually kick a knee kicker; kicking with your knee risks injury. Instead put the padded end of the knee kicker a few inches above your knee, then push firmly. This provides the pressure you need without harming your leg. Note that the knee kicker setting can be adjusted. Start by setting the dial at 3½, then adjust it higher or lower as necessary. Never use a kicker on one side of the carpet if the other side has been stretched. Use a power stretcher instead. In a room with obstacles, such as a radiator, a power stretcher may not reach from wall to wall. If that's the case, make a "deadman": Nail two lengths of tack strip to the face of a 2×10, teeth facing the same direction. Put the teeth of the strip into the carpet so that they slope away from the head of the stretcher. Have a helper stand on the 2×10. Put the foot of the stretcher against the deadman and push against it as if it were a wall.

Specialty tools and materials

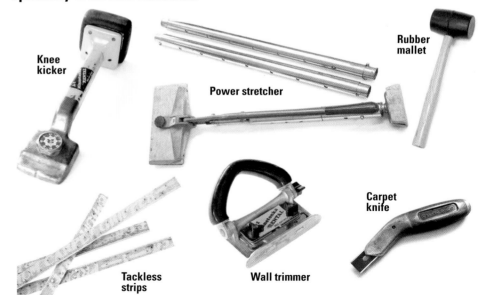

Knee kicker

Power stretcher

Rubber mallet

Carpet knife

Tackless strips

Wall trimmer

4 Starting at a corner lay out the carpet pad perpendicular to the direction you plan to install the carpet and staple it near the tack strips with a staple hammer. Staple the seams of the pad, alternating staple locations so that they are directly adjacent to one another.

5 Using a utility knife, trim the carpet pad so that it lays as close to the rows of tack strip as possible but without covering the strip. Measure the longest portion of the room. Add six inches to this measurement to allow for error and any areas where the walls may not be plumb.

Carpet padding

A quality carpet pad increases the durability and comfort of the carpet. The Carpet and Rug Institute recommends choosing a pad no thicker than 7/16 of an inch. Thicker padding makes the carpet flex more, which can cause the backing to break down more quickly. In most cases a pad with a 6- to 8-pound density is best—less may void the carpet manufacturer's warranty. Carpet padding is typically made from one of four materials:

■ **Rebonded urethane** accounts for 80 percent of carpet pads made today. These pads offer resilience and good performance and install with the mesh side up.

■ **Prime urethane** is less resilient than rebonded urethane and is substantially more expensive.

■ **Waffle-patterned rubber** is heavier in weight and is sometimes recommended for installations with high humidity levels.

■ **Synthetic fibers** are firmer underfoot and work better with level loops and berber carpets.

Carpet fibers

There are five basic types of carpet fibers:

■ **Nylon** accounts for 90 percent of all residential carpet. It's affordable, durable, colorfast, and resists dirt and mildew.

■ **Olefin** is the trade name for polypropylene and accounts for 80 percent of all commercial carpet and nearly all outdoor carpet. It's affordable, durable, colorfast, and resists dirt and mildew.

■ **Polyester** has a soft, luxurious feel, but polyester fibers crush more easily than other fibers. It's also affordable, colorfast, and resists dirt and mildew.

■ **Wool,** a natural carpet fiber, also has a nice texture and resists crushing. It's more expensive than the other fibers and can be harder to clean. It does not perform well in humid areas.

■ **Acrylic** mimics the look and feel of wool but costs less. It's affordable, durable, colorfast, and resists dirt and mildew but will wear quickly in high-traffic areas.

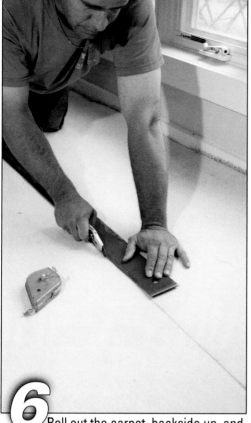

6 Roll out the carpet, backside up, and snap chalklines across the back of the carpet to this measurement. Put a piece of scrap wood under the marked carpet and, using a straightedge and carpet knife, cut the carpet along the chalklines.

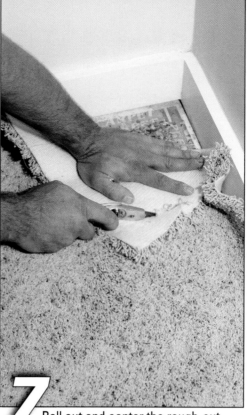

7 Roll out and center the rough-cut carpet in the room. Make relief cuts at the corners so that the carpet lies flat. Butt one end of the carpet against the long wall.

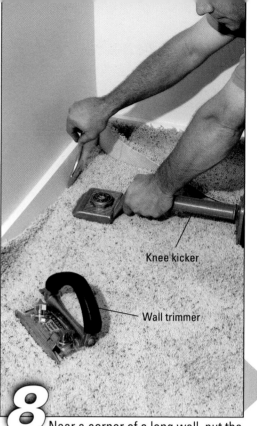

8 Near a corner of a long wall, put the toothed end of a knee kicker in the carpet about 3 inches from the wall. Strike the padded end to stretch the carpet over the tack strips. Trim excess carpet with a wall trimmer, which rests against the wall and provides a straight cut at the correct spot.

Knee kicker

Wall trimmer

Typical installation

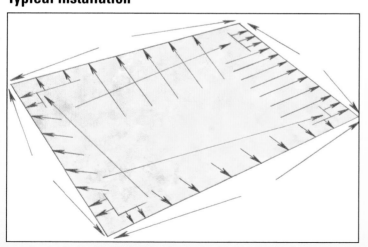

A typical carpet installation is diagramed here. The short arrows indicate where you push the carpet with the knee kicker. The long arrows show the angle and starting point of the power stretcher.

STANLEY PRO TIP

Install transition molding at carpet meeting another surface edge

Install transition moldings wherever the carpet meets other flooring. A binder bar, as shown here, is most commonly used. Other options in carpet transitions are shown on pages 168–169. Seal the edge of the carpet with latex seam sealer to prevent unraveling. Nail the binder bar to the floor and push the kicker to fit the carpet over the hooks in the binder bar. When the carpet is in place, hit the bar with a rubber mallet or put a block of

wood over the bar to protect it. Hammer the flange closed.

9 Use a stair tool to tuck the carpet between the tackless strip and the wall. Repeat this procedure to tuck the carpet along 3 feet of the wall. Repeat the anchoring procedure on the short wall of the same corner: Push the carpet over the tackless strips with the knee kicker, trim, and tuck the carpet. Once you have the carpet attached to the short walls, use the power stretcher to stretch the carpet between the two remaining walls.

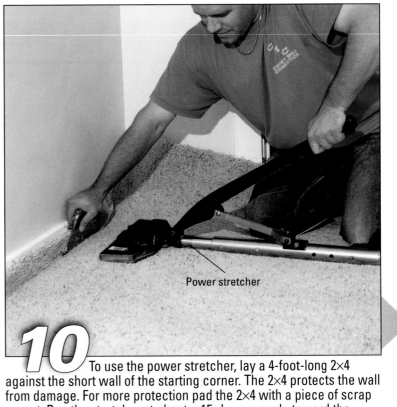

Power stretcher

10 To use the power stretcher, lay a 4-foot-long 2×4 against the short wall of the starting corner. The 2×4 protects the wall from damage. For more protection pad the 2×4 with a piece of scrap carpet. Run the stretcher at about a 15-degree angle toward the opposite corner. Set the head of the stretcher 6 inches from the wall. Push on the handle to stretch the carpet about 1 percent. This translates to around 1¼ inches over a 10-foot span.

Types of carpet

Most carpet is tufted. It comes in two broad types: cut and looped. Each comes in several varieties.

Saxony texture
This dense carpet has tightly twisted fibers and feels soft underfoot. It disguises tracks and is one of the best-selling carpets.

Saxony plush
This carpet has longer fibers that are lightly twisted. It readily shows footprints and vacuum lines.

Frieze
Pronouced free-zay this carpet has dense twisted fibers that curl in different directions. It disguises tracks.

11 Hook the stretched carpet along about 3 feet of both of the corner walls. With the knee kicker push the carpet the full length of the long wall.

12 Power-stretch the second corner. Run the stretcher at about a 15-degree angle to the corner as shown. Stretch the carpet along about 3 feet of both walls that form the corner.

13 Anchor the other short wall. Use the knee kicker to push the carpet against the short wall and attach it to the tackless strips. Continue using the knee kicker to work your way along the short wall.

Level loop
This carpet features tightly packed loops that are all the same height.

Berber
This level loop carpet is made with a thicker yarn. Its tight construction eliminates tracks. It's dirt resistant and cleans easily.

Multilevel loop
This carpet loops at different heights to create a pattern. It hides tracks and is dirt resistant; greater variations in height can cause dirt to accumulate on lower sections.

Cut and loop
A combination of cut and looped fibers creates the pattern. It hides dirt and track marks.

Installing seamless stretched carpet continued

14 Power-stretch the other long wall. Use the power stretcher to stretch the carpet from the long wall of the starting corner, running the stretcher at about a 15-degree angle. Hook and anchor the carpet over the tackless strips near the head of the stretcher. Moving the stretcher along the wall, stretch, hook, and anchor the carpet section by section.

15 Attach the carpet along the last wall. Push it in place with the kicker; anchor and tuck it with the stair tool.

WHAT IF…
You need to install a threshold?

Even threshold
A threshold provides a visual and mechanical transition between one type of floor and another. The threshold shown is curved; you can also purchase a flatter version.

Height change threshold
When the carpet meets a raised floor, such as a thick tile floor, use a threshold that screws down through the carpet and angles to provide a smooth transition.

Wedge threshold
Like the height change threshold this threshold connects flooring materials of two different heights.

Metal carpet edging
This transition joins carpet to an existing floor. Nail the edging to the floor and stretch the carpet over the barbs. For a snug fit tap down the curved edge.

16 Power-stretch the remaining corner. Stretch the carpet from the short wall of the starting corner, running the stretcher straight across the room. Attach the carpet to the tackless strips, then work your way across the wall with the knee kicker as shown.

17 Set a wall trimmer to the thickness of the carpet and guide it along the wall to trim the edges of the carpet. Use a plastic broad knife to tuck the edges into the space between the strips and the wall.

Marble threshold
An alternative option is to butt the carpet against the hard surface flooring and place a marble threshold over the edge. A special adhesive attaches the marble.

Faux-stone threshold
Like the marble threshold the faux-stone threshold provides another option for butting carpet against hard surface flooring.

Square-nose reducer
This wood molding covers the carpet and butts against a wood floor. Nail the piece to the subfloor.

INSTALLING SEAMED AND STRETCHED CARPET

If you must seam your carpet, plan to put the seam where it's least obvious and where there will be little foot traffic. Light shining across a seam can emphasize it, so run it in the same direction as the largest window in the room. Equally as important is matching the carpet grains. Join the pieces so that they both face in the direction that they came off the roll.

PRESTART CHECKLIST

☐ **TIME**
  20 minutes per square yard, not including subfloor preparation

☐ **TOOLS**
  Tape measure, carpet knife, straightedge, knee kicker, power stretcher, wall trimmer, hammer, chalkline, row cutter, seaming iron

☐ **SKILLS**
  Measuring, lifting, laying, cutting, and stretching carpet

☐ **PREP**
  Repair and level subfloor

☐ **MATERIALS**
  Carpet, pad, tackless strips, binder bar, transition moldings, hot melt seaming tape, seam sealer

1 Seam the carpet in a spot where there will be little foot traffic and so that each piece of carpet is at least 4 feet wide. Align the pieces so that the carpet nap and pattern (if any) will match. Once you have determined the best place for a seam, snap a chalkline on the subfloor where the seam will fall.

2 Using a carpet knife trim about 1½ inches off the seam edges of the existing carpet pieces (an existing cut edge of the carpet usually results in a visible seam).

STANLEY PRO TIP: **Seams and carpet types**

Some carpets are more difficult to seam than others. If you are working with a patterned carpet, you'll need to cut the pieces so the pattern matches across the seam. Because the density of the weaves vary, you'll also need to stretch the pieces so that the pattern aligns along the seam.

Berber carpets are often the most difficult to seam. The pile is made from long strands of yarn glued to a backing, and they can easily pull loose. This causes raveling. If you are planning to install a patterned berber, work with a pro who can give you a good, yet not invisible, seam.

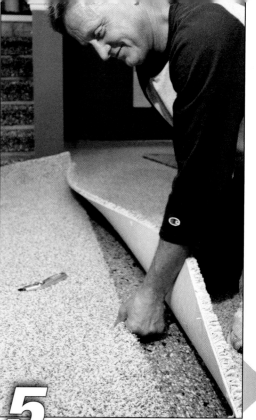

3 On the larger piece of carpet, put a pen or a screwdriver between two rows of tufts about an inch from the seam edge. Drag the pen or screwdriver the entire length of the seam, keeping it between the same two rows of tufts. This creates a visible valley in the carpet.

4 Using a carpet knife begin the cut in the valley and complete the cut with a row cutter. As you cut angle the row cutter about 5 degrees so that you are cutting away slightly more backing than tufted fiber.

5 Put the second piece of carpet in place, positioning it so the first piece overlaps it by about 2 inches. The left edge of the piece, as it came off the roll, should be against the right edge of the other piece as it came off the roll.

STANLEY PRO TIP: **Finding the right spot for a seam**

You cut and join carpet seams before you actually install the carpet. Once you create the seam, you'll install the carpet as if it were a single piece.

Resist the temptation to put the seam in the middle of the room. While it makes planning easier, it also makes the seam obvious. Given the choice between putting a seam below a sofa or near the doorway, place it under the sofa. Walking over a seam will cause it to show more and more over time.

Not all carpets are candidates for do-it-yourself seaming. Before purchasing your selection ask a carpet professional about the requirements for seaming pieces together.

An unavoidable problem with seams is seam peaking, also referred to as seam lifting. No matter what you or a professional carpet layer do, a seam has a tendency to lift slightly off the floor. This is because the carpet stretches everywhere except along the seam where it is backed by tape. Because the problem is unavoidable, the seam's location is all the more important.

The unavoidable seam in this carpet is tucked beneath the sofa.

6 As you did in Step 3, on the second piece of carpet put a pen or a screwdriver between two rows of tufts about an inch from the seam edge. Drag the pen or screwdriver the entire length of the seam. Align the cut edge of the larger carpet piece with this new valley. Using a carpet knife begin the cut in the second valley and then use a row cutter to complete the second cut.

7 Check for gaps, sliding the pieces back and forth as necessary to form a perfect seam. If you have to force edges together to make them fit, you may need to recut the seams.

STANLEY PRO TIP: **More seam help**

Saxony plush

Frieze

Some carpets require special seaming procedures, so check with the manufacturer before following these or any other seaming steps.

If the seams on the carpet you selected are certain to show, consider making a carpet border of another color that runs around the perimeter of the room. This may give you the allowance you need to make the largest piece of carpet seamless.

It is easier to hide a carpet seam in a plain pale-color carpet (without any pattern) that has longer carpet fibers, such as a frieze or a saxony plush as shown here.

Perfect match
The key to a nearly invisible seam is to make sure the cuts line up exactly. To do this overlap the edges of the carpet leaving 2 inches of excess carpet at the point where you want to seam the carpet and at the wall. To ensure a straight seam, snap a chalkline on the back of the overlapped carpet edges and trim a straight edge.

Overlap the straight edges and use a row cutter to cut the bottom piece. The edge of the top piece should be your guide in cutting the seam to fit.

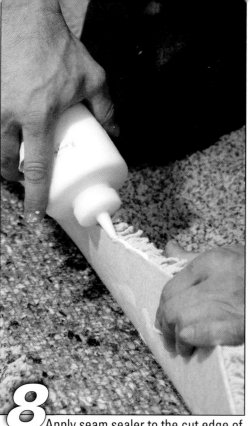

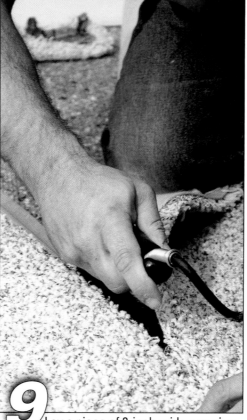

8 Apply seam sealer to the cut edge of the large piece of carpet, squeezing a bead the thickness of the backing onto the actual backing, taking care not to get any of the adhesive on the nap of the carpet. The sealer keeps the carpet from unraveling. The sealer must remain wet for the next step.

9 Lay a piece of 3-inch-wide seaming tape along the entire length of the seam. Slip a 4-foot-long board under the tape at the end of the seam where you are starting and melt the tape with a seaming iron. As you work move the iron down the length of the seam, pushing the edges into the hot adhesive.

10 Move the board down as you work. Once you have taped the entire seam, clean up any stray sealer with the recommended cleaner. Allow the seam to dry and then stretch and install the carpet as explained on pages 165-169.

STANLEY PRO TIP

More hiding places for seams

If the room you are carpeting is both wider and longer than 15 feet, a carpet seam is unavoidable. In this bedroom the necessary seam runs about 5 feet from the wall below the bed. A second alternative would be to run the seam to the left of the bed, 5 or 6 feet out from the wall.

INSTALLING GLUED AND SEAMED CARPET

Commercial-grade carpet almost always requires a glued-down installation. It features a dense, short nap designed to withstand heavy use and is an excellent choice for some home applications, such as over concrete or in a home office or hobby space. If you will be applying carpet glue on concrete, you'll need a special glue that adheres well to high-alkaline concrete floors. Check with the carpet manufacturer to ensure the product you are considering will adhere well to concrete.

Most outdoor carpets are made from olefin, a waterproof synthetic fiber. Outdoor carpeting has a special backing made of mildew-resistant fabric and, like commercial carpeting, requires a glue-down installation.

PRESTART CHECKLIST

☐ **TIME**
20 minutes per square yard, not including subfloor preparation

☐ **TOOLS**
Tape measure, carpet knife, straightedge, screwdriver, wall trimmer, hammer, chalkline, row cutter, seaming iron

☐ **SKILLS**
Measuring, lifting, laying, and cutting carpet

☐ **PREP**
Repair and level subfloor

☐ **MATERIALS**
Carpet, pad, tack strips, binder bar, transition moldings, hot melt seaming tape, seam sealer, duck bill napping shears

1 Seam the carpet in a spot where there will be little foot traffic and so that each piece of carpet is at least 4 feet wide. Align the pieces so that the carpet nap and pattern (if any) will match. Once you have determined the best place for a seam, snap a chalkline on the subfloor where the seam will fall.

2 Using a carpet knife trim about 1½ inches off the seam edges of the existing carpet pieces (an existing cut edge of the carpet usually results in a visible seam).

Specialty tools

Steel-wheel seam roller

Carpet trowel

Chalkline

Seaming iron

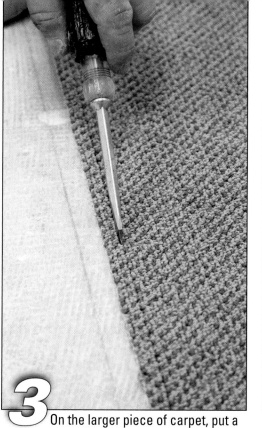

3 On the larger piece of carpet, put a a pen or screwdriver between two rows of tufts about an inch from the seam edge. Drag the pen or screwdriver the entire length of the seam, keeping it between the same two rows of tufts. This creates a visible valley in the carpet.

4 Using a carpet knife begin the cut in the valley and then use a row cutter to complete the cut. As you cut angle the row cutter about 5 degrees so that you are cutting away slightly more backing than tufted fiber.

5 Put the second piece of carpet in place, positioning it so the first piece overlaps it by about 2 inches. The left edge of the piece, as it came off the roll, should be against the right edge of the other piece as it came off the roll.

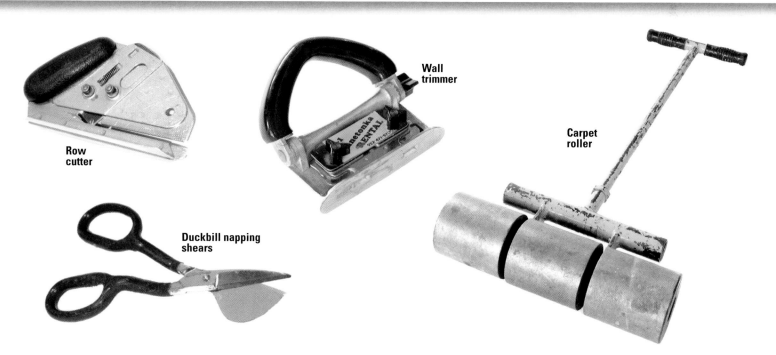

Row cutter

Wall trimmer

Carpet roller

Duckbill napping shears

Installing glued and seamed carpet continued

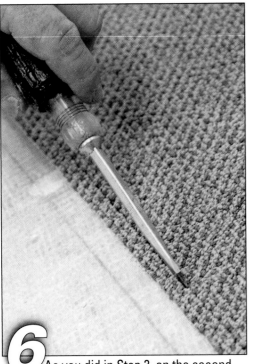

6 As you did in Step 3, on the second piece of carpet put a screwdriver or pen between two rows of tufts about an inch from the seam edge. Drag the screwdriver the entire length of the seam. Align the cut edge of the larger carpet piece with this new valley.

7 Using a carpet knife begin the cut in the second valley and then use a row cutter to complete the second cut. Check for gaps, sliding the pieces back and forth as necessary to form a perfect seam.

8 Fold back each piece about 3 feet from the seam line. If necessary weight down the carpet to hold it in place. Vacuum up any loose carpet fibers created during cutting.

STANLEY PRO TIP

For added durability choose a commercial-grade carpet

Glued-down, commmercial-grade carpets are typically not as soft underfoot as stretched carpets, but they clean up easily and withstand lots of wear and tear. Consider a commercial-grade carpet for a basement rec room or in a child's room where there is always lots of play action. Many commercial-grade carpets feature geometric patterns to help disguise dirt, but because patterned carpets can be hard to seam, choose these only in rooms where one dimension is smaller than 15 feet. If the room you are carpeting is small enough to avoid seams, you can start with Step 9 instead of Step 1.

Carpet adhesive

9 Using the trowel recommended by the carpet manufacturer, apply the carpet adhesive recommended by the manufacturer onto the bare floor on each side of the seam. Let the glue set for the proper length of time as directed by the manufacturer.

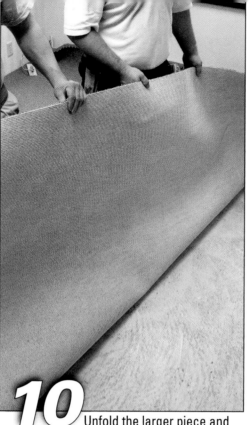

10 Unfold the larger piece and adhere it to the subfloor. If you are gluing a large piece of carpet, have helpers hold the ends of the folded back edge taut while you hold down the middle. To avoid wrinkles walk slightly ahead of them and work your way toward the edges.

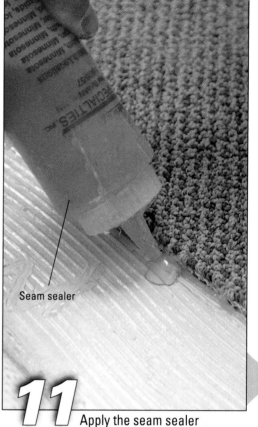

Seam sealer

11 Apply the seam sealer recommended by the manufacturer to the cut edge of the large piece of carpet, squeezing a bead the thickness of the backing onto the actual backing. Take care not to get any of the adhesive on the nap of the carpet.

STANLEY PRO TIP: **Below-grade installations**

Commercial-grade carpets adhere well to concrete subfloors and can withstand lots of wear and tear. However they are difficult to pull up should your basement ever flood. Before applying any carpet to a basement floor, perform a moisture test: Tape plastic trash bags every few feet across the basement floor and leave them in place for at least 24 hours. Lift the bags: If it's dry underneath you can proceed with the carpet installation. If not you'll need to remedy the moisture problem before installing carpeting.

12 Working quickly, fold the edge of the short piece of carpet into the adhesive. Work with helpers again, this time keeping the edge of the carpet in a straight line as you approach the seam. Do not apply additional seam sealer to this piece of carpet.

13 Using a seam roller, press the seam together while rolling along the seam to remove any bubbles and to ensure a firm seal.

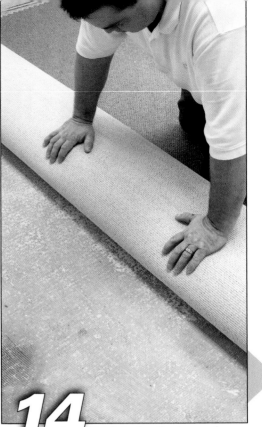

14 Finish laying the large piece of carpet. Roll up the unattached section, apply adhesive to the subfloor, and fold the carpet back into place. To ensure a firm seal, roll a floor roller across the entire width and length of the carpet as shown in Step 16.

WHAT IF...
I am installing a one-piece glued carpet?

Installing a one-piece glued carpet will save you time and effort. If seams are not required in your installation, begin with Step 9. This basement office is just 14 feet wide, so no carpet seams were necessary.

WHAT IF...
You are installing indoor/outdoor carpeting?

To install indoor/outdoor carpeting, follow the same steps as for other glued-down carpeting, but use an adhesive specifically approved for outdoor use and apply it with a notched trowel as recommended by the manufacturer. During installation the outside temperature should be within the range specified on the adhesive container.

15 Finish laying the small piece of carpet. Roll up the unattached section, apply adhesive to the subfloor, and fold the carpet back into place.

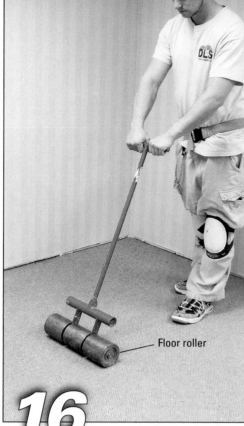

Floor roller

16 To ensure a firm seal, roll a floor roller across the entire width and length of the carpet. If any adhesive seeps up from the seam after rolling, you'll need to clean off the glue.

Duckbill napping shears

17 Brush the seam with a clean broom to raise the nap. Trim off stray fibers with duckbill napping shears.

CLEAN OFF THE GLUE

If any glue squeezed onto the carpet, remove it using a carpet cleaner as recommended by the manufacturer. Do not use a glue solvent as it will dissolve the glue that holds the carpet together. Once you have finished the installation, avoid walking on the carpet for at least 24 hours.

A high-quality carpet that is properly installed can last for years. To keep your carpet looking good, vacuum it at least once a week.

STANLEY PRO TIP: **Perfect cuts**

When cutting carpet make sure the knife blade is always sharp. This is especially important when making cutouts around poles and other obstacles. The cleaner the cut, the less noticeable the seams will be.

INSTALLING CARPET TILE

Carpet tile is one of the easiest flooring materials to install. It's lightweight, cuts with ease, wears well, and goes down quickly. When it gets worn in one place (as any flooring tends to do), you can pull up a tile or two and put down fresh ones.

Aside from quality differences carpet tile falls into two general categories: self-stick and dry-backed. The application of self-stick tiles is more or less self-explanatory. Installing dry-backed tiles (which are usually a little thicker) means laying down a mastic or using doubled-faced carpet tape. Mastic applications usually leave a little more time to finetune the layout and keep the joints straight. Double-faced tape won't gum up the entire floor, a factor to consider if there's a chance you'll one day remove the tile from a solid wood floor. In either case acclimate the tile to the room for 48 hours before you install it.

PRESTART CHECKLIST

☐ **TIME**
About 15 minutes per square yard, not including subfloor preparation

☐ **TOOLS**
Utility knife, tape measure, metal straightedge, chalkline, 100-pound roller

☐ **SKILLS**
Measuring, laying, and cutting tile

☐ **PREP**
Repair and level subfloor

☐ **MATERIALS**
Carpet tile, mastic or double-faced tape for dry-backed installation

1 Prepare the subfloor, then snap chalklines from the midpoints of opposite walls. Square the lines and dry-lay the tile on both axes. Move the rows back and forth until you have edge tiles that are at least a half-tile wide and equal at each end.

2 Carpet tiles are made with a certain "lay" to the pile, indicated by arrows on the back. Most manufacturers recommend setting the tiles at 90 degrees to each other to minimize wear appearance. With arrows in the same direction, the carpet will look more like a broadloom weave.

PREPARE THE SUBFLOOR

■ **Wood:** In new construction install ¾-inch plywood. On an existing wood floor, remove the finish and repair. On planks wider than 4 inches, install ⅜-inch underlayment. Fill depressions and sand smooth.

■ **Concrete:** Check for moisture by taping plastic sheets to the slab every 2 feet. If moisture beads under the plastic, don't install the tile. Remedy the moisture problem first. Clean and roughen the surface slightly to give it a "tooth."

■ **Vinyl tile or sheet goods:** If the existing material is cushioned, remove it and repair the subfloor. If you're installing tile over a wood floor, sand or strip the finish and repair.

■ **Ceramic tile:** Level the surface with self-leveling compound. Remove damaged tile.

■ **Carpet:** Remove carpet and repair wood or concrete subfloor as above.

Layout tips

Check the dye lot numbers on your carpet tile cartons. If you have different dye lots, install them in separate rooms to avoid a color transition in the same room.

Laying tiles with the arrows at 90 degrees will create a checkerboard pattern that greatly reduces the appearance of wear. Laying the arrows in the same direction helps the carpet look more like a broadloom weave. Laying tiles with arrows in a random pattern is not recommended.

To get the best visual effect, place the starting arrow so it points away from the largest source of sunlight.

Install each tile securely against the others but don't compress the edges. When cutting cut-pile tiles, brush back the pile at the edges to avoid trapping the piles in the joint.

3 Peel off the backing from self-stick tiles and set the tile squarely on the intersection of the layout lines. From this point you can set the tiles in repeated concentric squares around the center or in quadrants. Dispose of the backing. It's very slick and can cause a fall.

4 Lay the subsequent tiles in the same fashion, setting the tile with its leading edges against the previous tiles. Lay the tile, keeping the pressure against those in place. Don't slide the tiles. Set the tiles in a stair-step pattern so you have two points of reference for the next tile.

5 When you reach the edges, you will have to cut the tiles individually. Make sure you cut the tiles from the back. When you have installed all the edge tiles, roll the floor with a rented 100-pound roller.

Applying mastic-set tiles

Dry-backed tiles are set in mastic or adhered with double-sided carpet tape. Some tiles are suited to both applications. Check the manufacturer's directions before deciding on a method.

In either case you must snap layout lines in the center of the room and start the installation at the intersection of the lines. If you're laying mastic you'll use the quadrant method.

Apply the adhesive with a paint roller. Let the mastic become tacky if necessary, then line up your first tile on the lines. Push the tile into place or pull it up and reposition it. Most tacky mastics allow plenty of working time. Continue setting the tile in one quadrant, making sure the edges of the tiles are butted securely against each other.

CUT THE TILES

1 To mark a carpet tile for cutting, lay a loose tile upside down exactly on the last full tile already installed. Then lay a guide tile on this one and push it against the wall. Draw a line down the edge of the guide tile.

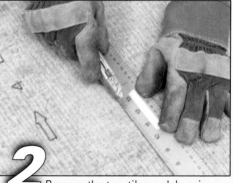

2 Remove the two tiles and, keeping the marked tile backside up, set a steel straightedge along the marker line. Make several light passes along the line with a sharp utility knife. When you have cut through the backing, bend the tile slightly and cut through it completely.

INSTALLING CARPET ON STEPS

A carpeted stairway quiets your home by softening footsteps and absorbing sound waves. Carpeted stairs are safer than hard-surface stairs, as they lessen your chances of slipping and pad your fall if you lose your balance.

Building codes control the dimensions of treads and risers. Treads are typically 10 to 11½ inches deep; the deeper the tread, the more comfortable the climb. Risers are generally no more than 7¾ inches tall. If your stairs' dimensions are not within these guidelines, for safety's sake you'll need to rebuild them.

Stairways get heavy wear, especially along the tread nosing, so choose a carpet that is durable and easy to clean. A carpet with an attached padded backing is easier to put down, but these carpets are not usually recommended for stairways as they have a tendency to wear quickly.

PRESTART CHECKLIST

☐ **TIME**
20 minutes per square yard, not including subfloor preparation

☐ **TOOLS**
Tape measure, carpet knife, hammer stapler, straightedge, wall trimmer, stair tool

☐ **SKILLS**
Measuring, lifting, cutting, and laying carpet

☐ **PREP**
Repair and level stair risers and treads

☐ **MATERIALS**
Carpet, pad, tackless strips, hot melt seaming tape, seam sealer

1 Measure each step individually and cut a quality carpet pad to fit each step and riser as shown. The pad should be cut to precisely fit between the tackless strips that you'll be nailing to the back of the tread and the bottom of the riser.

2 Carefully place tackless strips on the riser and back of each tread as shown. To determine how high to place the tack strips, use a spacer made out of two strips taped together.

WHAT IF...
What if your stairs curve?

If your staircase curves or if the walls are not plumb, you won't be able to use a template to cut the carpet pieces for each step. Instead you'll need to measure each step and cut the carpet to fit.

3 Using a hammer stapler and starting in the center of each stair tread, staple the pad in place. Staple across the entire length of the pad. (Staple the pad just in front of the tackless strip.)

4 Wrap the carpet pad around the front edge of the steps and down the riser. Smooth and stretch the pad so that it fits tightly against both the tread and riser, then staple pad to riser. When all the padding is attached you'll need to make a template and cut the carpet to fit.

5 Using a tape measure, measure the stair and riser and add 4 to 6 inches (or more if your steps are deeper) to the stair width to cover the edges.

USE A SPACER

Make a spacer by taping two tack strips together. This will help you properly position your tackless strips.

Specialty tools

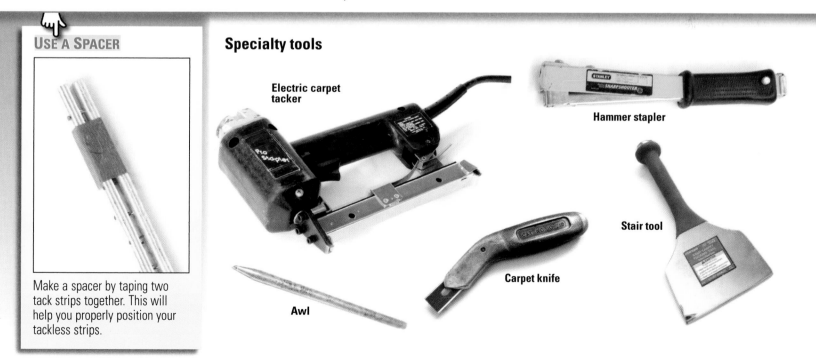

Electric carpet tacker

Hammer stapler

Awl

Carpet knife

Stair tool

Installing carpet on steps
continued

6 To make the template measure each individual step and riser, as they may not all be built to the exact same dimension. Using a tape measure and a straightedge, cut the carpet to template size.

7 Center the carpet on the bottom edges of the steps.

8 Use an awl to push the carpet onto the tackless strip. This creates a clean line between the bottom of the stairs and the flooring.

WHAT IF...
You are installing a runner?

Make hardwood stairs safer and more comfortable underfoot by installing a carpet runner. Purchase a ready-made carpet runner that is long enough to cover your stairs, or measure and cut a piece of carpet to the appropriate length and have a professional bind the edges at the appropriate width. If you want to install carpet padding below the runner, follow Steps 1 through 4 of "Installing Carpet on Steps," then install the runner as explained here.

1 Roll up the carpet runner backside facing out and center it a few steps from the bottom. Gently pull the end to the bottom, allowing some slack so the roll doesn't fall to the bottom stair.

2 Run a row of staples along the bottom riser where the carpet meets the floor. Wiggle the staple gun between the nap (tuff) to hide staple impressions.

3 Use a power stretcher to pull the carpet tight as you place another row of staples in the corner between the riser and the tread. Note: Do not use a knee kicker to stretch the carpet.

9 When you are satisified with the carpet placement, staple the carpet onto the riser just below the tread taking care not to staple through the fold. Wiggle the electric carpet tacker between the nap (tuff) to hide the staple impressions.

10 Using a knee kicker stretch the carpet into the seam between the tread and the riser. Start in the middle and work side to side.

11 Fold the edges around the step and use a stair tool and a rubber mallet to crease the carpet into the seam and secure it to the tackless strip. Repeat Steps 8 through 11 for each remaining step.

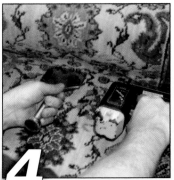

4 Use the stair tool to wedge the carpet into the corner and to create an even crease when you're folding the carpet over. Repeat the process as you work up the stairs.

STANLEY PRO TIP

Other stair types

If your stairs are open along the sides or at the treads, you'll need to modify the installation procedure to ensure that all the edges are finished.

The most common method for carpeting a stairway with a closed wall on one side and open balusters at the other is to roll both edges under, allowing about 1 inch from the wall with 1¼-inch rollunder at the edges. If your carpeting won't unravel at a cut edge, butt it against the sidewall without rollunder.

INSTALLING & STAINING CEMENT OVERLAYS

Topping your old cement with a cement-base overlay is a great way to facelift a worn, drab surface and level uneven spots. For flawed cement an overlay is simpler and cheaper to apply than breaking out an old slab and pouring a new one. This pourable layer—which is seamless, self-leveling, and equal in thickness to a credit card, up to about ⅜ inch—can also be applied over a wood subfloor as shown on the following pages.

Make it yours

A cement overlay can be custom colored using a number of techniques. Acid staining is an effective option when a handheld plastic-body sprayer is used in a well-ventilated room. Because you are working with an acid product, wear eye goggles and gloves.

You can also find overlay systems that are poured thicker to allow the surface to be textured for interest or stamped to recreate the look of brick, natural stone, tile, and other materials. Another decorative alternative is to inset other materials or objects into the overlay, such as metal medallions or tiles. Simply locate and secure the insets to the subfloor where desired and then pour the compound to a level that matches the thickness of the inset.

What to expect

The secret to a successful outcome overall is proper preparation of the surface prior to application and following the manufacturer's suggestions for mixing and applying the self-leveling compound. Manufacturers now boost longevity, bonding ability, and good looks for the overlay by blending the cement with polymer resins, usually acrylics or acrylic blends.

Maintaining the surface

Because a cement overlay, done right, is extremely durable, it can last a lifetime provided you finish the surface with the sealer recommended by the manufacturer. Keeping the sealed surface clean is as easy as regular sweeping or vacuuming and wiping up spots as they occur. Damp-mop periodically with mild detergent and water.

A cement overlay is more than a cover up for an old floor. Use it to express your style.

CHAPTER PREVIEW

Pouring a cement overlay
page 188

Acid staining
page 191

Cement floors can be stained in a range of colors. Sealing the surface is a critical finishing step to ensure easy maintenance and long-lasting color.

POURING A CEMENT OVERLAY

Before pouring a self-leveling compound, prepare the subfloor according to the manufacturer's directions so you'll achieve a sound bond between old and new.

For concrete remove loose pieces and sweep away dirt and debris. Repair large cracks. If the overlay manufacturer recommends it, clean the concrete and apply a bonding agent or primer for improved adhesion of the bonding layer.

A wood subfloor should be stable with plywood sheets or boards securely nailed so there's no give. These instructions are for pouring an overlay over wood. Felt helps ensure a good bond.

PRESTART CHECKLIST

☐ **TIME**
About 2½ hours for a 12×12-foot room to lay felt and pour compound; about 2 hours to trowel thin finish for the same-size room; about 3 hours to protect surfaces and apply acid stain

☐ **TOOLS**
Staple gun, aviation snips, drill equipped with a mixing paddle, gauge rake, squeegee, putty knife, trowel, plastic-body sprayer, paint roller equipped with an extension handle

☐ **SKILLS**
Using a staple gun and a gauge rake; troweling

☐ **PREP**
Prepare subfloor

☐ **MATERIALS**
#30 felt, metal lath, galvanized staples, self-leveling compound, colorant, concrete thin finish, painter's tape, masking paper, acid stain, ammonia, clear sealer

1 Carefully remove the baseboards so they can be reinstalled later; remove old flooring, if any, to expose wood subfloor. Roll out 30-pound felt paper and staple to secure. Overlap subsequent rows by about 2 inches.

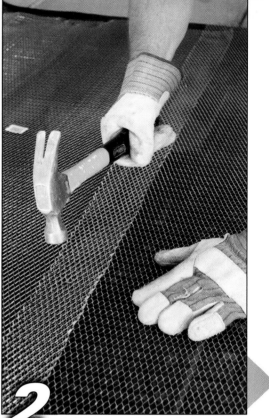

2 Install the metal lath so it runs perpendicular to the felt paper and overlap by 2 inches. (Cut metal lath to fit using aviation snips.) Use a hammer so lath lays flat. Secure lath so it lays tight against the subfloor, driving in 1½-inch galvanized staples every 2 inches with the pneumatic stapler.

STAPLE TO SECURE
Using a pneumatic staple gun

Securing the felt paper and metal lath to the wood subfloor with a pneumatic staple gun will make the job go much more quickly and will spare your knees. The secret behind this tool's ability to simplify the job is that the staples are propelled into the wood through the force of an air compressor. You simply position the tip of the gun where you want the staple and pull the trigger.

To secure the felt paper, roll it out starting in one corner of the room. Secure the felt to the wood subfloor at regular intervals using 1½-inch galvanized finish staples (so they won't rust due to moisture from the overlay).

3 Following the manufacturer's directions use the drill equipped with a mixing paddle to combine water and self-leveling compound in a 5-gallon bucket. Pour and spread the compound one bucket at a time.

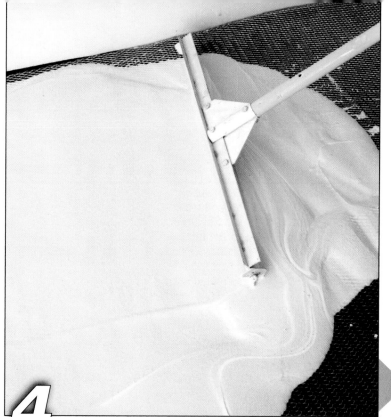

4 Begin pouring compound in the farthest corner of the room. Use a gauge rake, set at ¼ inch, to spread the compound over the metal lath. Push the compound into the corners using a squeegee or a putty knife if needed. This layer will need to dry 10 to 20 hours.

AVIATION SNIPS

Metal lath can be tricky to cut and can slice your fingers if your hands are unprotected (see Safety First, right). In addition to wearing thick gloves while cutting, select a sharpened tool that's designed for the job, such as these aviation snips.

It's worth noting that green-handled aviation snips, which generally cut clockwise curves best, are a good choice if you're right-handed. Left-handers will typically find red-handled aviation snips more comfortable to use. These are designed to make counterclockwise cuts through metal.

SAFETY FIRST
Grab your gear

As with any project invest in the proper protective gear before laying felt, cutting lath, pouring cement, or spraying on acid stain. Wear cushioned knee pads, for example, when laying felt and metal lath to protect your knees from wear and tear. You'll also want to put on heavy work boots and wear thick gloves to avoid cuts and scrapes as you cut lath. Because any cement-base product is caustic and can splatter, always wear eye goggles, gloves, and heavy boots as you mix, pour, and spread overlay materials or spray acid stain.

When using a pneumatic stapler, read the manufacturer's handbook and familiarize yourself with the safety precautions. Never point the staple gun at yourself or toward another person.

Pouring a cement overlay *continued*

5 Following the manufacturer's directions add colorant to 6½ quarts water in a 5-gallon bucket. (Select a hue that provides a compatible base coat for the stain.) Wear a dust mask and use the drill and mixing paddle to blend in a 55-pound bag of thin finish. This mixture will be thinner than the self-leveling compound. Dampen the floor with water using a plastic-body sprayer. Use a squeegee to spread the thin finish. Let dry.

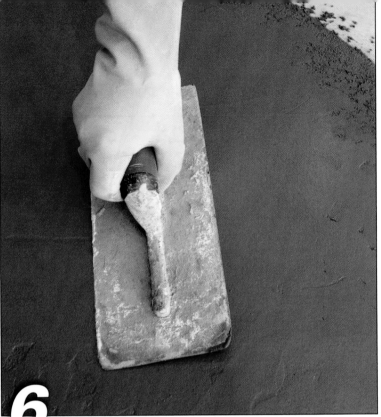

6 For the second layer of thin finish, mix the colorant into 5½ quarts of water and add the thin finish powder. Dampen the floor with water as before and use a trowel to spread the thin finish. Let dry overnight.

USE THE DRILL AND MIXING PADDLE
Mixing self-leveling compound

Wear a dust mask and pour about 1 gallon of water into a 5-gallon bucket, then pour in one-half bag of self-leveling compound powder. Blend the water and powder until all the lumps are gone using a drill equipped with a long-handled mixing paddle. Slowly add the remaining powder to achieve a pourable mixture similar to the consistency of a milkshake or pea soup. Add water if the mix becomes too thick. Have a helper begin mixing another batch in a second bucket while you pour and spread the first bucket.

About gauge rakes

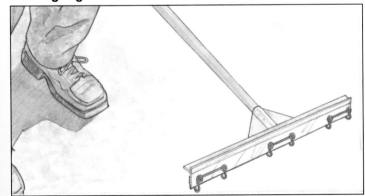

Use a long-handled gauge rake to spread self-leveling compound to a uniform depth across the floor. This wire-style gauge rake features six spring-steel wires or loops teamed with a bar that adjusts for spreading depths up to ⅝ inch. These multiple wires come in contact with the metal lath, maintaining a consistent height for the spreading bar, even on unlevel or pitted surfaces.

ACID STAINING

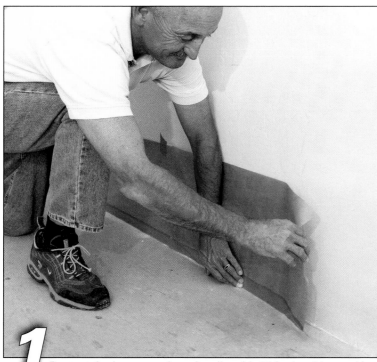

1 Protect the lower portion of walls with 12-inch-wide masking paper secured with painter's tape.

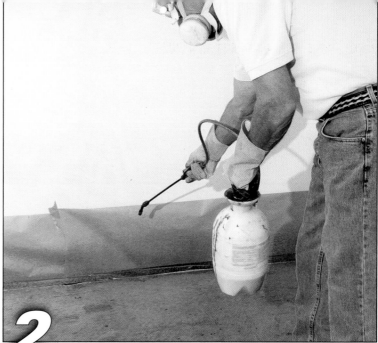

2 Working outdoors or in a well-ventilated room and wearing goggles and gloves, pour the acid stain into a plastic-body sprayer. Read the manufacturer's directions to determine if the stain should be diluted for a hand-troweled floor. You may also want to dilute the stain with water, depending on the intensity of the color desired. (Experiment with the color in an inconspicuous area.) Hold the wand about 18 inches above the surface of the floor as you apply the stain. Let dry 1 hour, spray on a second coat, and let dry.

3 To neutralize the acid use a clean plastic-body sprayer to apply a mixture of 1 part ammonia to 4 parts water. Let dry and mop the floor with clear water. Use a shop vacuum to remove excess moisture on the floor.

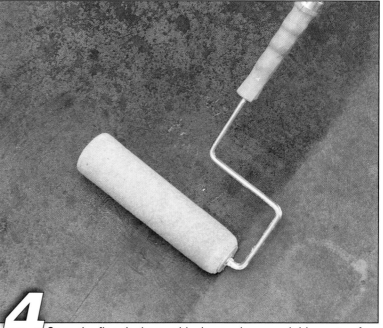

4 Once the floor is thoroughly dry, apply several thin coats of water-base sealer using a paint roller equipped with a long handle. The sealer helps protect the concrete and finish from stains.

INSTALLING & FINISHING BASEBOARDS

Baseboards, which are installed along the bottoms of walls, not only serve as architectural accents for the room, they also hide structural defects and rough edges.

Baseboards conceal the gap between the wall and the floor, whether you've selected wood, tile, carpet, or some other material. These moldings come in many choices of styles and contours but are often a simple design paired with a length of quarter round at the floor. Choose the wood for your baseboard according to the kind of finish you'll apply and to complement other woods used in the room.

Choices to consider

Trim lumber, as shown *right,* differs in several ways from lumber used in framing. It's drier (less subject to warping), has fewer defects (the number depends on the grade), and costs more.

Softwoods, such as redwood, cedar, pine, fir, and spruce, are cut from coniferous evergreen trees. They are light and easy to work with.

Hardwoods, such as oak, ash, poplar, walnut, and cherry, are produced by broadleaf, deciduous trees. They offer stability, strength, machining predictability, and resistance to abuse. As hardwood trees are not as abundant as softwood trees in North America, their lumber is more costly.

Neatly installed baseboards provide the finishing touch for any flooring project.

Baseboards are a beautiful finishing touch for any of your flooring projects. Select a baseboard molding style to complement the rest of your home or to boost architectural interest in an ordinary space.

INSTALLING BASEBOARDS

More than a convenient way to cover the joint between the floor and the wall, the baseboard is a hardworking piece of molding that protects lower wall surfaces from shoes and errant vacuum cleaners. Aesthetically it eases the transition from vertical to horizontal, adding visual appeal to the floor and the wall.

Accurate measuring and cutting skills are critical to achieving professional results for your baseboard installation. To accomplish a seamless joint, cope (or back-cut) the joint. Use miter cuts for smooth transitions around corners.

Or if you don't want to go to the trouble of coping the joints, install no-cope baseboards with corner pieces and butt joints.

For a look that's all your own, combine boards and various moldings to create a substantial custom baseboard.

PRESTART CHECKLIST

☐ **TIME**
About 45 minutes for an 8-foot section

☐ **TOOLS**
Hammer, nail set, stud finder, cordless drill, tape measure, pencil, combination square, miter saw, circular saw, wood file, caulk gun, coping saw

☐ **SKILLS**
Basic carpentry skills: measuring, marking, cutting, drilling

☐ **PREP**
Remove old baseboard, install finished flooring

☐ **MATERIALS**
Baseboard, 8d finishing nails, corner pieces, shoe molding, sandpaper, caulk

Install coped baseboards

1 Measure from the edge of the door trim to the nearest corner and cut a piece of baseboard to fit. Cut butt joints on both ends of the baseboard. Cut butt joints on both ends of the baseboard and predrill it for 8d finishing nails. Drive the nails into the studs and bottom plate of the wall.

2 Using a power mitersaw miter the end of the adjoining corner piece as if you were cutting it for an inside corner. Then set the baseboard on a firm work surface and outline the edge of the profile with a pencil.

PREDRILL
Drill pilot holes to avoid splitting trim

1 Using side cutters or diagonal cutters, snip the head of the 6d or 8d finishing nail. Insert the nail into the chuck of your cordless drill.

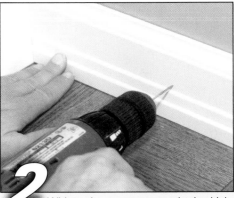

2 With moderate pressure and using high speed, drill guide holes into the baseboard. Then drive finishing nails through the pilot holes and into the wall. Use a nail set to drive the nails below the surface.

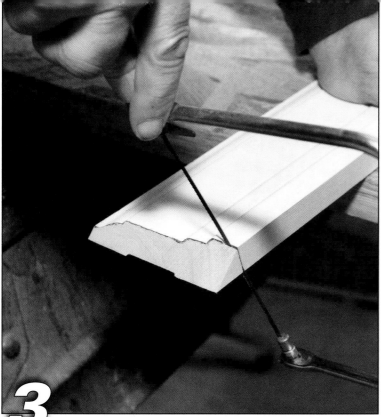

3 Clamp or steady the baseboard on a work surface and hold a coping saw with a fine-tooth blade at right angles to the mitered end. Carefully cut the board along your penciled outline. The goal is to create a thin edge at the front of the baseboard—one that follows its contour and will fit almost seamlessly into the profile of the adjoining corner piece.

4 Test fit the coped piece against the baseboard already in place (or a piece of scrap), sanding and filing to correct your contour until it mates with the baseboard. Use 80-grit sandpaper where it will fit the contour and a fine round wood file in tightly curved sections. Don't worry about small gaps—you can fill them with caulk. If you've made a larger mistake, miter the board again and start over.

STANLEY PRO TIP: **How to splice baseboards**

A scarf joint joins two identical pieces of molding end to end. The ends of the molding are cut at parallel 45-degree angles and fitted together, one end overlapping the other. A scarf joint should be made over solid backing, such as a stud. Drill pilot holes through both pieces and secure the joint with finishing nails.

Locating a stud for nailing is sometimes tricky, especially in older homes where door trim often extends beyond the studs. Wherever you know you'll have trouble anchoring the baseboard, lay a bead of construction adhesive on the back of it.

Install coped baseboards
continued

5 Cut the other end of the coped piece, if necessary, to fit its section of wall. If the board fits to the corner cut the end square. If another board is needed to complete this section, miter to finish a scarf joint. Fasten this piece with finishing nails, being sure to <u>nail to a solid base.</u>

6 Cut a piece of baseboard to fit the next wall. Then cut, miter, and cope the left corner, employing the same techniques you used for the first piece. Fit the final piece of baseboard against the door trim with a butt joint.

7 Cut shoe molding to length for each section of wall, duplicating coped and butt joints where they fall on the baseboard. Predrill the shoe molding and nail it at an angle into the baseboard. Make sure the bottom edge is flush with the surface of the finished floor.

NAIL TO A SOLID BASE

There may be times when you need to drive a nail into a baseboard to eliminate a gap, but a stud isn't where you need it. Drill a hole and drive a 16d finishing nail at a downward angle through the molding to catch the bottom plate.

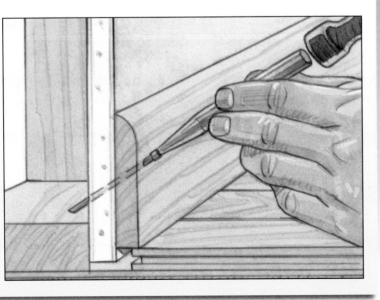

STANLEY PRO TIP
Know about nails

If you look closely at the tip of a common finishing nail, you will see that it is not symmetrical. Viewed point on the tip is diamond shape, not square. Nails are made this way for a reason. If you start the nail so the flatter side of the diamond is parallel to the grain of the board you are nailing it into, there will be less chance of splitting the wood than if the flat side goes against the grain.

Install baseboard outside corners

1 Stick a piece of masking tape on the floor at the outside corner (to protect the floor from the marks you will make). Set a piece of scrap baseboard against one wall and pencil a line along its outer edge past the corner. Pencil another line along the adjoining wall.

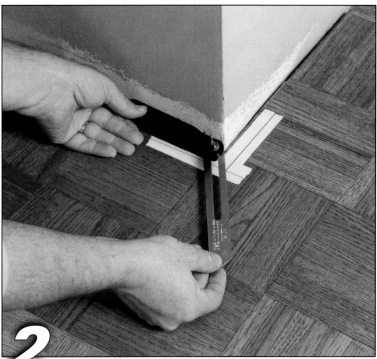

2 Hold an adjustable bevel against one wall and set it against the corner of the wall. Adjust the angle until the "T" intersects the penciled corner. Tighten the bevel screw. Transfer the angle to the top of the baseboard and line up the mark with the blade of your mitersaw. Clamp the board to the mitersaw fence. When you cut the piece, lower the blade slowly.

WHAT IF...
You're installing capped baseboards?

Install the baseboard. Using the pattern of your choice, measure, cut, and fasten the first piece of cap molding to the baseboard. Cope the remaining pieces. Predrill the stock. Use the heaviest finishing nail that does the job without splitting the cap pieces.

STANLEY PRO TIP

Setting nails

With thumb and forefinger hold the nail vertically and grip the hammer near the end of the handle. Lightly tap the nail until it stands by itself. Once the nail is set remove your hand. Keep your eye on the nail as you swing the hammer. Relax and let your whole arm move, swinging from the shoulder. Keep your wrist loose so you can give the hammer a snap at the end of each blow. Stop swinging when the nailhead is flush or nearly flush with the surface of the wood.

Use a nail set to gently sink the small head of the finish nail to just below the surface. Fill with wood putty (page 201) to cover the hole.

Install no-cope baseboard outside corners

1 Cut and install inside and outside corner pieces longer than the width of the baseboard (to the height of your choice). Hold a combination square against a corner piece and scribe a line on the baseboard. This line will conform to any out-of-plumb conditions in the walls. Scribe both ends of each baseboard section and cut the first piece.

2 Drive 8d finishing nails into the predrilled baseboard and use the same techniques to install the remaining pieces between the corners. Drive the nails below the surface with a nail set. Fill and sand them smooth, and stain, paint, or varnish.

STANLEY PRO TIP: **Getting a tight fit**

Mark and cut the piece about ¹⁄₁₆ inch longer than the space. If you are butting against a piece of casing, make sure the casing is well secured so it does not move when you press against it. Install the baseboard by bending it into position. This will give you a tight fit on both sides.

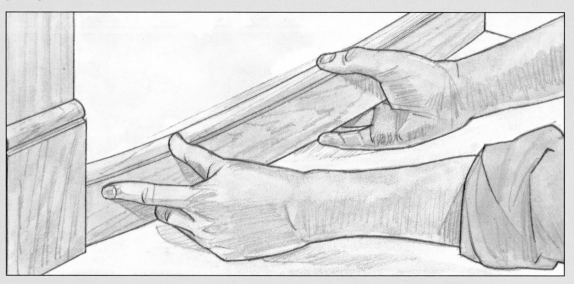

Install built-up moldings

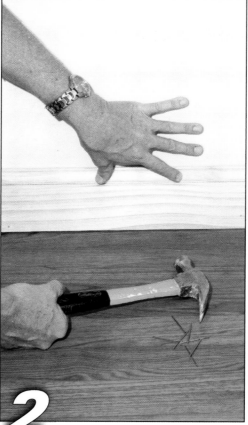

1 Create a unique baseboard by combining stock molding. Start with a flat or low-relief board that measures 4 to 6 inches high. Install it tightly against the flooring along the bottom of the wall.

2 Add the cap and other accent moldings, nailing them along the top into the main board or wall studs.

3 Nail the base shoe to the floor so that it can expand and contract with the flooring and prevent gapping.

WHAT IF...
You want to match historic moldings?

To design a molding profile or match an existing one, obtain a small sample piece from the room if possible. A custom woodworking shop may be able to recreate the profile. Or contact woodworking mail order outlets or Internet sites that cater to woodworkers.

STANLEY PRO TIP: **Using a preacher**

Wherever a piece of baseboard will meet a door casing, make a special jig (sometimes referred to as a preacher) to help mark the length of the board as shown. Fashion this notched piece from ¾-inch pine or plywood. Cut this U-shaped jig so the U is taller and wider than the baseboard. Cut one end of the baseboard as needed (a coped or miter cut) and put in place. The opposite end of the board should extend past the door casing. Slip the preacher over the end of the baseboard and snug the back leg of the U against the casing. Use the front leg as a guide for marking your cutting line.

PAINTING AND STAINING BASEBOARDS

When choosing new baseboards consider the finish. Whether it will be painted, stained, or left natural determines the material selection. Wood is the traditional choice, but it's not your only option. If you're planning to paint the trim, manufactured materials such as medium-density fiberboard (MDF) and plastic moldings (including urethanes and other synthetics) are good-looking, budget-conscious alternatives.

To save money when staining, select wood based on the appearance of the grain, and stain to personal preferences. Cherry, for example, is an expensive wood, but you can get the same look by buying birch and applying a cherry stain. The grain and hardness of cherry and birch are very similar.

PRESTART CHECKLIST

☐ **TIME**
About 45 minutes total (not including drying time) to sand, finish, and fill holes on an 8-foot length

☐ **TOOLS**
Sandpaper (fine and medium grits), sanding block, tack cloth, putty knife, paintbrush, lint-free cloths, disposable foam brushes, #0000 steel wool

☐ **SKILLS**
Using sandpaper and a paintbrush

☐ **PREP**
Fill knotholes, sand

☐ **MATERIALS**
Baseboard, wood filler, mineral spirits or paint thinner, paint, stain, clear polyurethane or varnish

Painting baseboards

1 Sand baseboards, whether unfinished or painted, with medium-grit sandpaper on a sanding block. Wipe away residue with a tack cloth.

2 Fill knots and nail holes with water-mix putty. Let dry. Lightly sand filled spots and wipe clean.

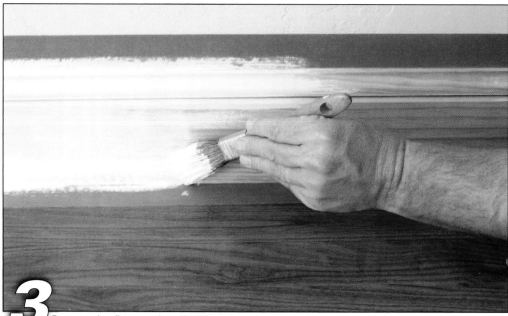

3 Protect the floor and wall with painter's tape before painting. Apply paint to the wood surface with short light strokes across the wood grain, laying down paint in both directions. Finish with longer strokes in one direction only—working with the wood grain. Use only the tips of the bristles to smooth out the paint.

Staining baseboards

1 It's easier to stain uninstalled baseboards as you can finish them on a waist-high work surface. Sand baseboards with sanding paper or a sanding block and wipe dust particles away with a tack cloth.

2 Mix stain before using. With a brush or a lint-free cloth, apply it with the grain. Slightly overlap your strokes so you don't miss any spots. Let the stain set according to the manufacturer's directions.

3 Before the stain begins to dry, wipe the entire surface with a lint-free cloth to remove excess stain. This forces the stain's pigment into the grain, enhancing contrast.

4 To apply clear sealer or varnish, use a disposable foam brush and work across the grain. For the second coat brush with the grain to avoid ridges. Once dry install baseboard and fill nail holes with wood putty.

FILL KNOTS AND NAIL HOLES

For small nail holes on baseboards you plan to stain, use a dough-type wood filler. (Since even filler made to accept stain never looks like real wood, limit its use along the length of the baseboard.) Filler can be applied before or after staining; experiment to find out which looks best. Begin by tamping a small amount of the filler into the hole with your thumb. Smooth it with a putty knife. Wipe away the excess with a rag dampened with water or mineral spirits depending on the type of putty (check the label).

If you plan to paint the baseboard, water-mix putty excels at filling shallow depressions. The putty sets up quickly, so don't mix more than you can use in 10 minutes. To fill cracks around a knot, mix the putty to a pastelike consistency and force it into all the cracks with a putty knife. Feather out the patch to the surrounding wood.

Once the wood filler or putty dries, sand the surface smooth.

APPLY CLEAR SEALER
A smooth finish

For a silky smooth finish, let the first coat of polyurethane dry thoroughly. Then lightly buff the surface with #0000 steel wool or fine (320-grit) sandpaper. Repeat this step between any additional coats you decide to apply.

Paint & Epoxy Finishes

Painting a floor is part science, part art. Because floors and subfloors are made of a variety of materials, you'll need to be familiar with a number of preparation methods, paint products, and application techniques.

Preparation of the surfaces you're painting is the key to success. Preparation will consume approximately 80 percent of the total time you'll devote to the project, but this time will pay off in the long run. Paint on a well-prepared surface can last for decades.

Quality primers and paints will adhere securely to the surface and won't easily fade, scratch, or scuff.

Dealing with lead-base paint

Prior to 1978 lead was a major ingredient in paints, but legislation that year banned its use because it is a carcinogen. Because you may be scraping, sanding, or otherwise removing existing paint in preparation for the new coating, you should determine if possible when that paint was applied. If that's not possible contact the Environmental Protection Agency (EPA) or your local health department for instructions on how to proceed where lead paint could be present.

To learn more about the hazards associated with lead-base paint, request a copy of the most recent literature from the EPA. It will provide information about how to test for the presence of lead paint, steps to take to minimize your exposure to lead where lead-base paint may be present, how to remove it safely, and in-place management of lead-base paint.

With the right products and preparation, a painted finish can last for decades.

CHAPTER PREVIEW

Applying an epoxy finish
page 204

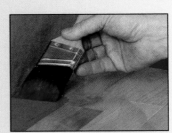

Painting a wood floor
page 208

Painting vinyl flooring and ceramic tile
page 210

Resistant to stains, an epoxy paint finish will keep your garage floor looking good for many years.

APPLYING AN EPOXY FINISH

Epoxy paint finishes resist grease, oil, and many other substances that would ruin an ordinary painted finish, making it easy to keep your garage floor looking clean and attractive for years.

Epoxy will not adhere to a damp floor, so test it for dampness as described in the Pro Tip *below right*. For optimum curing when you apply the paint, the concrete should be a minimum of 55 degrees and the air temperature should be between 60 and 90 degrees.

PRESTART CHECKLIST

☐ **TIME**
From 30 to 45 minutes per square yard to prepare the surface, plus another 15 minutes to paint each section

☐ **TOOLS**
Flat-edge shovel or scraper, vacuum, garden hose, power scrubber with brush attachment, stiff-bristle brush, rubber squeegee, wet vac, plastic sprinkler can, drill with stirring bit, brushes, 9-inch medium-nap roller

☐ **SKILLS**
Prepare and paint concrete

☐ **MATERIALS**
Duct tape, plastic bag, cleaning/degreasing solution, rubber gloves, respirator, water, muriatic acid, two-part epoxy paint

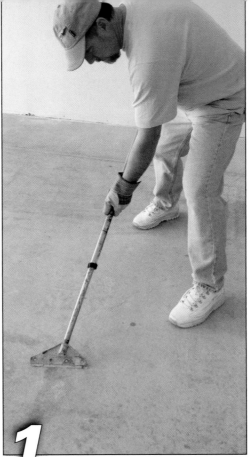

1 If necessary use a flat-edged shovel or scraper to remove any hardened debris, then vacuum the entire garage floor. Prepare a cleaning/degreasing solution according to manufacturer's instructions. Wearing rubber gloves use a stiff-bristle brush and the solution to scrub off any grease or oil stains.

Power scrubber

2 Wet the entire floor with a hose. Working in 5-foot-square sections, use a power scrubber with a brush attachment and the degreaser to clean the entire floor. Use the stiff-bristle brush to scrub the corners and along the walls where the machine can't reach.

STANLEY PRO TIP: **Checking for moisture**

Before you paint test your concrete for excessive moisture.

Using duct tape tape a plastic trash bag to the garage floor for 24 hours. Lift the bag; if it's dry underneath proceed with an epoxy coating. If you see moisture underneath the bag, don't paint the floor. The moisture will ruin the epoxy bond.

3 When the floor is clean, pool the soap mixture into smaller areas with a rubber squeegee. Vacuum up the solution with a wet vac. (Check with your county's environmental office to see if you are allowed to dispose of the solution by flushing it down the toilet.)

4 Pour a gallon of water into a plastic sprinkler can. Wearing a vapor respirator as shown *above,* pour 12 ounces of 32-percent muriatic acid (the most common formulation) into water (1 part acid to 10 parts water) in the sprinkler can. Mix the solution for a few seconds with a paint stirrer. Sprinkle the mixture evenly over a 10×10-foot area.

Choose the right epoxy

Epoxy floor paints are tough resin-base paints that come in two separate parts that are mixed together before applying. There are three different types of epoxy paint: solid, solvent-base, and water-base.

Solid epoxy

Epoxy that is solid is the purest form of epoxy. It doesn't contain solvents that evaporate. These products are expensive and difficult to handle because they harden very rapidly. This finish should be applied by a professional.

Solvent-base epoxy

Solvent-base epoxies contain from 40 to 60 percent solids. They penetrate the concrete surface and adhere well. They are available in wide range of colors. Because the solvents are powerful and potentially hazardous, you must wear a respirator when applying the finish. You'll also need to ventilate the garage and keep people and pets away from the garage.

Water-base epoxy

Like solvent-base epoxies water-base epoxies also contain from 40 to 60 percent solids. The benefit of this type of epoxy is there are no hazardous solvent fumes. These epoxy finishes are sold at most home-centers and hardware stores, and are becoming increasingly popular alternatives to solvent-based finishes.

Applying an epoxy finish
continued

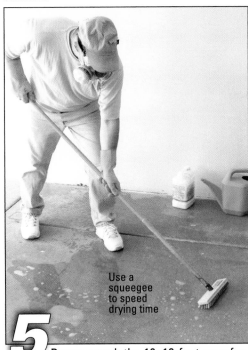

5 Power-scrub the 10×10-foot area for 10 minutes or, to save on equipment rental, use a long-handled acid brush. Repeat the sprinkling/scrubbing process until the entire floor is acid etched. When you're finished rinse the floor three times to flush the residue out. Let the floor dry overnight.

Use a squeegee to speed drying time

6 Following the manufacturer's instructions use a drill and stirring bit to mix together the two epoxy solutions. To ensure complete blending pour the mixture into a second bucket and power-mix the paint again.

7 Using duct tape tape the area directly beneath the garage door, then brush a 4-inch strip of epoxy against the tape and along the garage walls.

How much paint to buy

When working with solvent- or water-base epoxy, most manufacturers recommend applying two coats. For a two-car garage (450 square feet), you'll need 2 to 3 gallons of paint. The price per gallon ranges from $50 to $100. Check the cans for exact coverage.

STANLEY PRO TIP

Acid etching and rinsing is key

After etching the concrete with the acid solution and before allowing the surface to dry overnight **(Steps 4 and 5)**, use a garden hose to flood the garage floor, spraying the material out of the garage for 10 minutes or more. Check with your municipality, but in many areas muriatic acid can be rinsed into a storm sewer with large volumes of water. Rinse the power-scrubber brush, then scrub the wet floor one additional time for 5 to 10 minutes. Rinse the entire floor and driveway two to three more times. The concrete surface should feel like fine-grit sandpaper. If not repeat the acid-washing. To speed the drying process, squeegee out any pooled water. If possible leave the garage door open overnight for quicker drying.

8 Use a 9-inch-wide roller with a medium nap to paint the floor. Dip the roller into the bucket so only the bottom half of the roller is covered. (This loads the roller with the right amount of epoxy.)

9 Working in a 4-foot-square area, apply epoxy to garage floor in a large "W" pattern. Backroll to fill in the pattern and remove any roller marks.

10 Let the first coat dry according to manufacturer's instructions. If you don't want a glossy floor (they are slippery when wet), add a nonskid floor coating into the epoxy for the second coat. Stir with the drill and stirring bit. Repeat Steps 7 though 9.

STANLEY PRO TIP

Paint bottom 4 inches of garage wall

To protect the lower portion of your garage walls, consider covering the bottom 4 inches of the wall with the same epoxy used on the floor.

SAFETY FIRST
Paint vapors

To paint a basement floor, follow the same steps for painting a garage floor but choose an epoxy paint designed for indoor use. Whatever area you are painting, read the label and choose a paint with lower volatile organic compounds (VOCs).

VOCs are petroleum-base solvents used to thin oil paints. VOC vapors escape into the atmosphere and in a complex chemical reaction produce ozone, a component of smog. A lower VOC level means fewer emissions and typically less odor. This will make painting the room more comfortable and better indoor air quality.

When using an epoxy paint indoors, make sure the area is well-ventilated and for added protection wear a respirator as shown on page 205.

PAINTING A WOOD FLOOR

Although wood floors are commonly finished with stains and clear varnishes, painted floors can add a special touch to any room. Today's floor paints are durable and attractive and work well as a single-color element in the room or as a base for other decoration such as stenciling.

Painted floors require preparation, with similiar steps for varnished, already painted, or bare wood floors.

■ Remove mildew with a 3-to-1 water-bleach solution.

■ Scuff-sand glossy areas (mill glaze on new wood, gloss paints on painted floors, and varnished wood).

■ Remove deteriorated paint and make repairs to the flooring.

■ Clean the floor thoroughly to remove dirt and grease.

■ Prime the floor. Apply a primer recommended for floors—latex primer for latex floor paint or an alkyd primer for latex, alkyd, or polyurethane floor paint.

PRESTART CHECKLIST

☐ **TIME**
From 30 to 45 minutes per square yard to prepare the surface, plus another 15 minutes to paint each section

☐ **TOOLS**
4-foot level, sander, vacuum, screwdriver or cordless drill and screwdriver bits, putty knife, paintbrushes, roller with extension handle

☐ **SKILLS**
Using a level; cleaning, repairing, and painting wood

☐ **MATERIALS**
Bleach, sandpaper, primer and floor paint, patching compound

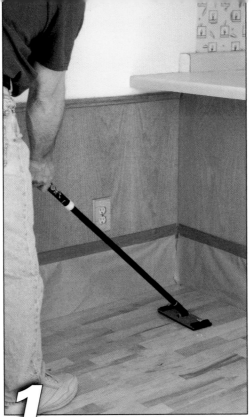

1 Remove mildew and let the floor dry. Scuff-sand glazed or glossy surfaces with 120-grit sandpaper and a pad sander. Make other repairs as necessary, then vacuum and clean the surface.

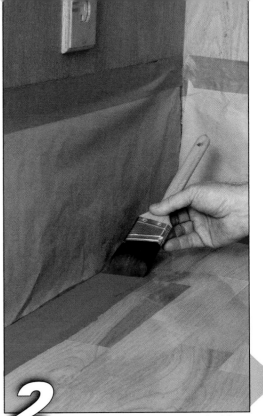

2 Using the primer recommended for both the kind of existing floor surface and the finish top coat, cut in the primer along the edges of the floor with a 3-inch brush. Start in a corner and on each leg of the corner, paint a band about 4 feet long.

PREPARING A WOOD FLOOR

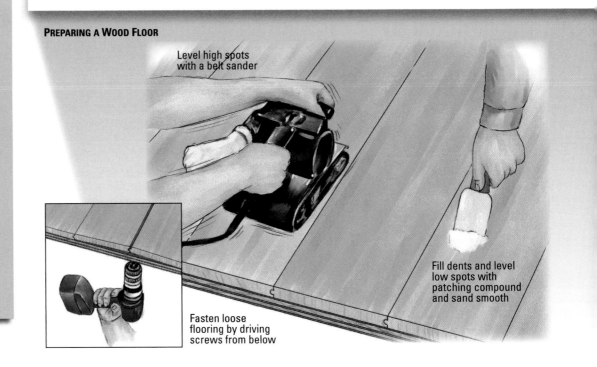

Level high spots with a belt sander

Fill dents and level low spots with patching compound and sand smooth

Fasten loose flooring by driving screws from below

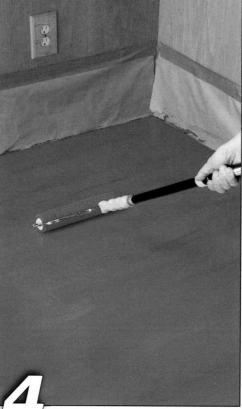

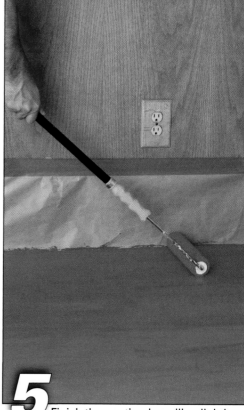

3 Using a medium-nap roller, apply the primer in the section you've just cut in, rolling the paint as close to the edge of the wall as possible and working with the grain.

4 Working in the same 4×4-foot section, roll the primer against the grain. This will spread primer into any floor irregularities.

5 Finish the section by rolling lightly with the grain, lifting the roller at the end of each stroke. Move to the next section, cutting in and rolling in the same fashion, and working toward a wet edge. When the primer is dry, use the same techniques to apply paint to the floor.

Decorative techniques

STENCILING

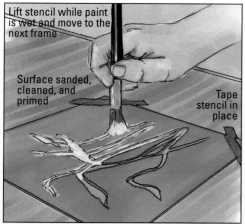

Lift stencil while paint is wet and move to the next frame

Surface sanded, cleaned, and primed

Tape stencil in place

COMB PAINTING

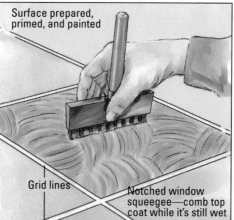

Surface prepared, primed, and painted

Grid lines

Notched window squeegee—comb top coat while it's still wet

SPATTER PAINTING

Spatter succeeding colors after each color has dried

Surface prepared, primed, and painted

A painted floor provides a literal canvas of opportunities for the application of decorative techniques. The three shown here are among the easiest of many different effects you can create on a painted floor. With some techniques, such as stenciling, it will help to sketch out your pattern first. With others, like spatter painting, you can exercise your creativity.

PAINTING VINYL FLOORING AND CERAMIC TILE

If your old vinyl flooring or ceramic tile looks tired, consider painting the surface.

You can easily paint both vinyl flooring (sheet flooring and tile) and ceramic tile with the proper preparation. Paint is much cheaper than the expense of tiling over the existing floor.

This treatment is not recommended for ceramic tile shower and tub walls, but it works well for other walls in the bathroom that don't get wet. The key to success is careful preparation and the use of the right primer and paint.

The preparation techniques and products shown here apply to both materials. You will not need to use a deglossing agent on ceramic tile.

Use high-quality primers and paints made specifically for vinyl or ceramic. Get recommendations from your paint supplier.

PRESTART CHECKLIST

☐ **TIME**
About 3 hours for a 10×10-foot floor, not including drying time for primer and paint

☐ **TOOLS**
Sanding block and/or pad sander, paint rollers and brushes, stencil pattern (optional)

☐ **SKILLS**
Preparing and painting vinyl or ceramic tile flooring

☐ **MATERIALS**
Bleach, cleaning solution, sandpaper, deglossing agent, primer, paint, sealer

1 Remove any mildewed areas by scrubbing them with a 3-to-1 water-bleach solution, letting it soak for 20 minutes before rinsing it. Then scrub the floor thoroughly to remove grease and dirt.

2 To provide a slightly roughened surface that will help the paint adhere, scuff-sand the flooring with 150-grit sandpaper and a pad sander. Wipe the floor with a damp rag. Then remove any remaining gloss with a deglossing agent (see below).

STANLEY PRO TIP: **Deglossing (for vinyl only)**

Almost all vinyl flooring, both tile and sheet flooring, is manufactured with some kind of pattern embossed in it. Because a major portion of this pattern lies slightly below the rest of the flooring, scuff-sanding may not reach and remove the gloss in the depressions. Since paint won't adhere to these small glossy indentations, you'll end up with a pattern of "holes" in your paint job. Use a deglosser to remove this final bit of gloss in the original flooring.

Because different products call for different application methods, read the instructions carefully. Wear gloves and protective glasses when working with caustic solutions.

Apply the solution full strength. Saturate a coarse cloth (an old terry-cloth towel makes a good applicator) and, working in sections, rub

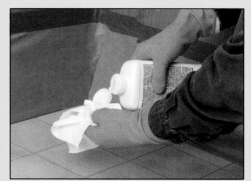

the surface in a circular motion. Fold and resaturate the cloth frequently to prevent redepositing grease or wax. When the deglossed surface is dry to the touch (about 10 minutes), it's ready for priming. For the best adhesion prime within an hour of deglossing.

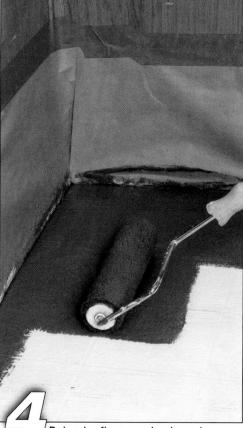

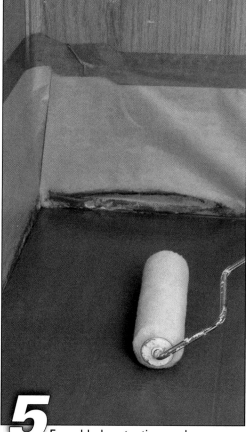

3 Apply a thick coat of latex stain-blocking primer, first cutting in the edges with a brush, then filling in the rest of the surface with a roller. Sand the primer when it's dry, then apply a second coat if necessary to further level the surface.

4 Paint the floor, cutting in and brushing. For walls use a quality latex kitchen and bath paint in a satin, semigloss, or gloss finish. For floors use a latex satin-finish floor paint or a semigloss oil-base or polyurethane floor paint.

5 For added protection apply an acrylic floor sealer. Check with your paint distributor to find a product compatible with the floor paint you applied.

Coloring the grout (for ceramic tile only)

If you don't want to paint an entire ceramic tile surface, color the grout instead. Colorants made specifically for grout can dramatically alter the color scheme of the floor. First chip out any loose grout with a hammer and cold chisel and vacuum the loose dust. Patch the repaired spots with the same grout as the original, finish it with a striking tool, and let cure. Mix up the colorant and apply it to the grout with a narrow brush. Repeat the application to make the color darker.

Stenciling a pattern over the final coat

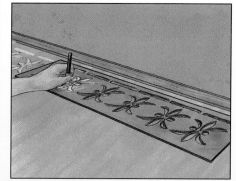

Painted floors provide perfect backgrounds for stenciled patterns. Tape the stencil to the floor and paint the pattern with a stencil brush. Stenciling will help hide areas that might show remnants of the vinyl or ceramic texture.

Your floors will last for years if you regularly clean and maintain them. Check with the manufacturer for specifics on caring for your floors.

Ceramic tile

Regular vacuuming and damp-mopping with a mild cleanser keeps tile in top condition. To clean stained grout joints, dip an old toothbrush into full-strength bleach and scrub to clean the grout joints. Rinse.

Stone or concrete

Keep hard but porous surfaces—such as marble, granite, slate, brick, and concrete—looking good by applying the manufacturer-recommended sealant.

Wood floors (including parquet)

Today's factory-applied polyurethane finishes make wood floors durable and easy to clean. Wipe up spills immediately. Dust the floor with a dust mop treated with a dusting agent. Wash the mop head regularly. For weekly or biweekly cleaning, vacuum with a floor brush attachment. Do not use a vacuum with a beater bar (or turn off the beater bar). To prevent grit damage place rugs at entrances and in front of appliances and sinks. Include a boot removal area to avoid damage from water and deicers. Use protective pads under furniture.

Resilient flooring

Remove dust and dirt with a broom, dust mop, or vacuum. A quick wipe with a damp mop works well between deep cleanings. Choose a nonabrasive all-purpose cleaner.

Carpet

Regular vacuuming protects the life of carpeting. Vacuum carpeted main living areas, stairs, and high-traffic areas of your home at least twice a week, more frequently if you have children or pets. Place doormats on both sides of each exterior door to trap dirt before it enters the house. Sweep and shake out rugs every day, particularly during inclement weather when more dirt can be tracked in.

Thoroughly clean carpet every 12 to 18 months, more often in high-traffic areas. Clean more frequently, two or three times a year, if you have children and pets or if you have light-colored carpet.

Cork

Cleaning cork means cleaning the finish, usually polyurethane or acrylic. For polyurethane clean with water and mild detergent or white vinegar; rinse well. Check with the manufacturer about recommended products. Avoid polishes if you prefer a matte finish; expect to refinish every 8 to 10 years. If the cork is unfinished or waxed, follow the cleaning instructions for polyurethane and apply solid or liquid wax.

Laminate

Dust laminate with a dust mop treated with a dusting agent to pick up dust, dirt, and pet hair. Never use abrasive cleansers and avoid using excessive amounts of water. To prevent grit damage place rugs at entrances and in front of appliances and sinks. Include a boot removal area to avoid damage from water and deicers. Use protective pads under furniture.

Regular cleaning keeps most flooring in top condition. Wipe up spills as soon as they occur.

CHAPTER PREVIEW

Cleaning and sealing tiles
page 214

Replacing grout
page 216

Repairing damaged ceramic tile
page 218

Porous stone floors, such as this tumbled marble, require a penetrating sealer to prevent staining. Wiping up spills immediately and regular dust mopping help keep the marble clean.

Caring for parquet
page 220

Staining or varnishing wood floors
page 222

Maintaining resilient tile
page 224

Maintaining carpet and cork
page 226

Caring for laminate tile
page 228

CLEANING AND SEALING TILES

Although regular cleaning will keep your ceramic tile in good condition, some surfaces, especially in kitchens and family rooms, may require stain removal.

When you need to remove a stain, start with the techniques outlined in the chart *below right*. If these solutions don't work, ask a tile supplier for a commercial stain-removal agent made for your tile. Stubborn stains often can be removed with a cleaning agent mixed with baking soda, plaster of Paris, or refined clay. Deodorant-free cat litter works well. Mix the ingredients into a wet paste and apply it to the stain. Tape a plastic bag over the paste and let it sit for a couple of days. Then brush off the paste and rinse.

Unglazed tile usually requires a sealer, and even presealed tile may need periodic stripping and resealing.

Penetrating sealers soak into the tile bisque and preserve the natural color of the tile. Topical sealers lie on the surface of the tile and may lighten or darken the tile colors or change its sheen. Topical sealers wear off and can require yearly reapplication. When tiles look dull it could be time to strip and reseal them.

Stripping tiles

1 To remove old sealer flow stripper on surface with a sponge or mop in an area that you can clean before the liquid dries (about 25 square feet). Scrub the area with a brush or with a floor-scrubbing machine. Do not let the stripper dry on the surface.

2 Remove residue with a sponge or rags. Some water-base strippers allow removal with a wet-dry vacuum. Rinse with clean water and wipe dry.

PRESTART CHECKLIST

☐ **TIME**
About 45 minutes to vacuum and damp mop a 15×20-foot kitchen, 90 minutes to strip it, about the same time to seal it

☐ **TOOLS**
Stripping: scrub brush and mop or scrubbing machine, vacuum
Sealing: vacuum, applicator, buffer

☐ **PREP**
Vacuum and clean surface

☐ **MATERIALS**
Stripper, sponge, sealer, bucket, rags, wax if needed

Removing stains from tile

Stain	Cleaner and method
Ink, coffee, blood	Start with a 3 percent hydrogen peroxide solution; if that doesn't work try a nonbleach cleaner.
Oil-base products	Use a mild solvent, such as charcoal lighter fluid or mineral spirits, then household cleaner. For dried paint scrape with a plastic (not metal) scraper.
Grease, fats	Clean with a commercial spot lifter.
Rust	Use commercial rust removers, then try household cleaner.
Nail polish	Remove with nail polish remover.

Always rinse the stained area with clear water to remove residue.

Applying sealers

1 On newly tiled floors wait 48 hours before sealing. On existing floors vacuum the surface thoroughly to keep dirt and dust from becoming embedded in the new sealer.

2 Clean the tile with a commercial tile cleaning product following the manufacturer's directions. Rinse with clear water.

3 Apply sealer with a sponge applicator, paint pad, brush, or mop, as required by the manufacturer. Do not let sealer puddle or run on walls. Some sealers can't be overlapped. Some may require wiping with a clean rag. Allow time to dry between coats. Apply one or two additional coats.

SAFETY FIRST
Floor care products can be toxic

Many strippers and sealers are solvent-base and highly caustic. Even water-base products contain harmful chemicals.

All floor care products are potentially dangerous—observe the manufacturer's safety precautions.

Wear rubber gloves, old long-sleeve clothing, pants, and eye protection. Wear a respirator to avoid breathing toxic fumes and put a fan in the window to provide adequate ventilation. Perform tile maintenance tasks when children are out of the house.

Working with waxes

Many unglazed tile surfaces lend themselves to waxed finishes. Some waxes contain pigments that enhance the color of the tile.

To properly renew a waxed floor, strip the old wax and wash the surface thoroughly with a mild detergent. Rinse with clear water and let it dry completely. Wax the surface in successive thin coats with the applicator recommended by the manufacturer. Allow each coat to dry and buff in between. Repeated thin coats leave a brighter shine than one thick coat; they also reduce wax buildup.

A dull shine doesn't necessarily call for rewaxing. Clean the floor with a soap-free cleaner and buff with a cloth or rented machine. When using a buffer start in the middle of the floor with the brush level. Tilt the handle up or down slightly to move it from side to side. Don't push the machine. Buff across the surface.

REPLACING GROUT

Replacing grout on an entire floor is a monumental job, but if you've inherited an installation that is crumbling, you probably have no other choice. Make the task easier by using a rotary hand tool.

Don't be deceived by grout—it is a remarkably hard material. If you need to cover a large section and don't own a rotary hand tool, buy one. Kits that come complete with bits are well worth the investment when removing large areas of grout. Although the process is shown here on a wall, it is the same technique you'll use for floor grout.

If the grout is stained or mildewed, don't replace it—clean it. Most home centers carry cleaning solutions formulated for grout. Wear eye protection, gloves, and old clothes (long-sleeve shirts) when using them. Provide adequate ventilation.

Before you tackle even small repairs, find out what caused the grout to deteriorate. A few small areas may not indicate a problem, but large cracks may have been caused by a structural problem and may have let water behind the tile. In this case remove the tile and start over.

PRESTART CHECKLIST

☐ **TIME**
About 30 minutes per square foot

☐ **TOOLS**
Rotary hand tool, grout saw (for small repairs), hand brush, margin trowel, mixing paddle, bucket, grout float, sponge

☐ **SKILLS**
Using power tools, floating and cleaning grout

☐ **MATERIALS**
Water, grout, sealer

1 Use a rotary hand tool with a diamond grinding burr to remove large amounts of damaged grout. Choose a bit that is slightly smaller than an empty grout joint and work the tool with two hands. Take care to keep the shank of the bit in line with the joint so you don't snap the bit or chip the tile.

2 Brush the joints with a hand brush and rinse with clear water. Let the joints dry overnight. Mix up the amount of grout you can apply before it sets up. Apply the grout with a grout float, forcing it into the joints at a 45-degree angle and working diagonally.

WHAT IF...
You're removing only a small amount of grout?

If you have only one or two small sections that need repair, you might be able to use a grout saw—a small handheld tool available at local hardware stores.

To remove the grout from the joint, hold the tool so the blade is flat against the joint. Work the tool up and down (or back and forth) in the joint until you have removed about half the grout. For wide grout lines use a rotary hand tool. Chip out mortared joints with a cold chisel.

MIX UP THE AMOUNT OF GROUT
Handle grout easier and faster

Although it's important to follow the manufacturer's directions when mixing up a batch of grout, there's one item you might not find printed on the bag—the size of the mixing container. The task will go much faster if you can scoop the grout out of the container and onto the wall with the grout float. Mix the grout in a medium-size plastic dishpan or similar container that makes its removal easy.

3 When you have completed one section of the installation, scrape off the excess grout with the grout float, holding the float just short of a 90-degree angle. Don't press too hard to avoid drawing the grout out of the joints. Let the grout set up, then dampen a sponge and clean the grout residue from the surface. When the first section is clean, grout and clean the remaining sections with the same methods.

4 Once you have grouted and cleaned the entire installation, let the grout set up. Using a soft rag wipe the haze from the surface. Some grouts leave a haze that requires a bit of work to remove. Use pressure and a scrubbing motion if necessary. Seal the grout (and the tile if necessary) with the product recommended by the manufacturer.

Matching the color

Generally you will want to replace the grout with one of the same color. If you're replacing an entire installation, that's not a problem. The new grout can be slightly "off hue" from the original and no one will notice.

If you're replacing the grout in only a few joints, try to remove a chip (not dust) from a damaged section to match to the new grout. Use a utility knife or small screwdriver, taking care not to damage the tile.

If necessary mix two grouts of a similar hue to get the best possible match.

LET THE GROUT SET UP

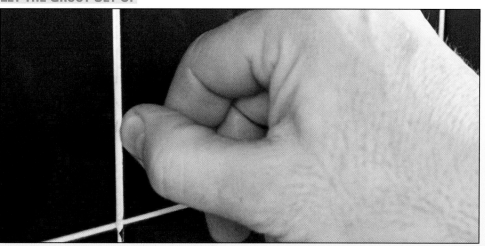

To avoid pulling the grout out of the joints while you clean them, wait until it sets up. To determine if the grout is hard enough to withstand cleaning, push your thumbnail into it. When your thumbnail makes no impression, you can start cleaning.

REPAIRING DAMAGED CERAMIC TILE

Tile is the most durable floor covering, although not impervious to damage. Improper installation, poor adhesives, and falling objects can cause cracks or chips.

Repairing the problem begins with removing the grout and tile. Determine if you need to make a structural repair before installing new tile.

Cracked joints are most often caused by an improper grout mix or the absence of expansion joints. If the grout is soft and powdery, remove it and regrout. If the cracked grout is hard, remove it and fill the joint with a matching colored caulk.

Cracked tiles on a long length of floor are caused either by a faulty adhesive or an underlying crack. Before you remove the tiles, tap them lightly with a wrench. If you hear a hollow sound, the bond is probably at fault and a thorough cleaning and new mortar will solve the problem. If the wrench "rings," the bond is probably solid; you may need to isolate the crack with a membrane.

Although tile replacement is shown here on a wall, it is the same technique for flooring.

PRESTART CHECKLIST

☐ **TIME**
About an hour and a half to remove and replace grout and tile, at least a day to regrout a large area

☐ **TOOLS**
Grout saw or utility knife, sledgehammer and cold chisel, putty knife or margin trowel

☐ **SKILLS**
Breaking tile with a hammer and cold chisel, troweling

☐ **MATERIALS**
Heavy paper, replacement tiles, thinset, grout, tape

Removing and replacing damaged tile

1 Before removing a damaged tile protect the surrounding area with heavy paper. Score the grout around the damaged tile with a carbide grout saw or utility knife. Scoring reduces the tendency of other tiles to crack when you remove the damaged area.

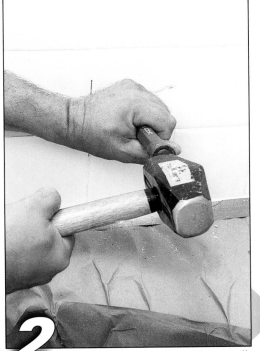

2 Break the damaged tile with a small sledgehammer and cold chisel, starting from the center of the tile and working to the edges.

Finding replacement tiles

It's unlikely that you have extra tile laying around from the original installation job, so you'll need to find replacement tile that will match. One manufacturer's tile may not look like another, so you may have a challenge. Start by seeing if the name of the manufacturer is written on the back of the tile. If it is you can narrow your field fairly quickly. If not take the old tile to your supplier; they will help you find a tile that will match. Don't forget about matching the grout. Cleaning the old grout will help you match it more effectively.

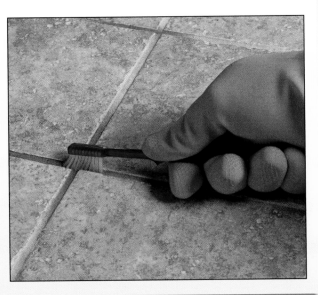

3 Remove the broken pieces, prying them out with a putty knife or margin trowel if necessary. Scrape the old adhesive from the wall.

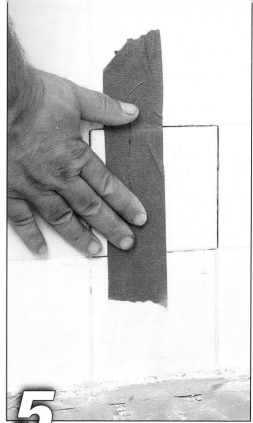

4 Backbutter the new tile with a sufficiently thick coat of mortar. If possible purchase the adhesive or mortar used originally. Apply thinset if you don't know what mortar was originally used.

5 Firmly press the new tile in place. Make sure it's level with the rest of the surface. Remove the tile and adjust the layer of mortar if necessary. Center the tile in the recess. Use nails or spacers to keep it aligned. Tape the tile until the mortar cures, then apply grout.

Repairing tile on a cracked slab

1 Remove grout from the joints along the entire length of the crack, including at least one tile beyond those damaged. Following the manufacturer's directions apply adhesive and an isolation membrane.

2 Trowel thinset into the recess and backbutter each tile. Replace the tiles and level them. Grout and clean when the mortar is dry.

APPLY GROUT
Regrouting a small area

When regrouting a small area or a single replacement tile, dig out the old grout with a utility or grout knife. Unless you are replacing the entire section of grout, try to match the color of the existing grout. Mix a small batch and let it dry; then compare it with the existing grout.

If grouting a large area, apply the grout with a float. On a small area or a single tile, use your finger to press the grout into the joint. Shape the grout with a wet sponge.

CARING FOR PARQUET

You'll get good results if you treat your parquet floor as you would fine furniture. Use a cleaner that is made or recommended by the manufacturer. Never clean the floor with water or water-base products.

Wipe up spills immediately with a damp cloth and dry the area with a dry cloth. Old T-shirts are excellent for this purpose. Do not use cleaners that contain abrasives, caustic chemicals, bleach, or ammonia. For routine cleaning use a solvent-base cleaner or a one-step cleaner/polish combination.

Most prefinished parquet tile is manufactured with a durable acrylic or polyurethane finish. Some finishes are no-wax, others benefit from waxing. Check the manufacturer's directions before you purchase cleaning products. Acrylic waxes generally are not recommended for wood floors, and some polyurethane finishes should not be waxed.

Almost all wood finishes change color over time. You can slow this process by keeping the draperies closed. Areas covered with rugs won't be subject to color changes, so the color difference will be revealed if you decide to move the rugs.

PRESTART CHECKLIST

☐ **TIME**
An hour to vacuum and clean a 15×20-foot floor; an hour to remove, replace a damaged tile

☐ **TOOLS**
Cleaning: vacuum, cleaning product applicator
Repairing: circular saw, chisel, hammer, notched plastic scraper, trowel, putty knife, utility knife, backsaw

☐ **MATERIALS**
Cleaning: manufacturer's cleaning solution
Repairing: replacement tile, mastic

1 To remove a damaged parquet tile, set your circular saw to the thickness of the tile and equip the saw with a fine-tooth blade. Make a series of parallel plunge cuts about 2 inches apart, stopping just short of the adjacent tiles.

2 Using a ¾-inch or 1-inch chisel with the bevel down, cut out the sections of parquet between the lines. Keep the chisel as flat as possible—you may have to remove the first section one layer at a time. Clean out any wood scraps and scrape off the old adhesive with a putty knife.

Refinishing a parquet floor

Parquet tile, especially tile with a thick veneer, is an excellent candidate for refinishing. Using a pad sander and a medium-grit sandpaper, start sanding along the diagonal of the room. Work the sander from one side of the room to the other. Shift direction and sand along the other diagonal length of the room. Make a final pass parallel to and along the longest wall of the room. Repeat this three-pass process with succeedingly finer grits of sandpaper.

Stain and varnish the floor with the product of your choice, either a penetrating or surface finish. Penetrants sink into the wood pores; they won't wear away unless the wood does. Surface finishes don't soak into the pores of the wood; they stay on top and generally are less durable.

STANLEY PRO TIP
Cut the tongue

To remove the tongues so a new parquet tile can replace a damaged unit, clamp the tile to a work surface and cut the tongues with a backsaw. Use two hands and keep the saw vertical and lined up on the edge of the tile.

3 If the parquet is tongue-and-groove (and most quality tiles are), the tongues will be in the way when you replace the tile. When you remove the damaged tile, cut the tongues on the surrounding tiles. Cut the tongue from the replacement tile and press it into freshly laid adhesive. Spread the adhesive with a notched plastic scraper and press the new tile flush with the old tile.

4 Clean excess adhesive that seeped through the joints and weigh down the tile with heavy books or exercise weights. Let the adhesive dry overnight. If the replacement tile is prefinished, it may look more glossy than the originals. Reduce the new-tile gloss with a light burnishing with #0000 steel wool. If the tile is unfinished, stain and finish it to match the surrounding floor.

Preventive maintenance

Regular vacuuming is parquet's best friend. It helps keep tracked-in grit from scratching the floor and dirt from being ground into the joints.

To keep the grit to a minimum, place slip-resistant nonstaining mats at entrances, use casters or felt pads under furniture legs, and avoid walking with any kind of spiked shoes (athletic or heels).

Floor mats in front of stoves, refrigerators, and sinks help prevent stains. Use them in the bathroom too.

Always use the cleaner that the manufacturer recommends. Generally these are solvent-base solutions, but several new environmentally friendly cleaners are on the market.

Maintaining parquet

Problem	Remedy
Bubbles in finish	For light damage sand and recoat; if heavy sand, stain, and refinish.
Chewing gum, crayon, candle wax	Freeze with ice in a bag, scrape with plastic scraper.
Cigarette burns	Burnish with fine steel wool or scrape charred area; wax or sand, stain, and refinish.
Dents	Cover with dampened cloth and press with an electric iron.
Scratches	Wax the area or hide the scratch with a thin coat of dusting spray rubbed into scratch.
Seasonal cracks	Increase humidity in dry season—install humidifier, boil water, open dishwasher after rinse.
Surface stains	Remove with sandpaper or steel wool, feathering edges; or clean with one of the following solutions:
Heel marks	Wood cleaner or wax
Oil and grease	Try wood cleaner first. On waxed floor use TSP or soap with high lye content. On surface finish use TSP.
Pet stains	Wood cleaner, followed by mild bleach or household vinegar for up to an hour. A remaining spot is not likely to sand out. Cover damage with rug or remove, replace, and refinish.
Ink	Use procedure for pet stains.
Water spots	Buff lightly with #0000 steel wool, then wax. If necessary sand with fine paper, stain, and recoat.

STAINING OR VARNISHING WOOD FLOORS

Finishing a wood floor requires a number of preparation steps, but the result is a wood floor with all its warmth and richness.

If you're planning to refinish an existing floor, pull up a floor register to make sure you have enough wood for another sanding. Standard hardwood strip flooring can be sanded several times, but if your floor is only slightly more than ½ inch thick, consult a professional. The same goes for engineered flooring. It can be refinished, but its top layer is quite thin.

Take inventory of the existing floor and mark and repair popped nails and damaged areas. Because depressions in an old floor are inevitable, they'll show up as you're sanding them. Mark them so you can resand them if necessary.

Even if your floor is brand new and unfinished, it will require sanding and preparation. In almost all cases it's easier to use a pad sander rather than a drum sander.

PRESTART CHECKLIST

☐ **TIME**
  2 to 4 days, depending on conditions and size of the floor and your skills and experience

☐ **TOOLS**
  Pry bar, putty knife, hammer, pad sander, random orbit sander, vacuum, finish applicator, paintbrush

☐ **SKILLS**
  Preparing, sanding, and finishing wood

☐ **MATERIALS**
  Finishing nails, wood putty, stain, sandpaper, varnish

Finishing a wood floor

1 Remove <u>shoe molding</u> and baseboard (if desired). Rough-sand the floor with a heavy-grit paper, keeping the sander moving and working with the grain. Change sandpaper often to keep the cutting surface fresh. A sander equipped with a dust-removal system will speed the work.

2 When the floor is sanded to a rough-cut smoothness, fill the entire surface with a wood filler as recommended by your floor products retailer. Let the filler dry.

SHOE MOLDING
Save the moldings

Shoe molding (and baseboards) invariably suffer damage from the sanding machine. To avoid replacing the moldings and baseboards with new material (which will also require finishing), remove them with a flat pry bar.

STANLEY PRO TIP
Down to the nitty gritty

When you're refinishing a wood floor, begin sanding with a heavy grit and work with successively finer grits until the floor is smooth enough to accept a finish. (An improperly sanded floor will show scratches immediately after application of the finish.)

On existing floors with dents and other signs of wear, you may need to use the following grits in succession—36-grit, 50-grit, and then 80-grit. On new floors start with a medium paper such as 100-grit and move up to finer grits such as 150-grit and higher. Run your hand over the floor surface as you work to locate any slight imperfections. Although you will want to increase the grit as you sand, using abrasive finer than 220-grit can create a burnished surface that won't accept stain evenly.

3 Rough-cutting the floor will leave the edges slightly higher than the main body of the floor. To even out this difference in floor levels, scrape down the edges so they're level with the sanded surface. Change blades often and pull the scraper toward you with firm pressure on the wood.

4 Buff the floor with a 100-grit screen to remove any remaining imperfections and to bring the floor to a consistent level from edges to center, leaving the surface at its finished smoothness. Vacuum thoroughly and remove dust with a tack cloth.

5 Stain the floor (optional) with a rag or the applicator recommended, removing the excess if required. Let the stain dry. Using a lamb's wool or other suitable applicator, apply the finish coats, letting each coat dry. Scuff-sand and vacuum each dry coat before applying the next one.

USING A DRUM SANDER

1. Start here and sand a section two-thirds the width of the floor.

2. Sand the remaining one-third on the other side of the room.

Drum sanders require a specific technique to produce a smooth surface. Start about two-thirds of the way along the length of one wall and sand with the grain, pulling the sander towards you. Then, push the sander forward and overlap its next path slightly. After sanding the section turn the sander around and repeat the process.

Choosing the right finish

Interior stains are generally wiping stains applied to bare wood with a protective clear coat.

Wiping stains:
- Apply to bare wood with a rag or brush in maximum 2-foot sections. Let stand 5 minutes; wipe excess with rags; allow to dry overnight.
- Darkness will depend on stain, color, porosity of wood, time left on before wiping, how hard it is wiped, and number of coats.

Oil finishes are based on drying oils such as tung or linseed oil.
- Apply to bare wood, often over wiping stain, with brush or rag. Let stand for 5 minutes; wipe excess with rag; dry overnight.

- Provide a rich satin finish and moderate water resistance.

Varnishes—solvent base
- Applied to bare or stained wood with natural bristle, nylon, or polyester brush.
- Stir matte finishes without making foam; do not shake.
- Let first coat dry 24 hours. Sand first coat to ensure adhesion.

Varnishes—water base
- May be milky white in the container but dry clear.
- May appear more like plastic than solvent-base varnish.
- To remove whiskers that come up when applying the coating, predampen bare wood.

MAINTAINING RESILIENT TILE

Modern resilient tile is so easy to maintain that the biggest problem you're likely to experience is the tendency to overdo it. Too much maintenance causes premature wear and dulling.

A regular schedule of vacuuming (not with an upright model or beater-bar attachment) and damp-mopping keeps a resilient floor in tip-top shape. If you need to address an unusually soiled spot with a cleaning solution, use a product recommended by the manufacturer. Steer clear of generic products made for all floors.

The chemicals in vinyl tile are prone to interact with the chemicals in other synthetic products, especially the rubber backings of area rugs. Many rubber backings stain vinyl. Don't use a rubber-backed rug unless the manufacturer or retailer gives the OK.

Be wary of felt or fiber scratch guards that self-stick to the bottom of furniture legs. They work initially but gradually accumulate grit and scratch the floor. Check them periodically and replace when they fill up with dirt.

You can remove some minor scuffing with a tile cleaner and #0000 steel wool. Rub gently.

PRESTART CHECKLIST

☐ **TIME**
   About 45 minutes to vacuum and damp-mop a 15×20-foot kitchen; about 30 minutes to remove and replace a damaged tile

☐ **TOOLS**
   Cleaning: vacuum, sponge mop
   Repairing: hair dryer, putty knife, notched trowel or plastic scraper, rolling pin

☐ **MATERIALS**
   Cleaning: manufacturer's cleaning solution
   Repairing: adhesive, replacement tile

Replace a damaged tile

1 To remove a damaged resilient tile, set a hair dryer on high heat and concentrate the heat for a minute or so on one edge of the tile. Insert the blade of your putty knife and work it back and forth, pushing forward to break the adhesive bond.

2 Don't expect the tile to come up in one piece. It will tear and leave small pieces stuck in the adhesive. Warm and scrape each piece until you have removed all of them.

Maintaining no-wax floors

No-wax floors are manufactured with a vinyl or polyurethane coating applied to their surface. Of the two the urethane is tougher, but for both no wax means no wax. If you start waxing one of these materials, you'll dull the finish, make it dangerously slick, increase its tendency to collect dust and dirt, or all three. To maintain the shine of a no-wax floor, just keep it clean.

Once a week vacuum the floor and damp-mop it with a mild detergent solution—even if the floor doesn't look dirty, it is, and those microscopic dust particles will wear away the sheen. Make sure you rinse the floor thoroughly. Occasional buffing will also bring back the shine. If you have to "refinish" a no-wax floor, use a product made by the manufacturer especially for this purpose.

3 Using a notched trowel spread adhesive into the recess left by the damaged tile. If a regular trowel proves unwieldy, notch the end of a plastic scraper and use it to comb the mastic. Spread the adhesive to the edges.

4 Before you set the replacement tile make sure its orientation conforms to pattern. The arrow won't help because you can't see the other tiles' arrows; instead eyeball the pattern. Set the tile at an angle with one edge tight against the other and lower the tile into place.

5 Adhere the new tile tightly to the adhesive by rolling with a rolling pin. Warm the surface slightly before you roll it. The heat will soften the adhesive and help bond the tile.

Removing stains from vinyl tile

Stain	Remove with
Asphalt, shoe polish	Citrus-base cleaner or mineral spirits
Candle wax	Scrape carefully with plastic spatula
Crayon	Mineral spirits or manufacturer's cleaner
Grape juice, wine, mustard	Full-strength bleach or manufacturer's cleaner
Heel marks	Nonabrasive household cleaner; if stain remains use rubbing alcohol.
Lipstick	Rubbing alcohol or mineral spirits
Nail polish	Nail polish remover
Paint or varnish	Wipe with water or mineral spirits while still wet. If dry scrape carefully with a thin plastic spatula. If stain still shows dab with rubbing alcohol.
Pen ink	Citrus-base cleaner, rubbing alcohol, or mineral spirits
Permanent marker	Mineral spirits, nail polish remover, or rubbing alcohol
Rust	Oxalic acid and water (1 part acid to 10 parts water); extremely caustic; follow all directions.

After removing the stain wipe the area with a damp cloth to remove residue.

Preventing dents and scratches

Resilient flooring is more prone to dents, scuffs, and scratches than other flooring. Unlike spots they can't be removed. Here are some ways to prevent dents:

■ Protect the floor when moving appliances. Lay plywood panels on the floor and "walk" the appliance across the panels.

■ Use floor protectors to keep furniture legs from denting the floors; the heavier the furniture, the wider the protector should be.

■ Avoid furniture with rolling casters. If you must have casters, use double rollers.

■ Keep dust and dirt outside the house— use mats or rugs at entrances but avoid rubber-backed rugs. They can discolor resilient flooring.

■ Keep the floor clean with regular sweeping or vacuuming but don't use vacuums with beater bars.

MAINTAINING CARPET AND CORK

Carpet requires periodic deep cleaning because no matter how frequently you vacuum, dirt and grime eventually work their way down into the fibers.

Most cork products are finished with a varnish that requires periodic reapplication and keeps the cork from soaking up the dirt.

Both materials benefit more from routine preventive maintenance than from occasional deep cleaning. Regular vacuuming helps keep tracked-in grit out of the fibers and joints.

Nonstaining mats at entrances control dirt, and casters or cups under furniture legs minimize dents. Floor mats in front of stoves, refrigerators, and sinks help prevent stains.

When deep-cleaning carpet vacuum first to remove as much loose soil as possible and apply a spot removal agent to heavily soiled sections. Remove all the furniture you can and put plastic bags around the legs of everything you can't move. Ventilate the room with fans to speed drying.

Although these pages feature a cleaning powder, some carpet can stand up to steam and water-base cleaning methods. Ask your supplier which cleaning methods are compatible with your carpet's weave.

PRESTART CHECKLIST

☐ **TIME**
About 2 hours for an 8×10 floor

☐ **TOOLS**
Vacuum cleaner, floor brush or carpet machine, sponge mop, utility knife and putty knife (for tile removal), scissors for carpet repair

☐ **MATERIALS**
Manufacturer's cleaning agents, varnish for cork tiles, sponge or applicator

Deep cleaning carpet

1 Read the manufacturer's or retailer's recommendation before purchasing a carpet-cleaning solution. Sprinkle the cleaning powder evenly across the surface of the floor. Properly applied it should appear as a thin layer on the carpet.

2 Using a short-bristled floor brush or rented carpet machine, work the powder into the fibers. To avoid the possibility of premature wear, do not brush too heavily in any area. Leave the powder in the fibers for the recommended time.

WHAT IF...
The carpet has sprouts or dents?

1 From time to time even the best carpet tiles will have a fiber or two that comes loose from the backing. If your carpet shows "sprouts," don't pull them—you'll create holes in the fabric. Gently pull the sprouted fibers up and trim them flush with the others.

2 Dents in carpet are more difficult to remedy than other maladies. Start by using the back of a tablespoon to work the fibers up in the dent. If this doesn't work try wetting the area by allowing an ice cube to melt on the spot or warm the spot slightly with a hair dryer.

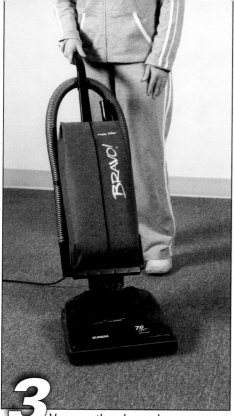

3 Vacuum the cleaned area thoroughly using a high-quality vacuum with beater bars. Go over each section both with and against the grain in order to ensure removal of all the cleaning powder and soil.

Cleaning cork

1 Vacuum a cork floor with a high-quality canister vacuum. Don't use an upright vacuum or canister attachment with beater bars—doing so risks tearing up the surface of the tile.

2 Using either a cotton string mop or a synthetic sponge mop, damp-mop the floor. Don't overwet or flood the surface—you'll warp the tile and weaken the adhesive bond. For deeper cleaning purchase a cleaner recommended by the manufacturer.

WHAT IF...
You have to replace a carpet tile?

The procedure illustrated *below* works equally well for both carpet tiles and cork tiles. The removal of cork tiles is more difficult because of the reciprocating glue. Always work from the center of the tile outward. Working from the edges will damage them.

1 Using a metal straightedge (optional) and a sharp utility knife, make several passes in the center of the tile until you have cut through to the subfloor.

2 Insert a 3-inch putty knife under the cut you've made and remove one-half of the tile by prying and seesawing the putty knife back and forth to break the adhesive bond. Repeat the procedure on the other half of the tile. Replace the adhesive, press in the tile, and roll.

Refinishing cork tiles

Although a wear-layer varnish protects modern cork products, the cork's surface still needs to be renewed periodically. Clean the floor as described *above* and let it dry. Then use a sponge or lamb's wool applicator to reapply the varnish. Never use a generic product—always use a solution made especially for cork.

CARING FOR LAMINATE TILE

As durable as laminate tile is, laminate products are not indestructible. Laminates (especially the thicker, more expensive products) are more subject to denting than scratching. The dents are impossible to remove.

To keep the surface from scratching take the precautions listed in "Preventive Maintenance for Laminate Tile" *(below right).* In addition don't drag heavy appliances or furniture across a laminate floor. Use an appliance dolly or air pad when resetting the refrigerator, and ask friends to help move sofas, dressers, and other large pieces of furniture.

Plastic furniture casters seem deceptively safe for laminate floors. Small pieces of grit embedded in the roller over time abrade the surface of the floor. If you have plastic furniture rollers, replace them with rubber rollers.

Humidity also plays a role in laminate maintenance. Keep the room humidity at 50 percent to ensure the joints stay closed, thus preventing an accumulation of dirt between tiles.

PRESTART CHECKLIST

☐ **TIME**
About 45 minutes to vacuum and damp-mop a 15×20-foot floor; about 20 minutes to repair a tile and 30 minutes to remove and replace a damaged tile

☐ **TOOLS**
Cleaning: vacuum, sponge mop
Repairing: utility knife, vacuum, plastic spatula, circular saw, chisel, hammer

☐ **MATERIALS**
Cleaning: manufacturer's cleaning solution
Repairing: masking tape, patching compound, replacement tile, mastic

Repairing a damaged tile

1 If the damaged area lies in a woodgrain or other straight pattern, square the damaged area with a sharp utility knife. If the pattern is irregular, you may want to leave the outlines of the patch slightly irregular. The wear layer on laminate tile is extremely hard—use a sharp blade. Don't cut clear through the layers of tile. Only remove the top layer. Vacuum up the chips and dust from the area to be patched.

Preventive maintenance for laminate tile

Sweeping will do for daily cleaning, but vacuuming is necessary before you damp-mop a laminate floor. Don't wax the floor. Wax leaves a film that deadens the shine.

Laminate tile is among the easiest of floor materials to care for, but no material maintains itself. The best thing you can do to keep its surface shiny is to use area rugs or mats at home entrances to trap as much loose dirt as possible. Use felt pads on furniture legs and check them periodically—you will have to change them regularly because they pick up dirt and can act like small circles of sandpaper.

Sweep or vacuum the floor daily to remove loose dirt and grit. If something gets spilled wipe it up immediately and clean the residue with a spray cleaner product recommended by the manufacturer.

Damp-mop the floor once a week with a mild cleaning solution and a sponge mop. Don't flood the floor; wring the mop until it's just damp.

2 To make cleanup easier apply tape around the damaged area. Squeeze a small amount of the manufacturer's repair compound into the damaged area and press it into the recess with the edge of a plastic spatula. Smooth the compound level with the tape. If the compound comes out of the area when you smooth it, lower the angle of the spatula. Let the repair dry thoroughly.

3 When the repair compound has dried thoroughly, carefully remove the tape. Most compounds are made to shrink as they dry, so the repair should now be level with the surface of the surrounding tile. If some putty got on the floor, wipe it with a damp cloth.

Removing stains from laminate tile

Stain	Remove with
Candle wax	Scrape carefully with plastic spatula.
Crayon, rubber heel marks	Rub out with a dry cloth or acetone if needed.
Grape juice or wine	Rub with a dry cloth or concentrated cleaner.
Lipstick	Paint thinner or acetone
Nail polish	Acetone-base nail polish remover
Paint or varnish	Wipe with water or mineral spirits while still wet. If dry scrape carefully with a plastic spatula. If the stain still shows, clean with rubbing alcohol.
Pen ink	Acetone or paint thinner
Shoe polish	Acetone or paint thinner
Tar	Acetone
Others	Start with concentrated cleaner, then acetone

After removing the stain wipe the area with a damp cloth to remove residue.

Removing a tile

In the unlikely event that the damage to a laminate tile is so severe that it warrants removal, you have two options.

If the floor is a glueless installation, you may be able to unsnap the tiles up to and surrounding the damaged tile. Then replace the tile and reassemble the floor.

If disassembly is not possible, or if the edges of the tile are glued, you'll have to cut the tile out.

Mark the perimeter of the damaged tile with masking tape (blue tape provides a more visible line). Set a circular saw to the thickness of the tile and insert a fine-tooth blade. Cut the tile along the taped line. Chisel out the corners and remove any pieces of tongue or groove. Using a sharp utility knife, cut the tongue and protruding groove edges from the replacement tile and glue it in place.

GLOSSARY

A

Actual dimensions: The actual size of a flooring material as measured with a tape or ruler. *See also* Nominal size.

Awl: A sharp-pointed tool used to make small starter holes for screws or to scribe lines.

B

Back-butter: To apply mortar or adhesive to the rear face of a file before setting it.

Backerboard: Any of several cement or gypsum-based sheets used as substrate for setting tile. Also called cement board.

Baseboard: Trim running along he bottom of a wall to cover gaps between the wall and floor and to protect the bottom of the wall.

Beam: In framing, a horizontal support member.

Bearing wall: An interior or exterior wall that helps support the roof or the floor joists above.

Beating block: Used to press tiles evenly into adhesive. Can be a store-bought rubber-faced model or a piece of plywood that you've covered with terry cloth.

Bedding: A layer of mortar into which tile is set.

Bisque: The clay-and-liquid mixture that forms the body of the tile.

Blind-nail: To nail so that the head of the nail is not visible on the surface of the wood.

Board: Any piece of lumber that is less than 2 inches thick and more than three inches wide.

Bond: The cementing action of an adhesive.

Building Codes: Community ordinances governing the manner in which a hom emay be constructed or modified. Most codes primarily are concerned with fire and health; some have sections relating to electrical, plumbing, and structural work.

Bullnose tile: Also called cap tile. Tile shaped to define an edge of a surface.
Butt joint: A joint where ends of the two adjoining pieces are cut square and the pieces are simply placed against each other.

C

Casing: Trim around a door, window, or other opening.

Caulk: Any compound used to seal seams and joints against infiltration of water and air.

Cement board: A backerboard with a mesh coat that acts as a surface for setting tile.

Cement-bodied tile: Tile whose bisque is formed of mortar as opposed to clay.

Ceramic tile: Made from refined clay usually mixed with additives and water and hardened in a kiln. Can be glazed or unglazed.

Chalk line: A reel of string coated with colored chalk, used to mark straight lines by pulling the string taught and snapping it, leaving a line.

Chamfer: A bevel cut made along the length of a board edge.

Concrete nails: Hardened steel nails that can be driven into concrete.

Coped cut: A profile cut made in the face of a piece of moulding that allows for butting it against another piece at an inside corner.

Corner lead: The first few courses of tile laid in stair-step fashion in a corner to establish position for the remaining tiles in those courses.

Counterbore: To drive in a screw below the surface of the surrounding wood. The void created is filled later with putty or a wooden plug.

Countersink: To drive the head of a nail or screw so that the top is flush with the surrounding surface.

Course: A row of tile or other units. Most projects consist of several courses laid beside one another and separated by grout.

Crosscut: A cut across the grain that reduces material to a desired length.

Cupping: A type of warping that causes the edges of a board to curl up along its grain.

D

Dado (groove): A channel cut in wood that runs across the grain. A groove is a channel that runs with the grain.

Dado joint: A joint formed when the end of one member fits into a groove cut partway through the face of another.

Dimension lumber: Lumber that is 2 to 5 inches in nominal thickness and up to 12 inches in nominal width.

Dowel: A cylindrical piece of wood, often a joint reinforcement.

Dry-fit: Preliminary joining of wood or other materials without glue or adhesive to check fit.

Drywall: A basic interior building material consisting of sheets of pressed gypsum faced with heavy paper on both sides. Also known as wallboard, gypsum board, plasterboard, adn Sheetrock(r).

E

End grain: The ends of wood fibers that are exposed at the ends of boards.

Expansion joint: A space between structures or materials, filled with a flexible material, to allow for expansion and contraction during temperature changes without damage.

F

Field tiles: Flat tiles with unrounded edges used within the edges of a tiled installation. In contrast to trim tiles that are shaped to turn corners or define surface edges.

Filler: A pastelike compound used to hide surface imperfections in wood. One type, pore filler, levels a surface that has a coarse grain.

Finish coat: the final coat of paint, varnish, or other finishing material in an application.

Flush: Having the same surface or plane as an adjoining surface.

Framing: The skelatal or structural support of a home. Sometimes called framework.

G

Glazing: A protective and decorative coating that is fired onto the surface of some tiles.

Grade: Ground level. Also, the elevation at any given point.

Green bisque: Clay that has not been fired (not a reference to color).

Grain: The direction of fibers in a piece of wood; also refers to the pattern of the fibers.

Granite: A quartz-based stone with a tough, glossy appearance; granite is harder than marble.

Grit: The adhesive material bonded to sandpaper. Grit is designated by numbers, such as 120-grit. The higher the number, the finer the abrasive.

Grout: A thin mortar mixture. Also, the process of applying grout. *See also* Mortar.

Grouting float: A rubber backed trowel used for pressing the grout into the joints.

Gypsum board: *See* Drywall.

H

Hardwood: Lumber derived from deciduous trees, such as oaks, maples, and walnuts.

Heartwood: In a log, the wood between the pith and the sapwood. Usually full of resinds, gums, and other matierals that make it dark in color and resistant to decay.

I

Impervious tile: Tiles least likely to absorb water; they are generally used only in commercial locations.

Inside corner: The point at which two walls form an internal angle, as in the corner of a room.

Isolation membrane: A sub-surface later for tile installations. Chlorinated polyethylene (SPE) sheets are used for an isolation membrane.

J

Jamb: The top and sides of a door, window, or other opening. Includes studs, frame, and trim.

Jig: A device that holds a workpiece or tool in a certain way to efficiently and accurately saw or shape wood.

Jointing: The smoothing or straightening of the edges of boards so they fit together precisely. A machine for this purpose is called a jointer.

Joists: Horizontal framing members that support a floor and/or ceiling.

K

Kerf: The void created by the blade of a saw as it cuts through a piece of material.

Knot: A hard, dark-colored area with a circular grain structure in a piece of wood; formed where a branch grew on the tree.

L

Laminate flooring: A type of manufactured flooring with a hard plastic decorative veneer on its top surface.

Lap joint: The joint formed with one member overlaps another.

Latex-modified thinset: Thinset mortar mixed with latex additive to increase its flexibility, resistance to water, and adhesion.

Layout: Any drawing showing the arrangement of structural members or features. Also the act of transferring the arrangement to the site.

Level: The condition that exists when a surface is at true horizontal. Also, a hand tool used to determine level.

Linear foot: A term used to refer to the length of a board or piece of molding.

Load-bearing wall: A wall that supports a wall or foof section on the floor above.

M

Marble: A hard and durable limestone characterized by varied patterns and colors of veins.

Mastic: A viscous material used as an adhesive for setting tile or resilient flooring.

Mexican paver: Unglazed tile used most often on floors.

Miter: An angle, often 45 degrees, cut across the grain on a piece of wood.

Moulding: Shaped wood used as trim.

Mortar: Any mixture of masonry cement, sand, water, and other additives. Also describes the action of applying mortar to surfaces or joints.

Mosaic tile: Small (1- or 2-inch) vitreous tiles, mounted on sheets or joined with adhesive strips.

Mud: Trade jargon for cement-based mortars.

Natural finish: A transparent finish—usually a sealer, oil, or varnish—that protects wood but allows the natural color and grain to show through.

N

Nominal dimension: The designated size of a piece of tile or lumber. It varies slightly from the actual size.

Nonvitreous tile: Porous ceramic tiles for use indoors in dry locations.

O

OC (on center): The distance from the center of one regularly spaced framing member to the center of the next. Studs and joists commonly are 16 or 24 inches)C.

Open time: The interval between application of adhesive and when it can no longer be worked; also called working time.

Organic mastic: One of several petroleum or latex-based adhesives for setting tiles. Exhibits less strength, flexibility, and resistance to water than thinset adhesives.

Oriented Strand Board (OSB): A panel material of specially produced wood flakes that are compressed and bonded together with phenolitic resin. Used for many of the same applications of plywood.

Outside corner: The pint at which two walls for an external angle, the corner you can usually walk around.

P

Panel: A large, thin board or sheet of construction material.

Parquet: A type of wood flooring in which small strips of wood are laid in squares of alternating grain direction.

Particleboard: Panels made from compressed wood chips and glue.

Partition wall: Unlike a load-bearing wall, a partition supports no structure above it and can therefore be removed.

Pavers: Vitreous floor tiles, usually 3/8-inch thick and glazed or unglazed.

Pennyweight: A system of measuring the size of a nail. Originaly derived from a unit of weight, pennyweight is represented by the letter "d." For example, a "10 penny" nail would be designated 10d.

Pllot hole: A small-diameter hole that guides a nail or screw.

Plank: A broad piece of lumber, usually more than 1 inch thick.

Plumb: A surface that lies on a true vertical plane.

Ply: A term used to refer to a layer in a multilayered material.

Plywood: A wood product made up of layers of wood veneer bonded together with adhesive. It is usually made up of an odd number of plys set at a right angle to each other.

Polymer-modified: A substance like grout or martar to which an acrylic or latex solution has been added to increase its strength and workability.

Primer: A first coating formulatedto seal raw surfaces and hold succeeding finish coats.

Q

Quarry tile: Ungladed, vitreous tiles, usually ½-inch thick, used on floors.

Quarter-round: A convex molding shaped like a quarter circle when viewed in cross section.

R

Rabbet: A channel sawed or formed on the edge of a board or panel.

Radiant heating: Electrically heated panels or hot-water pipes in the floor that radiate heat to warm the room's surfaces.

Radius trim: A trim tile whose edge turns down to form a smooth, glazed border.

Register: In a floor, the device thorugh which air from the furnace or air conditioner enters a room.

Rip-cut: To reduce a wide board by sawing with the grain; a cut along the long dimension of a sheet or panel.

Rod saw: A strip of tungsten carbide that fits into a standard hacksaw body. It is used for cutting tight curves in tile.

Roughing-in: The initial stage of a project, when all components that won't be seen after the second finishing phase are assembled.

Rout: Shaping or cutting wood with a router and bit.

S

Sanded grout: Grout containing sand, which increases the strength and decreases the contraction of the joint.

Sanding: Rubbing sandpaper or similar abrasive material over a surface to smooth it or prepare it for finishing.

Sapwood: The wood near the outside of a log; contains the living cells of a tree. Usually lighter in color than the heartwood and more susceptible to decay.

Scribe: To use a geometry compass or scrap of wood to transfer the shape or dimension of an object to a piece of wood or other material to be cut.
Sealant: Coatings used to protect tile and grout from water infiltration.

Semivitreous tile: Tile of moderate density that exhibits only a partial resistance to water and other liquids.

Set: The process during which mortar hardens.

Setting nails: Driving the heads of nails slightly below the surface of the wood.

Settlement: Shifts in a structure, usually caused by freeze-thaw cycles underground.

Shoe molding: Strips of molding commonly used where a baseboard meets the floor. Sometimes known as base shoe.

Sill: The lowest horizontal piece of a door or wall framework.

Slab: A concrete foundation or floor poured directly on the ground.

Slake: To allow a masonry mixture additional time after initial mixing. Allows the liquid to thoroughly penetrate the solids.

Slate: A rough-surface tile that has been split, rather than sliced, from quarried stone.

Sleepers: Boards laid directly over a masonry floor to serve as nailers for plywood, or strip or plank flooring.

Snap cutter: Cutting tool for tile. Resembles a glass cutter, except that it is mounted on a guide bar.

Sole plate: Bottommost horizontal part of a stud partition. When a plate rests on a foundation, it's called a sill plate.

Softwood: Lumber derived from coniferous trees, such as pines, firs, cedars, or redwoods.

Spacers: Small pieces of plastic that are used to ensure consistent grout-joint width between tiles.

Span: The distance between supports.

Square: Surfaces exactly perpendicular or at 90 degrees to another. Also describes a hand tool used to determine square.

Stone tile: Marble, granite, slate and flagstone. Dimensioned (or gauged) stone is cut to uniform size. Hand-split (or cleft stone) varies in size.

Straightedge: A metal or wood implement clamped to the workpiece to ensure a straight cut, used to mark a line on a material, or to determine if a surface is even.

Strip flooring: Wood flooring material consisting of narrow strips.

Stud framing: A building method that distributes structural loads to each of a series of relatively lightweight studs.

Subfloor: A layer of wood sheet material, generally plywood, used to proved a stable foundation for other flooring materials.

Sweep: A flexible strip placed on the bottom edge of a door for insulation and to prevent drafts.

Substrate: Any of several layers, including the subfloor, beneath the finished floor surface.

T

Template: A pattern from which parts of a structure can be made.

Terrazo tiles: Bits of granite or marble set in mortar, then polished.

Thinset mortar: A setting adhesive for tiles.

Three-four-five method: An easy way to check whether a corner of a large area is square. Measure 3 feet along one side and 4 feet along the other. If the corner is square, the diagonal distance between those two points will equal 5 feet.

Threshold: The plate at the bottom of some—usually exterior—door openings. Sometimes called a saddle.

Throw mortar: To place mortar using a trowel.

Tile-backing units: Waterproof units made of fiberglass mesh and concrete; produced specifically as an underlayment for ceramic and dimensioned stone installed in the thin-set adhesive method.

Tile nippers: A cutting tool for making small notches and curves in tile. It resembles pliers but has carbide-tipped edges.

Toe-kick: The wood part that is recessed beneath a cabinet base.

Toenailing: Driving a nail so it enters the first wood surface diagonally.

Tongue-and-groove joint: A joint made using boards that have a projecting tongue on the end of one member and a corresponding groove on the other member.

Trim: Any finish materials in a structure that are placed to provide decoration or to dover the joints between surfaces or contrasting materials.

Trowel: Any of several flat and oblong or flat and pointed metal tools used for handling and/or finishing mortar.

Trim tile: Tiles that are shaped to turn corners or define the edges of an installation. Includes cove trim, bullnose, V-cap, quarter round, inside order, and outside corner.

U

Underlayment: Cement-like product that is used to level floors prior to laying down the surface material. Sometimes used to refer to the subfloor mateiral or material laid on top of the subfloor. Usually some type of plywood installed below the surface material of the floor.

Utility knife: A razor-blade knife with a long handle and retractable blade.

Vapor barrier: A waterproof membrane in a floor, wall, or ceiling that blocks the transfer of condensation to the inner surface.

V

Veneer: A thin layer of decorative wood or other material laminated to the surface of a more common material.

Vitreous tile: An extremely dense ceramic tile with a high resistance to water absorption.

W

Warp: Any of several lumber defects caused by uneven shrinkage of wood cells.

Wet saw: A power tool for cutting tile. A pump sprays water to cool the blade and remove chips.

INDEX

METRIC CONVERSIONS

U.S. UNITS TO METRIC EQUIVALENTS			METRIC EQUIVALENTS TO U.S. UNITS		
To Convert From	Multiply by	To Get	To Convert From	Multiply by	To Get
Inches	25.4	Millimeters	Millimeters	0.0394	Inches
Inches	2.54	Centimeters	Centimeters	0.3937	Inches
Feet	30.48	Centimeters	Centimeters	0.0328	Feet
Feet	0.3048	Meters	Meters	3.2808	Feet
Yards	0.9144	Meters	Meters	1.0936	Yards
Square inches	6.4516	Square centimeters	Square centimeters	0.1550	Square inches
Square feet	0.0929	Square meters	Square meters	10.764	Square feet
Square yards	0.8361	Square meters	Square meters	1.1960	Square yards
Acres	0.4047	Hectares	Hectares	2.4711	Acres
Cubic inches	16.387	Cubic centimeters	Cubic centimeters	0.0610	Cubic inches
Cubic feet	0.0283	Cubic meters	Cubic meters	35.315	Cubic feet
Cubic feet	28.316	Liters	Liters	0.0353	Cubic feet
Cubic yards	0.7646	Cubic meters	Cubic meters	1.308	Cubic yards
Cubic yards	764.55	Liters	Liters	0.0013	Cubic yards

To convert from degrees Fahrenheit (F) to degrees Celsius (C), first subtract 32, then multiply by ⅝.

To convert from degrees Celsius to degrees Fahrenheit, multiply by ⅖, then add 32.

KNOWLEDGE IS THE BEST TOOL

FREE DVD INSIDE PLUMBING AND WIRING BOOKS!

STANLEY COMPLETE **PLUMBING**
EXPANDED EDITION FREE DVD INSIDE!
REPAIRS AND REPLACEMENTS
UPGRADES FOR INSIDE AND OUT
STEP-BY-STEP INSTRUCTIONS

STANLEY COMPLETE **WIRING**
EXPANDED EDITION FREE DVD INSIDE!

STANLEY COMPLETE **BASEMENTS**
HOW TO CREATE LIVABLE SPACES
DESIGN IDEAS AND PLANNING ADVICE
STEP-BY-STEP INSTRUCTIONS

STANLEY COMPLETE **Trimwork** & Carpentry
STEP-BY-STEP INSTRUCTIONS
REMODELING TIPS & IDEAS
FROM FRAMING TO TRIMMING

STANLEY COMPLETE **BATHS**
PLANNING & DESIGN
PLUMBING & LIGHTING
FLOORING, FRAMING, CABINETS, COUNTERTOPS

CONSTRUCT   REJUVENATE   PLAN & REPAIR   ENHANCE   MAINTAIN